Perpetrators

Perpetrators

The World of the Holocaust Killers

GUENTER LEWY

OXFORD
UNIVERSITY PRESS

OXFORD
UNIVERSITY PRESS

Oxford University Press is a department of the University of Oxford. It furthers
the University's objective of excellence in research, scholarship, and education
by publishing worldwide. Oxford is a registered trade mark of Oxford University
Press in the UK and certain other countries.

Published in the United States of America by Oxford University Press
198 Madison Avenue, New York, NY 10016, United States of America.

Library of Congress Cataloging-in-Publication
Names: Lewy, Guenter, 1923– author.
Title: Perpetrators : the world of the Holocaust killers / Guenter Lewy.
Description: New York : Oxford University Press, [2017] | Includes
bibliographical references and index.
Identifiers: LCCN 2016053104 | ISBN 9780190661137 (hardback : alk. paper)
Subjects: LCSH: Holocaust, Jewish (1939–1945) | Jews—Persecutions—Germany—
History—20th century. | War crimes—Germany. | National socialism—Moral and
ethical aspects. | Good and evil.
Classification: LCC D804.3 .L523 2017 | DDC 940.53/18—dc23
LC record available at https://lccn.loc.gov/2016053104

1 3 5 7 9 8 6 4 2
Printed by Sheridan Books, Inc., United States of America

CONTENTS

PREFACE

More than seventy years after the collapse of the Third Reich, the Nazis' attempt to annihilate the Jewish people, known as the Holocaust, continues to raise a disturbing question. During the course of a few years, about six million defenseless men, women, and children were murdered for no reason but their ancestry. Close to two million Jews were killed in mass shootings under the most horrific circumstances, and the remainder were asphyxiated in gas chambers and mobile gas trucks or worked and starved to death. The name "Auschwitz" in particular stands for a crime without precedent. How could such terrible deeds happen in the heart of Christian Europe and among a nation known for its poets and thinkers—a people that had produced Schiller, Goethe, Bach, Beethoven, and Brahms? What had converted so many seemingly ordinary people into killers, willing participants in what is probably the worst crime in modern history? That is the question I seek to answer in this book.

The source material for such an inquiry, it turns out, is readily available, even as much of it has remained untapped. Many soldiers and officers kept diaries. German archives have collected some fifty thousand letters written by the men serving in the East, and a good number of these missives describe the murder of Jews. Because the writers were close to the events, these communications are an important counterweight to the selective memory of defendants in postwar trials. We have the recollections of Jewish camp survivors, many of whom had lived with their tormentors for many months and therefore were able to provide valuable information about them. Finally, and most importantly, there is the record of the trials of hundreds of Nazi functionaries, beginning with Nuremberg in 1945–1946 and including German court proceedings that continue to the present day.

Most useful for this study has been the forty-nine-volume collection of 929 German trial verdicts published between 1968 and 2012 by Amsterdam University Press. (The absence of such a collection for Austrian court cases is the reason why this book deals with German wrongdoers only and does not include Austrian Nazi criminals.) This Dutch series, *Justiz und NS-Verbrechen* (Judiciary and Nazi Crimes), is focused on Nazi crimes between 1939 and 1945 that resulted in death and thus provides a unique opportunity to study the personal profiles of Nazi killers. SS guards generally did not write memoirs, and they preferred to lie low in postwar society. Hence the trial records are a highly valuable source of information about Nazi perpetrators.

Under applicable German law, the only crimes not subject to a statute of limitations have been murder or being an accessory to murder, and under German criminal law, deeds of murder require the perpetrators to have acted with malice or cruelty or from a base motive. The need of the courts to prove a bad intent produced important details of the killing process. The judges went out of their way to ascertain the state of mind of the defendants and the mainsprings of their actions. They collected information about the killers' personal backgrounds and their political records, though this knowledge was not always used to the disadvantage of the defendants. At the same time, the verdicts describe in detail the deeds committed by the convicted Nazis, utilizing interrogation reports, affidavits, and the testimony of witnesses, as well as archival documents. None of these sources, taken alone, is infallible, but taken together they provide a reliable picture. This material allowed the courts to check and cross-check what the defendants chose to tell or remain silent about. The result is a wealth of information about the Holocaust in all its horrible particulars and about those who carried out these hideous deeds. For those not familiar with the German language, this book will be the first work in English to make use of this valuable body of knowledge.

As the necessary context for the question of "Why did they do it?" I describe the "it"—the actual killing process of the Holocaust. However, this book is not another history of the Shoah. The work focuses on how and why this unprecedented series of events could happen, on the role played by individuals in the unfolding program of murder, and on the issue of personal responsibility. Why did so many Germans become mass killers? Why did so few opt out when such evasions were possible and did not endanger their own lives? This book is meant for all those seeking an answer to these questions.

Some readers will find this material, especially the photos, disturbing and may consider that it caters to sensationalism and obscene voyeurism. Much of the book, unfortunately, reads like a catalogue of horrors. I offer several reasons for this. First, as the Russian author and war correspondent Vasily Grossman stated in connection with his dreadfully realistic dispatches, "It is infinitely painful to read this. The reader must believe me when I say it is equally hard to write it." I plead for the same indulgence. Even though I am not a newcomer to the history of the Holocaust, I was able to create this book only by developing a quasi-clinical attitude to the terrible material I had to work with, analogous to that of the surgeon who learns to live with the smell and sight of blood as part of his profession. Second, and more importantly, it is my firm conviction that a detailed description of what happened to the hapless victims of the Holocaust is essential for the kind of inquiry I have taken on here. Only a full account of the horrors and cruelties enables us to address the issue of individual participation. Pictures in particular convey a reality that mere words can never produce.

The German-Jewish scholar Max Horkheimer has argued that it is the task of Jewish intellectuals who have escaped death to help ensure that these horrors never return and are never forgotten. I grew up in Germany and lived some six years under Nazi rule. During the November 1938 pogrom known as Kristallnacht (the night of broken glass), I was on the receiving end of storm-trooper brutality, and my father, together with thousands of other adult male Jews, was taken to the Buchenwald concentration camp. He survived a three-month ordeal, but just barely. Hence taking up the subject of why so many ordinary Germans participated in Nazi crimes was for me of more than theoretical interest. It illuminates a chapter in my personal life that I cannot and should not forget.

I want to thank my historian-friends Abraham Ascher and David Large for their comments on an earlier version of this work. I am grateful to my daughter Barbara for her careful reading and constructive editorial suggestions, which greatly improved the readability of the book. Most importantly, I am indebted to Nancy Toff, vice president and executive editor at Oxford University Press. Amazing as it may sound, in many years of scholarly work, she is the first editor I have had who actually edits, that is, who is willing to spend time attending to and improving the manuscript of her author. Nancy Toff's eye for clarity of expression and her attention to detail are exemplary, and I have been fortunate to benefit from her commitment to the book.

Perpetrators

Introduction

Shortly after the Germans and their local helpers had shot more than thirty-three thousand Kievan Jews in September 1941, Iryna Khoroshunova, a resident of the city, recorded in her diary that for hours on end she had witnessed naked people being driven to the ravine of Babi Yar. Trying to make sense of what she had heard and seen, she wrote, "I know of only one thing, there is something terrible going on, something inconceivable, which cannot be understood, grasped or explained."[1] After seeing thousands of unburied, emaciated dead bodies in the liberated concentration camp Bergen-Belsen, a correspondent for the *London Times* wrote in April 1945, "It is my duty to describe something beyond the imagination of mankind."[2] To this day, all this abomination seems beyond comprehension. The survivor Elie Wiesel is one of many who called the Jewish tragedy forever unexplainable. A scholar speaks of "a black hole in the understanding of humankind."[3] The radical evil exemplified by Nazi concentration and extermination camps, Hannah Arendt argued, represents a demonic element that "stands outside of life and death."[4] Yet if we are to have any success in preventing another such occurrence, we must seek to understand what led to such horrendous evil.

In 1945, twenty-two leading Nazis were charged at Nuremberg with war crimes. Given the grievous offenses involved, it is not surprising that pathological explanations of their motives and conduct were prevalent. The terrible deeds shown to have been committed by the Gestapo and the SS (the Nazi party's elite force commanded by Heinrich Himmler), two organizations that were declared to be criminal enterprises, prompted many people to assume that sadists or otherwise mentally deranged individuals had been responsible for these acts. Such monstrous violations of decency and morality could surely only have been carried out by monsters. Dismissing the heinous crimes as the work of satanic evildoers enabled many Germans to believe that not they but members of another species bore the responsibility for the horrors that had occurred.[5]

Clinical studies of the Nuremberg defendants, undertaken by several psychiatrists and psychologists, soon disproved the pathological explanation of Nazi evil. The prison psychiatrist Douglas Kelley initiated a series of Rorschach diagnostic tests as part of his assignment to ascertain the competency of the defendants to stand trial. By present-day standards, the administration of these tests left something to be desired, but the near-unanimous conclusion reached by the interpretations and reinterpretations has been that the leading Nazis were neither unique personalities nor insane. They had no diagnosable impairments that could account for the atrocities committed on their orders.[6] All of them knew the difference between right and wrong. Gustave Gilbert, the Nuremberg prison psychologist, spoke German fluently and had regular access to the defendants. In 1947 he published his *Nuremberg Diary*, concluding that there was no reason to question the sanity of these men.[7] The psychiatrist Henry Dicks conducted in-depth interviews with some lower-level SS killers and reached the same conclusion: these men were not insane in any generally accepted clinical sense.[8]

In the trials of Nazi criminals by German courts, the German public often looked upon the defendants as evil persons fundamentally different from ordinary Germans.[9] Moreover, by attributing these deeds to a few leading Nazis and to the members of Himmler's black corps, it became possible to exculpate the German population as a whole. The German edition of Gerald Reitlinger's book *The SS: Alibi of a Nation*, published in English in 1956, was retitled *Die SS: Tragödie einer deutschen Epoche* (The SS: Tragedy of a German Epoch), and a postscript added by the German publisher criticized Reitlinger's view that large numbers of Germans had been implicated in Nazi crimes.[10] The German soldier—insisted prominent politicians in postwar Germany, including Chancellor Konrad Adenauer—had conducted himself honorably.[11] German Christian soldiers, declared Bishop Galen in June 1945, had risked their lives for the fatherland while keeping "their hearts and hands clean of hatred, plundering and unjust acts of violence."[12] "The German people did not do it," argued the writer Walter von Molo in a letter to Thomas Mann in 1945.[13] And Adenauer opined in September 1951, "The German people, in its overwhelming majority, abhorred the crimes perpetrated against the Jews and did not participate in these crimes."[14]

Germany tried to escape its own history. It saw itself as a nation of victims, helpless in the face of totalitarian terror and therefore incapable of opposing Nazi policies. This view showed an interesting similarity to the official position of the East German communist regime, which regarded German fascism as a special form of monopoly capitalism that had subjugated the German people. The belief in German victimhood was widespread in the first years of the postwar period. It found expression in the black joke current at the time: "The Germans will never forgive the Jews for Auschwitz." As late as 2006, on his visit to Auschwitz, Pope Benedict XVI (the former Joseph Ratzinger) described himself as a "son of a nation once caught in the sway of a band of criminals," a nation that "was used and abused as an instrument of their destructive rage and domination."[15] The questionable thesis of the collective guilt of Germany thus was superseded by the even more inappropriate notion of the collective innocence of the Germans.[16] As an answer to the charge of collective guilt, a traumatized society invoked the excuse, "We did not know this!"[17] Hardly anyone recognized that the affirmation of the ignorance of the horrors was seriously weakened by its twin excuse—the impossibility of resistance to these crimes. How was it impossible to act against that which one did not know?[18]

Other misconceptions followed. For the first two decades after the defeat of Nazi Germany, the Holocaust was often described as the work of an efficient extermination machine, a crime, as it were, without criminals. What became known as the structuralist or functionalist approach to the Holocaust concentrated on the regime's bureaucratic machinery to the exclusion of individual perpetrators. The murder of the Jews was seen as the work of faceless bureaucrats, who had been cogs in an anonymous apparatus of destruction. This perspective helped deflect the delicate question of the involvement of large numbers of Germans in the Final Solution and the responsibility of German society for what had occurred during the Nazi era. And yet, the murder of the Jews was not carried out by a bureaucracy or any other "structure." Jews were done to death not by the SS or any other organization but by specific individuals. These perpetrators are the subject of this study—the actual killers, who acted in concentration camps, in mass shootings, or in extermination camps such as Auschwitz.

By the 1960s, a new generation showed the willingness to confront Germany's Nazi past with greater openness and honesty. A series of groundbreaking trials of Nazi killers played an important role in this transformation. The historian searches for the objective causes of events; the jurist pursues the guilt or innocence of individuals. Both contribute to illuminating the past.[19] Prosecutors and judges in the trials of Nazi criminals almost always followed a didactic course, seeking to account for the stunning atrocities that they confronted and to clarify their significance. The testimony of survivors at the 1961 trial of Adolf Eichmann, the man who had organized the deportation of Jews to the extermination camps, provided a detailed picture of the day-to-day reality of the Holocaust that shocked the world. In her book *Eichmann in Jerusalem*, Hannah Arendt referred to Eichmann as a symbol of the "banality of evil," a characterization that by now has been fully discredited. Whatever the merits of the concept of the "banality of evil," it was inappropriate for Eichmann, an ardent Nazi and convinced anti-Semite, and, it is completely inapt for the actual killers whose odious deeds the trial had illuminated.

On August 29, 1958, a court in Ulm passed judgment on ten members of *Einsatzgruppe A* (Task Force A), a mobile killing unit that had murdered thousands of Jewish men, women, and children in Lithuania.[20] German judges told the German public of the reality of Nazi horrors; these proceedings thus could not be dismissed as what many Germans called "victor's justice." The trial not only revealed gruesome crimes but also showed that many of the worst perpetrators had lived normal lives in postwar German society, often rising to positions of responsibility.

Of particular importance in the task of *Vergangenheitsbewältigung* (coming to terms with the past) faced by the new Germany was the Auschwitz trial in Frankfurt, which for the first time revealed authoritative information about this place of abomination. Lasting from December 20, 1963, to August 20, 1965, Germany's longest jury trial convicted twenty members of the Auschwitz camp personnel. Seventeen men were found guilty of murder or being an accessory to murder, and six received life imprisonment, the greatest penalty under German law.[21] Experts from the Institute for Contemporary History in Munich presented detailed analyses of the concentration camp system. More than four hundred witnesses, about half of them survivors, told what it had been like to live and die in Auschwitz, the place that has to come stand for the symbol of Nazi depravity.[22] The trial also revealed that some men had found ways not to participate in murder and that not one of them had suffered serious punishment for these acts. The argument of many defendants—that they had killed because otherwise they themselves would have been killed—turned out to be self-serving and false. There were opportunities to choose how to conduct oneself even in the most murderous environments, though few availed themselves of this choice.

Another milestone in the acknowledgment of Nazi crimes by the wider German public was reached in early 1979, when the American television series *Holocaust* was shown in Germany. The film was seen by twenty million people, half the adult population of the German Federal Republic, and an article in the magazine *Der Spiegel* summed up its tremendous impact: A Hollywood soap opera "accomplished what hundreds of books, plays, films, and television programs, thousands of documents, and all the concentration camp trials have failed to do in the more than three decades since the end of the war: to inform Germans about crimes against Jews committed in their name, so that millions were emotionally touched and moved."[23] People identified with the family of Dr. Josef Weiss because it had an identity every German could recognize—solid, educated, and middle-class. "Death is a master from Germany," the Holocaust survivor Paul Celan had written in his poem "Death Fugue," published in 1948.[24] Now for the first time, some thirty years later, large numbers of Germans said that they felt ashamed of what their country had done.[25] The idea that seeking redress for Nazi crimes amounted to *Netzbeschmutzung* (fouling your own nest) was finally being abandoned.

For a long time, historians debated the role of Hitler in the Final Solution. So-called Intentionalists argued that Hitler from early on had his sights on physically destroying the Jews. "Functionalists" stressed the inner dynamic of a bureaucratic system. The question of Hitler's responsibility for the Holocaust is important. However, from the 1990s on, as Holocaust research began to focus on the conduct of the individuals doing the actual killing, the intentionalist-functionalist debate receded into the background. Attention now shifted to the perpetrators in the narrow sense of the term—the personnel of the concentration and extermination camps, the members of the firing squads, the drivers of gas trucks, and similar culprits.[26] Their number, it turned out, was in the tens of thousands. By mid-1939, the personnel of the concentration camps had reached 22,033, and early in 1945 it numbered about 40,000 men and women.[27] At the war's end, the combined concentration and extermination camp Auschwitz alone had 4,481 male and 71 female personnel.[28] Some 6,000 men rotated through the Einsatzgruppen. They were assisted by about 15,000 men in police battalions and 25,000 Waffen-SS troops.[29] Studies of the role of the armed forces revealed that the Wehrmacht had been deeply involved in the murder of the Jews.[30] Inasmuch as the Wehrmacht was a mass conscript army, the recognition that these soldiers had perpetrated numerous crimes amounted to a powerful charge against German society as a whole (or at least its male part).[31]

Two books in particular played an important role in the emergence of this new perspective. Christopher Browning's *Ordinary Men: Reserve Police Battalion 101 and the Final Solution in Poland*, published in 1992, demonstrated the willingness of regular policemen to engage in wholesale murder, even though they had the opportunity to opt out. And Daniel Goldhagen's book *Hitler's Willing Executioners*, which appeared in 1996, carried the telling subtitle *Ordinary Germans and the Holocaust*. The perpetrators had acted the way they did, Goldhagen argued, because they were Germans. The German people as a whole, not just the Nazis, had become obsessed by a pervasive "eliminationist anti-Semitism." Browning and Goldhagen developed different explanations for the events they described, but common to both works was the concentration on the conduct of the perpetrators.

During the following years, the work of Browning and Goldhagen became the subject of prolonged discussion. Browning's emphasis on the social-psychological processes of obedience and conformity was held to have neglected the role of anti-Semitism and ideology generally. Goldhagen was criticized for his simplistic monocausal approach and the broad brush with which he had painted his picture of Nazi conduct. The present book takes up this debate and carries it forward. It broadens the discussion by making use of the large number court decisions as well as archival and other materials that have become available since the 1990s. It aims at developing a systematic answer to the question "Why did they do it?" that is based on these manifold sources. The extraordinary evil that men commit to this day will not be prevented by a disquisition of the kind presented here, but without accurate knowledge of how and why these horrors took place, we have no hope of averting such human catastrophes.

1

Jews in Concentration Camps

Nazi concentration camps (known as KZs, *Konzentrationslager*) evolved during the early months of 1933 for the purpose of dealing with the new regime's political enemies—functionaries of left-wing parties as well as lawyers and journalists who had opposed the Nazis during the Weimar Republic. Inmates were imprisoned not on the basis of ordinary legal proceedings but on orders of the Gestapo, the new secret police that came into being on April 26, 1933. That same authority decided the length of what was called "protective custody."

Since Jews had played a prominent part in this opposition, they were overrepresented in relation to their share in the population at large. It is estimated that before 1938, Jews made up 5 to 10 percent of all concentration camp inmates, whereas they represented less than 1 percent of the German population.[1] The KZs Dachau and Oranienburg had so-called *Judenkompanien* (Jewish companies), the members of which were treated especially brutally.[2]

The early months saw considerable lawlessness and arbitrary killings. When the SS took over the administration of the concentration camp Dachau in April 1933, the SS men celebrated this act by brutalizing Jewish inmates in particular. During the first two months of their control of Dachau, they murdered twelve prisoners.[3] The relatively small number of deaths was the result of the fact that during the early months of the regime, courageous public prosecutors still occasionally brought charges for particularly brutal killings. Very soon, however, the concentration camps gained their independence from judicial authority. In the few court cases that did occur and resulted in convictions, Hitler personally pardoned the offenders. Such an act of clemency benefited twenty-three storm troopers whose conduct in the Hohnstein concentration camp had been denounced by Minister of Justice Franz Gürtner as "cruelty resembling oriental sadism."[4]

In late June 1933, the SS officer Theodor Eicke was appointed commandant of Dachau. Eicke had joined the Nazi party in 1928, and two years later he had transferred from the SA (the paramilitary organization of the Nazi party) to the SS, where he rapidly rose in rank. In July 1934, Eicke became head of all SS units manning the camps, and the "Eicke system" became the model for all concentration camps.[5] Eicke's way has been called "an academy of violence where guards were schooled in steely resolution and the techniques of terror."[6] From here on, detailed rules regulated the behavior of the guards. Their attitude toward the inmates was shaped by indoctrination in Nazi ideology and was dictated by the prisoners' alleged hostility toward the National Socialist state. In a speech in 1937, Himmler declared that the inmates of the concentration camps were nothing but criminals and misfits. Hermann Göring called them the "trash of the nation" who deserved to be burned. Hence in dealing with these worthless individuals, the SS man had to be tough, ruthless, and show no pity.[7]

Individual motives for joining the SS varied. Some recruits were true believers. There were intellectuals who saw the SS as an instrument for reshaping German society to conform with National Socialist ideology. Many belonged to the generation that had learned violence in the rightist *völkisch* milieu of the 1920s, including service in the Freikorps, units of volunteers who fought the Weimar Republic and carried out political assassinations. For these men, hardness, brutality, and killing were proof of courage and strength.[8] Others were hangers-on whose ideological commitment was superficial or non-existent. Many of these entered the SS because it promised a secure job. One of them was Josef Kramer, who rose to the rank of camp commandant, and who has entered history as one of the beasts of Belsen. Still others were men who had failed at previous occupations or even were asocial or gangster types.[9] Most of them possessed mediocre education.[10]

At the end of 1934, the SS guards were taken out of the general SS and were consolidated into *SS-Totenkopfverbände* (Death's Head units). Members wore a badge with a skull and bones on their uniform. According to Eicke, "he who joins our ranks enters into comradeship with death." Volunteers for these units had to be born between 1914 and 1919 and be racially unobjectionable.[11] By 1935, there were seven concentration camps, with Dachau alone having about 2,500 inmates. The camps no longer contained only political enemies but also those considered harmful but not subject to legal sanction, such as asocials (Gypsies), homosexuals, Jehovah's Witnesses, and repeat criminal offenders. During the war years, the number of camps and subcamps increased steadily, swelled by the large number of foreigners sent there for slave labor. By April 1944, there existed twenty concentration camps with 165 attached labor camps.[12] The total number of such subcamps was far larger; Auschwitz alone had about fifty satellite camps.[13] Reliable estimates put the number of concentration camp inmates between 1933 and 1945 at 1,650,000. When the concentration camp Bergen-Belsen was liberated on April 15, 1945, it held fifty-five thousand emaciated inmates and some thirteen thousand naked and unburied bodies in various stages of decomposition. Another thirteen thousand people died during the following days despite medical aid. A doctor inmate related that he had witnessed numerous cases of cannibalism.[14] Similar conditions prevailed in the other camps.

Days in the concentration camps were marked by forced labor. Some inmates worked in quarries, mines, or construction projects, while others, especially during the war years, toiled in producing armaments and ammunition. The work was hard, the hours long, and food completely inadequate for the effort expended. The hot meal of the day consisted of a thin soup devoid of nourishment. Inmates weakened quickly; those who did not die became the emaciated figures who were revealed to the world upon the liberation of the camps. At the conclusion of the workday, the prisoners were marched back to the camp for the evening roll call. The survivor Eugen Kogon called it the terror of the inmates. Exhausted from work and regardless of the weather, they had to stand in ranks for hours on end until the SS guards had completed their count of the prisoners and had satisfied themselves that nobody had escaped. Whenever the count was not correct, the whole camp was kept on its feet until the culprits were captured, which was often a matter of many hours. During evening roll call in Buchenwald on December 14, 1938, two prisoners were missing. The temperature was thirty-six degrees, but the thinly clad inmates had to stand in the roll-call area for nineteen hours. By the next morning, twenty-five had frozen to death, and by noon the number had reached more than seventy.[15]

Rules usually imply the opposite of arbitrary action, but this was not so in the Nazi concentration camps governed by the Eicke system, where abuse of the prisoners governed the conduct of the SS. Here random brutality became the norm. The code of rules provided personnel with a handle for arbitrary actions. The guards had unlimited power over what they defined as negligence, refusal to work, or disorder, and these offenses could be punished by violence or the imposition of penalties. These rules have been called "terror incorporated."[16] The most trifling offenses, such as a missing button or a mess dish deemed insufficiently clean, could lead to retribution. Lashings could range from five to fifty. The prisoner was tied to a rack (known as the *Bock*), and the beatings were carried out with canes or bullwhips. The first few blows usually lacerated the skin. The inmate had to count the blows as they landed, and if he made a mistake, the torture would commence again from the beginning. Another extremely painful punishment was tying the prisoner's hands behind his back and for an hour or more hoisting him up so that the entire weight of the body rested on the twisted shoulder joints. Those who lost consciousness were revived by being doused with cold water. Most of the inmates incurred permanent injuries from these torturous practices and not a few died. Such deaths were supposed to be reported to higher authorities, but if the reports were filed at all, their content falsified the cause by camouflaging it as "shot while trying to escape."[17]

Every three months, the camp guards had to sign a declaration that forbade the mistreatment of inmates. "It is the Führer who makes decisions regarding life and death. Hence no National Socialist is entitled to raise his hand against enemies of the state and to subject them to physical abuse. The punishment of inmates is decided by the commandant."[18] Despite this order, capriciousness and brutality dominated the life of the prisoners.[19] SS guards regarded violence as their birthright and continued to torment inmates. A secret order issued at Dachau instructed the guards to record all violence against prisoners as self-defense.[20] Commandants signed official orders of punishment while at the same time they abused inmates without recourse to the official rules. According to the SS judge Konrad Morgen, rules limiting the power of the camp commandants were seldom enforced.[21]

SS personnel got into trouble only for acts that caused disorder or threatened the autonomy of camp discipline. This is what happened to Paul Seidler in the Sachsenhausen concentration camp. In February 1937, Seidler, known for his sadistic tastes, had been one several guards who had murdered Friedrich Weissler, a leading official of the Protestant church, in a particularly vile manner. Word about his killing reached foreign newspapers and caused alarm in Protestant church circles and abroad. When the Weissler case threatened to implicate other Sachsenhausen officials, Seidler was made a scapegoat and sentenced to one year of imprisonment. As far as is known, Seidler was the only SS guard convicted for abuse of a camp inmate.[22]

Guards were under orders to shoot anyone who approached the camp's barbed wire fence, and not a few inmates lost their lives in this way after having been forced near the camp perimeter. Rochel Hugo, a *Kapo* (an inmate functionary used to supervise other inmates), did just that in the Flossenburg concentration camp to a prisoner who showed insufficient effort during forced labor. While being severely beaten, the prisoner had lost his cap. Hugo picked it up, threw it toward the fence, and ordered the prisoner to retrieve it. When the prisoner hesitated to approach the fence, Hugo struck him repeatedly and drove him forward. When the prisoner finally picked up his cap at the fence, he was shot by a guard at the nearest guard tower. The commandant of the camp, who appeared at the scene, was told that the prisoner had been shot while trying to escape.[23]

Many punishments were life threatening, if not fatal. *Strafexerzieren* (punishment drilling), called *Sport* by the SS, consisted of chasing the victims across the parade ground and forcing them to hop, roll, and bend their knees until they collapsed. In the winter, "misbehaving" inmates sometimes were doused with water until they had frozen into a block of ice. Being sent to the punishment company multiplied all of these potentially deadly penalties, and few prisoners taken to the camp jail, the dreaded *Bunker*, returned alive. For deterrent effect, many punishments and all executions were carried out in public with the prisoners forced to watch. Execution by hanging usually involved being strung up in order to prolong the agony of death.[24] An undeterminable number of inmates were killed in the "euthanasia" program known as 14 f 13, which targeted the handicapped and those no longer able to work. At the Mauthausen camp between 1939 and 1945, once or twice a month up to twenty weakened prisoners were weeded out during regular selections and then killed by an injection into the heart.[25] Reska Weiss, who survived this selection process in Auschwitz, relates how the women had to undress while SS men stood by, laughed at their embarrassment, and made obscene remarks. "Overwhelmed by shame, we did not know which parts of our bodies we should cover with our hands."[26]

Nazi doctors used the inmates of the concentration camps for medical experiments. In Dachau in 1944, the doctors Hermann Becker-Freyseng and Wilhelm Beiglböck carried out research about the potability of seawater requested by the air force. The human guinea pigs were divided into several groups. One group was deprived of food and drink, a second was given only seawater, a third seawater with an additive that eliminated the salty taste of the water, and a fourth a liquid in which the salt had been neutralized by the addition of silver nitrate. The victims soon manifested symptoms of starvation and severe thirst. They rapidly lost weight and became increasingly agitated; those who started to scream and rave were tied to their beds. When they were close to death, they were injected with a preparation that was supposed to keep them alive longer. The two doctors who ran these experiments were ultimately sentenced by an Allied military court to lengthy terms of imprisonment.[27]

In Buchenwald, Dr. Sigmund Rascher used women inmates from Ravensbrück in experiments on how to revive sailors and airmen pulled out of the freezing ocean. Eight male prisoners were placed in a tank of near-freezing water and left there until they passed out. The men were then removed from the tank and each placed between two naked Ravensbrück women who were directed to snuggle up to the unconscious men in a large bed. In none of the cases was the re-warming more effective than if the men had been placed in a hot bath. One man had a cerebral hemorrhage and died.[28] Experiments in other concentration camps involved sterilization, a new vaccine against typhus, exposure to gas, and more. All of them were carried out with the utmost ruthlessness and usually ended in a torturous death for the unfortunate inmates.

Despite the proclaimed intent to "reform" inmates, as well as pressure during the war years to supply a productive labor force, mortality in the camps, the result of systematic mistreatment, malnutrition, and disease, was extremely high. In December 1942, Himmler urged Oswald Pohl, who was in charge of all work projects for the camps, to improve the nutrition of the inmates and to lower the death rate. The commandants of the concentration camps were to be held personally responsible for carrying out this order.[29] According to a regulation issued by Pohl that became effective on May 15, 1943, inmates who excelled at production were granted additional food and tobacco rations, and those demonstrating "extraordinary achievement" were given the right to visit the camp brothel once a week.[30] But to convert the camps into efficiently organized places of war never proved possible. The commandants of the camps were neither willing nor able to put an end to the routine of abuse.

Violence and death characterized life in the camps until the very end. Of the estimated total of 1.65 million camp inmates, approximately two-thirds lost their lives. Long-term survival depended on finding a special position such as work in the kitchen, in a repair shop, or as a clerk. Primo Levi recalled that of the few hundred Jews still alive in the work camp of Auschwitz in 1944, not one was an ordinary inmate.[31] For those not fortunate enough to find a niche of this sort, the average life span between 1934 and 1944 was one or two years, and during some periods it was shorter. Records recovered after the war show that during the second half of the year 1942, no less than 60 percent of the total number of inmates died within six months.[32] At the war's end, survivors were moved away from the advancing Allies in death marches, during which thousands more perished of exhaustion or were killed by the guards who accompanied them.[33]

Even though there existed no explicit policy to annihilate all the Jews before the fall of 1941, their treatment in the concentration camps was especially brutal and resulted in a large number of deaths. Different classes of prisoners in the camps were identified through the use of colored triangles attached to their clothing—red for political prisoners, green for common criminals, and so forth. Jews wore yellow triangles and the Star of David, and Jewish criminals green and yellow tags. Different groups of prisoners were treated differently, with Jews assigned to the lowest category, known as Level III. Their barracks were more crowded, they were assigned to the most back-breaking or unpleasant work, their bread rations were smaller, they were not allowed to receive packages, in most camps they were not admitted to the camp hospital, and they were more likely to die. It is estimated that some three hundred thousand Jewish prisoners were worked to death under a regime known as "destruction through labor."[34]

In Esterwegen, Jews made up 5 to 10 percent of the prison population but about 25 percent of those who died.[35] In Dachau, too, the *Muselmann*—the term used in the camps for an apathetic prisoner who had given up the will to live—was usually a Jewish inmate. "The Jews," one former inmate recalls, "were the target of Nazi bloodlust from the very outset."[36] Of the twenty-one prisoners murdered in Dachau in 1933, two-thirds were Jewish. In 1937, 10 percent of the inmates in Dachau were Jews, but among those who were killed that year, 20 percent were Jews.[37] Orders issued by Himmler in early 1935 forbade "individual actions" against Jews, but, like the orders against excessive violence, the precept was ignored.[38] The especially harsh treatment meted out to Jews in the concentration camps was the clear result of the SS translating anti-Semitic ideology into deadly practice.[39]

In February 1937, the Gestapo gave orders to concentrate Jews from other concentration camps in Dachau. The reason for this action appears to have been the desire to prevent the "corrupting influence of Jews on German-blooded prisoners."[40] By early 1938, Dachau held some 2,750 Jewish prisoners. Most of them had served a jail term for *Rassenschande* (race-defilement) under the

Nuremberg laws of 1935 and then were transferred from prison to the concentration camp. More Jews arrived in Dachau after the annexation of Austria in March 1938, most of them individuals associated with left-wing parties. Others had been seized during the wave of arrests of "asocials" in June 1938 known as "Operation Work-Shy."[41]

A new large influx of Jews to the concentration camps followed the assassination of the German consul in Paris on November 8, 1938, by the seventeen-year-old Polish-German Jew Herschel Grynszpan. During the November pogrom known as *Kristallnacht*, broken glass from the windows of destroyed synagogues, homes, and Jewish-owned businesses littered the streets of German cities. At the same time, the Gestapo arrested some thirty thousand Jewish men and took them to Buchenwald, Dachau, and Sachsenhausen. The treatment of the new inmates was even more brutal than usual. During the first week in Buchenwald, the SS would raid the barracks during the night and beat up the helpless and terrified prisoners.[42] By February 1939, 187 of the 10,911 Jews imprisoned at Dachau were listed as dead.[43] In all, about 1,000 of the Jews arrested following *Kristallnacht* lost their lives in the camps, died after release as the result of mistreatment, or committed suicide. The aim of this incarceration was to extort money and to put pressure upon the imprisoned Jews to leave Germany.[44] My father was one of the arrested men. Upon release, he was a mere shadow of his former self.

Events outside the concentration camps served the SS as pretexts to abuse Jewish prisoners. Thus, after the failed assassination of Hitler in a Munich beer hall on November 8, 1939, twenty-one Jewish inmates in Buchenwald were shot as a reprisal on the orders of the commandant of Buchenwald, Karl Otto Koch. The assassin, Georg Elser, was not Jewish and had acted alone, and official Nazi propaganda blamed the British secret service. Yet Koch used the opportunity to go after "his" Jews. Koch reported to Berlin that the Jews had "attempted a mutiny" and had "been shot while trying to escape."[45]

During the war years, Jews destined for a concentration camp were sent predominantly to Mauthausen, a Category III camp from which few emerged alive. The inmates had to toil for eleven hours a day in a quarry. A board was placed upon their shoulders and loaded down with extremely heavy stones. Then the prisoners had to ascend a steep series of 186 steps cut into the rock that was known as the "stairway of death." Stones fell off the boards and crushed those climbing up behind; many lost their balance or were given a shove by the guards. In the midst of this "sport," the SS men shouted, "Watch out! Parachutists!" while the victims hurtled to their deaths. Between 1941 and 1943, 2,600 Jews arrived in Mauthausen. All but a handful died there the year of their arrival. After the closing of Auschwitz in the face of the approaching Soviet forces, some 9,000 inmates, the majority of them Jews, were sent to Mauthausen. As many as 1,500 of the Auschwitz transport were unloaded dead at the Mauthausen railroad station, and some 500 more died after having been forced to stand long hours while awaiting registration.[46]

The euthanasia program 14 f 13, designed to murder the physically and mentally impaired, was also used to kill Jews in the concentration camps. Jewish inmates usually were in bad physical shape, and at times they were included simply because they were Jews. A member of one of the teams of doctors who visited the camps to select inmates wrote to his wife on November 23, 1941, from Buchenwald that he had chosen 1,200 Jews without an examination, simply on the basis of their files.[47] It is estimated that between April 1941 and April 1942, at least 10,000 Jewish prisoners were deported to the euthanasia killing centers located in asylums such as Bernburg and Hartheim.[48]

The advances of Soviet troops in the summer of 1944 led to the evacuation of concentration camps in the East. Some 47,000 Jewish prisoners were brought to the concentration camp Stutthof near Danzig. Those deemed unable to work— men, women, and children—were sent to Auschwitz, where most of them were killed.[49] Jewish inmates also died in large numbers during the death marches that began at that time. One of the most brutal massacres took place in East Prussia, where almost 7,000 Jews convoyed there from the Stutthof camp were shot on January 31, 1945. In the camps that continued to operate, conditions became chaotic. In Bergen-Belsen, for example, the camp administration no longer provided even minimal food rations, and thousands died of starvation and disease shortly before the arrival of rescuers.[50]

When Auschwitz was liberated on January 27, 1945, a large number of Jewish children, probably destined for medical experiments, were still alive. On November 29, 1944, twenty children, ten boys and ten girls between the ages of five and twelve, had been transferred to the Neuengamme concentration camp near Hamburg, where they were used by Dr. Kurt Heissmeyer in experiments on the prevention of tuberculosis. The East German court that condemned the doctor to life imprisonment on June 30, 1966, noted in its verdict that Dr. Heissmeyer had seen no difference between a guinea pig and a Jewish child.[51] By April 1945, the twenty children, covered with scars and festering sores, were seriously ill and listless. With the British only a few miles from Hamburg, an order arrived from Berlin to kill the children in order to cover up the experiments. On April 20, the children were thus taken to the Hamburg primary school Bullenhuser Damm, a subcamp of Neuengamme. After they had fallen asleep, an SS doctor injected them with morphine in order to keep them sleepy. Then one by one they were taken to a room in the cellar and hanged. The first of the children, a boy of twelve, emaciated from disease and mistreatment, was so light that the noose of the rope failed to tighten. Thereupon, one SS man, Johann Frahm, applied his own weight to the body of the boy until he had been asphyxiated. By the morning of April 21, the gruesome task of hanging the twenty children one by one was complete. A British military court condemned five of the SS men responsible for this atrocity to death. They were hanged on October 8, 1946.[52]

With the outbreak of the war in 1939, large numbers of SS guards from the concentration camps were transferred to the Waffen-SS, the SS units deployed for military service. Their places in the camps were taken by older men and later by the wounded of the Waffen-SS. Their ranks were joined by ethnic Germans (*Volksdeutsche*) drafted into the armed SS over the course of the war. In 1944, some twenty thousand regular soldiers who were no longer fit for frontline service became guards in the camps, and the personnel of the camps became increasingly heterogenous.[53] All of the newcomers adjusted quickly to the brutal routine of the camps. Until 1939, membership in the Death's Head units had been voluntary, and it had been possible to leave service in the camps. During the war, being a guard in a concentration camp, whether as part of the Death's Head units or the Waffen-SS, was considered "military service" from which one could not resign.[54]

Given the importance of the leadership principle (*Führerprinzip*) in the Nazi system and for the culture of the guards, it is not surprising that the degree to which the most brutal treatment dominated the conditions of a camp depended primarily upon its commandant. The SS officer Hans Loritz was successively commandant of the concentration camps Esterwegen, Dachau, and Sachsenhausen. In all of these camps, his arrival meant a noticeable deterioration in the situation of the inmates.[55] During the time that Rudolf Höss was commandant of Auschwitz, the survivor Hermann Langbein recalled, his officers knew that Höss had no objection to the daily torturing and killing. His successor in November 1943, Arthur Liebehenschel, on the other hand, did not reward cruelty and even halted some extreme brutalities. The result was a marked change in the camp's atmosphere.[56]

The camp personnel were of three basic types—sadists, those who simply followed the brutalizing routine of the camps, and a very small number of guards who actually refrained from abusing inmates or even occasionally helped them.

Survivors of the camps have estimated that only about 5 to 10 percent of the guards were sadistic personalities who enjoyed inflicting harm on their victims. Sadists suffer from deficient impulse control, a lack of a conscience, as well as a failure to experience empathy.[57] It appears that in psychopaths the part of the brain that is important for emotion, the amygdala, is smaller, and this may account for the fact that they do not respond to someone's fear or distress in the way that other humans do. There is no scientific consensus as to whether such psychopathological behavior is rooted in genetics or is at least in part induced by environmental influences.[58] The percentage of sadists in the concentration camps has been held to be more or less the same as in society at large.[59]

Josef Schwammberger was an Austrian who moved to Germany in 1933 in order to join the SS. Several years of service in this elite force made him into an ardent Nazi and a hater of Jews. During the war, Schwammberger became head of a concentration camp in Poland as well of a forced labor camp nearby.

Even though these camps were not extermination camps per se, large numbers of Jews died in both because of Schwammberger. Inmates called him a "beast in human form" because of his extreme cruelty. Schwammberger not only killed but sought to degrade and torture his victims. He was known for ordering lashings for naked inmates. Those who received fifty lashes and emerged from this punishment near death were usually shot by him personally. He also ordered his dog Prince to attack prisoners and forced men to eat excrement. His fury could be unleashed simply by seeing a Jewish prisoner. Hence when the cry "Schwammberger" was heard, Jewish inmates hid as best they could. The German court that sentenced him to life imprisonment in 1992 established that the SS officer had been responsible for at least 25 murders and 641 instances of being an accomplice to murder.[60]

An even more brutal SS guard, if that is possible, was Martin Sommer, who served in Buchenwald from 1937 to 1943 and rose to become the warden of the camp's prison, the dreaded *Bunker*. The survivor Eugen Kogon recalls that of "at least one hundred Jews who passed through the Bunker between 1940 and 1941, not one left alive." Some of the tortures Sommer inflicted, such as suspending inmates head down or applying a clamp to the victim's head and crushing it slowly, Kogon concludes, were "nightmares of sadism."[61] Men were "hanged" with their arms tied tightly behind their backs for up to five hours, and Sommer would hit the helpless inmates in their faces and genitals. The tortured victims cried out for water, for their wives and children, and asked to be shot in order to end their misery.[62] As a result of acting on his own and at times against the explicit orders of the camp commandant Hermann Pister, in 1943 Sommer was convicted by an SS court of "military disobedience" and sentenced to serve in a penal battalion on the Eastern front.[63] Here he was wounded, taken prisoner, and released in 1955.

The German court, which convicted Sommer of at least twenty-five murders by injection and sentenced him to life imprisonment in 1958, noted that Sommer appeared to have derived pleasure from lashing inmates. He was known to take the whip from guards, who in his view did not hit hard enough. Camp Commandant Karl Otto Koch liked to use Sommer for this punishment because he was known as the most brutal beater.[64]

Karl Chmielewski joined the SS in 1932. He served as a guard in the concentration camps Sachsenhausen and Mauthausen, eventually being promoted to commandant of Gusen, a subcamp of Mauthausen. Evaluations by his superiors described him as a dedicated National Socialist and therefore an especially valuable commandant, who treated his inmates in the manner they deserved. The German postwar court that sentenced him to life imprisonment found him guilty of 282 murders, carried out with brutality and cruelty. Chmielewski was responsible for initiating the killing of prisoners through *Totbaden* (death by bathing). The victims were prisoners no longer able to work and undesirables, including Jews. Inmates were herded into a room that had more than fifty showerheads with extremely forceful water pressure, and they were made to stand in these showers under the cold water until they collapsed. For some this took twenty minutes, for others more than two hours. Those who tried to dodge the water were pushed back and forcibly drowned. Others had their heads forced into water containers until they were dead. In none of these cases was the true cause of death listed in the camp records.[65]

Sexual relations between guards and inmates, especially Jews, were strictly forbidden, yet we know that they took place regularly. A female prisoner's refusal to yield to a guard could have deadly consequences and at times unleashed the most brutal propensities of a guard. Friedrich Heinen had volunteered for the Waffen-SS and in early 1943 became a guard in a forced labor camp in Lemberg. It appears that one day he made advances to two good-looking young Jewish girls but was rebuffed. The German court, which sentenced him to life imprisonment for murder, described what followed: Heinen ordered the two girls to undress, lie on the floor, and spread their legs. He then shot into the genitalia of the first girl and killed her with a shot into the mouth. The second girl was likewise shot, though the specific cause of death could not be established. The two murdered girls were taken away by inmates assigned to the job of removing corpses, and that was the end of the affair for Heinen until he finally received his appropriate punishment in 1978.[66]

Oswald Kaduk began his military career as a volunteer in the Waffen-SS, and after falling ill in 1941 became a guard in Auschwitz. Tried in 1965, Kaduk was sentenced to life imprisonment for numerous murders of inmates. The court described Kaduk as "one of the most cruel, brutal and gross SS-men in Auschwitz." It was dangerous for inmates to encounter him, for they could expect to be beaten, abused, or killed for the pettiest of reasons. When drunk, Kaduk was completely unpredictable and capricious. In numerous cases, he killed inmates by stamping on them with his heavy boots until they were dead.[67] No defendant at the Auschwitz trial appeared to be more "brutish."[68] When Kaduk was interviewed in prison by the German film producer Ebbo Demant, he confirmed that he never had had scruples about abusing or killing inmates, especially Jews, whom he had come to regard as *Untermenschen* (subhumans).[69]

Wilhelm Boger was a member of the Political Department at Auschwitz and was notorious for the brutality with which he conducted the interrogation of inmates. Boger enjoyed spreading fear and terror. His most dreaded instrument of torture was known as the "Boger swing." It consisted of an iron bar to which prisoners were tied with their heads down. They then were beaten until their buttocks were covered with blood. If their answers were unsatisfactory, the beating continued until they lost consciousness.[70] The Auschwitz trial convicted Boger of murder in at least 114 cases and for aiding and abetting the murder of 1,000 more persons. He was given a life term plus five years.[71]

The SS officer Josef Schm.[72] in Lagisha, a subcamp of Auschwitz, was known for taking his pleasure in brutalizing camp inmates, which included forcing them to do "sport." In late 1943, Schm. singled out a Jewish prisoner of about fifty years, who already had reached the condition of a *Muselmann*. When the prisoner, unable to do the "exercises," screamed for mercy, Schm. hit him repeatedly and stamped on him with his heavy boot. Witnesses confirmed that this beating and stamping lasted about twenty minutes, during which Schm. laughed and called his victim a "dirty Jew." When the prisoner finally stopped moving, Schm. ordered water to be poured over him, but this failed to revive the man. Schm. was convicted of murder by a postwar German court.[73] Another sadist who killed with apparent pleasure was Amon Goeth, the commandant of a concentration camp in occupied Poland, who amused himself by target-shooting inmates from his balcony. His murderous deeds were made widely known in the film *Schindler's List*. Goeth was tried by a Polish court in 1946 and hanged on September 13 of that year, not far from the Plaszow camp he had terrorized.[74]

The large majority of the guards abused the inmates because cruelty was the routine of the camps and therefore expected. The guards flogged, tormented, and killed prisoners because they were allowed and expected to do so.[75] Violence and brutality were considered proof of commitment. Being rough with prisoners could further one's career in the camp system, whereas being soft would hurt it and expose the SS man to derision and mockery from his fellow guards. Some guards harassed prisoners because they were bored or because it gave them a feeling of power. Many of the guards had little education, and the ability to have a member of the intellectual or professional class at their mercy provided a ready way to overcome a feeling of inferiority. By brutalizing a prisoner, recalls an inmate, the guard was able to feel strong and important.[76] Or, as a survivor of Auschwitz put it, being a guard in a concentration camp made it possible to experience "one's own dominance and strength, the right to decide life and death, the right to dispense death personally and at random, and the right to abuse one's power over the prisoners."[77]

We know relatively little about the background of these men and women. Wilhelm Schubert took pleasure in wearing a uniform and joined the SA, the Nazi party's paramilitary organization, in 1933 when he was seventeen years old. A bit later, in order to find a job with a secure income, he enrolled in the SS and became a guard in the Sachsenhausen concentration camp. Fellow officers described him as apolitical but ambitious. Medals were more important to him than the fates or lives of inmates. Seeking to impress his colleagues, he would treat prisoners especially cruelly when he knew that he was being observed. The postwar court that sentenced him to life imprisonment called him immature and unpredictable. "Men like Schubert were the most useful servants of the Nazi regime," the verdict noted.[78]

The career of the SS officer Otto Heinrich Kaiser was very similar. Unemployed at age nineteen, he joined the SS in 1936 and became a guard in Sachsenhausen. The court considered him politically immature and certainly not a fanatic

National Socialist. However, in a setting where inmates were treated with cruelty as a matter of course and his superiors told him that the inmates were enemies of the fatherland and therefore deserved no better, Kaiser willingly harassed and bullied prisoners and came to consider himself all-powerful.[79]

The effectiveness of the camp routine in coarsening the guards is especially visible in the case of female guards, who constituted about 10 percent of the concentration camp personnel. Most of them had volunteered for service in the camps in order to benefit from the higher wages and greater job security that came with being a concentration camp guard. This work also looked to be more interesting than the monotonous assembly lines in the armaments factories. The women went through a period of training during which they were taught to regard the camp prisoners as inferior and to treat them harshly. They then became civilian employees of the SS, carrying clubs and whips as well as pistols. In Ravensbrück, a concentration camp for women only, they were also given dogs.[80] Margarete Buber-Neumann, a survivor of Ravensbrück, recalls that it usually took no more than fourteen days for these young women, some from good families, to behave as if they had grown up in a military barracks and to begin to abuse and beat prisoners.[81] Germaine Tillion, another inmate who came to Ravensbrück in 1943 and published her recollections in 1946, concurs with this assessment. She notes that she knew of only one woman who could not adjust to the brutal camp routine and managed to get released from camp duty.[82] The female guards of the Majdanek concentration camp likewise exceeded their assigned responsibilities and duties and willingly abused their charges.[83]

Some of the women overseers became known for their extreme cruelty, among them Maria Mandl, the head of the female guards in Ravensbrück. Survivors relate that Mandl was responsible for the death of hundreds of inmates. In Auschwitz, where she held the same position, she ordered beatings and did some flogging herself.[84] Together with the camp's physicians, Mandl selected weak and sick female prisoners for death in the gas chamber. In 1947, she was sentenced to death by a Polish court.[85] Also serving in Auschwitz was Luise Danz, whose reported specialty was to finish every roll call by killing a few inmates.[86] Irma Grese served in Ravensbrück, Auschwitz, and Bergen-Belsen and became known as the "Beast of Bergen-Belsen." The daughter of an agricultural worker, Grese was only twenty-one when she was tried in 1945 before a British military court for having beaten, tormented, and killed an indeterminate number of inmates. She was hanged on December 12, 1945.[87] Five days before her execution, she declared, "I did my duty for the fatherland."[88]

Many of the Kapos (common criminals recruited from the ranks of the inmates to serve as supervisors of barracks or work details) also mistreated and killed prisoners because it was expected of them. The camp environment invoked their worst instincts, and not a few conducted themselves with more cruelty than the SS guards did. Otto Locke served as a Kapo in Auschwitz. He always carried a heavy club, with which he beat inmates at every opportunity.

The court that tried him in 1957 was able to find proof of seven killings. In none of these cases did the administration of the camp investigate the murders. The corpses were burned, and Locke could continue to reign with impunity as a strong-arm bully.[89] The Buchenwald Kapo Johann Herzog was found guilty of homicide resulting in death or serious damage to health in at least fifty cases. Here too Herzog was able to carry out his reign of terror because harassing and abusing inmates was the norm of the camps.[90]

In a system that rewarded brutality, there were, however, a few guards who defied this norm. When Johann Sosnowski went on trial in 1965 before a German court for his service in the concentration camp Sachsenhausen, former Jewish inmates described him as a "humane SS man." Though a volunteer for the SS and a National Socialist, he seldom used force against prisoners. Sosnowski also refused to participate in the lashing of inmates, arguing that he did not beat his dogs, let alone human beings. The postwar court sentenced Sosnowski to a prison term of one year.[91]

The Auschwitz survivor Shlomo Venezia recalls a Dutch SS man who had volunteered for the SS because he had admired the rigor and efficiency of the Germans. By the time he realized what this efficiency had wrought, it was too late to leave his deadly assignment. Still, he tried to act humanely. When he had to hit someone, he used a cane of bamboo that was split in the middle. The resulting pain was minimal, but the noise of the two tips as they came together made it sound like a whip being loudly cracked.[92]

In the Dachau concentration camp, SS personnel who treated inmates with humanity were known as "white ravens." One of the few individuals to belong to this category was Hans Mursch, who served on the Dachau administrative staff in various positions for twelve years from September 1933 onward. He never insulted or mistreated a prisoner, and he was known to warn inmates when they were scheduled to be called for interrogation by the Political Department of the camp. The prisoner Karl Röder, who survived an eleven-year stay in Dachau, praised Mursch, whom he called "one of us." According to another inmate, Mursch at one time was locked up for several weeks for failing to beat a refractory prisoner.[93]

In a class by himself was the SS medic Wilhelm Flagge, a man around fifty, who served in Babitz (Babice), a subcamp of Auschwitz. Because of Flagge, this small camp, with some 180 women prisoners doing agricultural work in the summer of 1944, became, in the words of the Austrian inmate Dr. Ella Lingens, an "island of peace." Flagge shared his food with the inmates and made sure that the schoolrooms where they were housed were heated. One time Dr. Lingens asked Flagge how a man with his attitude could remain in Auschwitz. He replied with the question, "Would you prefer a brute in my place?" Oddly enough, writes Dr. Lingens, he did not get into trouble. "He acted unobtrusively and never became conspicuous. He was never promoted either. His case exemplifies how much depended on the individual and his actions, and how untrue was the excuse of the others who claimed that they could not help having to do their acts of vileness. They had no courage, Flagge had courage—that is all."[94]

The longtime Auschwitz inmate Hermann Langbein, who served as camp scribe, agrees with this finding. There were several instances of SS men saving the lives of new arrivals who were from their home town. Some SS men, most of them former Social Democrats or Communists, declared that their nerves did not allow them to carry out certain assignments. There were indeed several documented cases of guards suffering a nervous breakdown. One of these, Richard Böck, who had driven disabled selectees from the ramp to the gas chamber, indicated that he could no longer do this job. He was excused and thereafter assigned to transporting food. The SS officer Emanuel Schäfer testified at the Auschwitz trial that there were other cases of men who were transferred to duties with less strain on their nerves and emotions.[95] These men were never promoted, but they were not punished either. Another way of getting away from the dreadful routine of Auschwitz was to volunteer for frontline duty. By transferring to active military service, SS officers lost whatever rank they had attained, but, as one such man testified at the Auschwitz trial, they were glad of no longer having to witness or participate in the horrors of the camp.[96]

Actively helping inmates carried risks. Langbein reports three cases of SS men assisting prisoners in escaping. In several cases, guards were punished for favoring inmates. Arthur Breitweiser, who was in charge of the clothing depot, had to serve a prison term because he had given a female inmate three meters of fabric. Ladislav Gura, an ethnic German from Slovakia, was imprisoned several times and finally sentenced to two years in jail by an SS tribunal in Kattowitz because he had been caught drinking alcohol with some inmates. Ludwig Karl Schmidt, who had facilitated a meeting between a male and female inmate, received a suspended prison sentence with a probationary period at the front. It appears that the number of humane acts increased in 1944 as the fortunes of war turned decisively against Germany. Morale reached a new low as Soviet troops approached Auschwitz. The survivor Heinrich Dürmeyer testified that on Christmas 1944, an SS roll call leader approached him in a drunken state, embraced him, and said, "Hey, if things ever change, you're gonna help me, aren't you? I'm already doing whatever you want."[97]

Most Nazi criminals standing trial after 1945 claimed that they had to carry out their deadly assignments for fear of being killed themselves. The evidence from the history of the concentration camps is one of several sources that prove this claim to be false. When Dr. Lingens testified at the Auschwitz trial, the judge asked her, "Do you wish to say that everyone could decide for himself to be either good or evil in Auschwitz?" and Lingens answered, "That is exactly what I wish to say."[98] There were choices, though the number of those availing themselves of the right choice was, unfortunately, very small.

2

Massacres by Shooting

The factory-like killing in the gas chambers of Auschwitz has created the idea that the Holocaust was an anonymous mass murder. This view needs correction. About 1.8 million Jews were killed in mass executions under the most horrible circumstances, and these shootings were carried out by specific individuals, many of them known to us by name. Germans being orderly people, the officers presiding over these massacres compiled detailed reports about the way in which these shootings proceeded and about the number of Jews eliminated. These reports are preserved. They reveal a machinery of murder that functioned with frightful efficiency. Memoirs and letters of soldiers from the East provide additional particulars. Finally, hundreds of the killers eventually were tried for these crimes, and the record of these legal proceedings gives us a close-up view of the perpetrators of these horrors.

There exists no specific written order from Hitler initiating the Final Solution. Otto Ohlendorf, the head of Einsatzgruppe D, testified about such an order at the Nuremberg trial, and many defendants tried to invoke it in their defense. However, this stratagem collapsed after Bruno Streckenbach, the Waffen-SS officer who was said to have transmitted Hitler's order, unexpectedly returned from Russia in 1955 and denied the existence of this alleged *Führerbefehl* (order of the Führer).[1] After much searching for such an instruction, we can now say with confidence that this kind of order was never issued. This is not to say that Hitler was uninvolved or that this role was not important in the development of the policy of extermination that began with the invasion of the Soviet Union in June 1941 and became more and more radical during the following months. Hitler, concludes the Führer's biographer Ian Kershaw, was the supreme spokesman for an ideological imperative to which his followers gave enthusiastic consent. "Without Hitler's fanatical will to destroy Jewry, which crystallized only by 1941 into a realizable aim to exterminate physically the Jews of Europe, the Holocaust would almost certainly not have come about."[2] The Final Solution represented Hitler's will. Hitler was the supreme architect of the Jewish catastrophe.[3]

As Karl Schleunes has pointed out in an important book entitled *The Twisted Road to Auschwitz*, the path that led eventually to the gates of the extermination camps was not necessarily charted in advance.[4] Nevertheless, Hitler's obsession with solving the Jewish problem was never in doubt. Time and again, Hitler set the tone in hate-filled public speeches in which he declared the Jews to be Germany's eternal enemies, who would have to be confronted and fought to the death. On January 30, 1939, speaking before the *Reichstag*, the German parliament, he declared that if the Jews "in and outside Europe should succeed in plunging the nations once more into a world war, then the result will not be the Bolshevization of the earth, and thus the victory of Jewry, but the annihilation of the Jewish race in Europe!"[5] After such a war had actually broken out, Hitler repeated this "prophecy" on more than a dozen occasions, thus making clear to his followers the deadly destiny he had in mind for the Jews.

Hitler's leading retainers took it from there, converting the Führer's threats into reality. Kershaw has called this process "working toward the *Führer*."[6] It consisted of fulfilling Hitler's known wishes without waiting for specific instructions. With regard to the Jews, it was Himmler and Reinhard Heydrich, the heads of the German police and SS, who eagerly turned the will of the Führer into concrete directives. "If one wants to know what Hitler was thinking," the historian Christopher Browning has suggested, "one should look at what Himmler was doing."[7] At a lecture in Koblenz on March 13, 1940, Himmler declared, "I do nothing which the Führer does not know."[8] On another occasion, he stated that the measures against the Jews in Poland were based on Hitler's orders, but that "the person of the Führer may under no circumstances be linked to these actions."[9] Himmler repeatedly affirmed that in organizing the extermination of the Jews he was acting on Hitler's authority. "The Führer has placed the implementation of this very difficult order on my shoulders," he wrote in a memo of July 28, 1942, to Gottlob Berger, the head of the *Reichssicherheitshauptamt* (RSHA—the head office of the security services).[10] Eichmann has maintained that he heard from Heydrich that Hitler had ordered the physical destruction of the Jews.[11]

Lower-ranking SS leaders, in turn, considered the orders coming from Himmler, involving an increasingly more radical approach to the Jewish Question, as fulfilling the wish of the Führer. And they were correct. The argument offered by many of these men at their postwar trials—that they had followed the orders of their superiors—was not only a plea designed to minimize their own culpability. There is no doubt, concludes Kershaw, that "Hitler's authority—most probably given as verbal consent to propositions usually put to him by Himmler—stood behind every decision of magnitude and significance."[12]

This does not mean that the officers directing the killing of the Jews in the field did not have considerable freedom of action. They were not just obeying orders. In their eyes, the Jews were the arch-enemy who had to be fought with firmness and persistence. Most of these men were dedicated Nazis who implemented the orders concerning the murder of the Jews with dedication, not to say enthusiasm, often on their own initiative applying them with extreme cruelty. Many of these orders were vague enough to allow Himmler's underlings to push the anti-Jewish measures in an increasingly more radical direction, culminating eventually in the murder of every Jewish man, woman, and child they could find.

The orders concerning Operation Barbarossa (the code name for the invasion of the Soviet Union on June 22, 1941), issued to the armed forces on March 3, 1941, spoke of the need to annihilate the "Jewish-Bolshevist intelligentsia," but provided no explanation of who was to be included in this category.[13] Prior to the invasion, the commanders of the *Einsatzgruppen*, special task forces that became mobile killing units, were convened for a series of orientation meetings at which they listened to exhortations by Heydrich defining their forthcoming mission. According to the recollections of several participants, they were told that Hitler had ordered the liquidation of Jews and Communist functionaries who endangered the security of the troops.[14]

There exists no written copy of these orders, but we do have a letter Heydrich sent on July 2, 1941, to the Higher SS and police leaders in the Eastern territories, recapitulating the oral instructions. This letter shows that Heydrich's orders too were less than precise, commanding the execution of "Jews in party and state positions" and "other radical elements."[15] Heydrich also counseled the promotion of pogroms by local elements, while taking care not to reveal the instigators. None of this constituted an order to kill all male Jews, a practice followed by both the Einsatzgruppen and the police units supporting them soon after the beginning of the war in the East. In short, the fate of the Jews that developed in the wake of the German invasion was not only the result of orders from above but also the consequence of more and more violent actions initiated at lower echelons of command. These initiatives were taken in the secure knowledge, communicated orally, that a radical solution of the Jewish Question had been decided.[16]

The Einsatzgruppen made their first appearance during the annexation of Austria and Czechoslovakia in 1938 and 1939. They took on a more extensive and sinister role during the Polish campaign of 1939, when they were assigned the task of eliminating real or imagined enemies of the Reich. It is estimated that in the part of Poland annexed to Germany through the end of 1939, more than sixty thousand civilians were killed, including an unknown number of Jews.[17] After a Waffen-SS unit had executed fifty Jewish civilians on September 18, some Wehrmacht officers recommended that the Waffen-SS men involved be court-martialed. General Walter von Reichenau, commander of the 10th Army, thereupon telephoned Hitler and was told that the matter fell within the jurisdiction of Himmler. And that was the end of the matter. On October 4, 1939, on occasion of the victorious conclusion of the Polish campaign, Hitler issued a "decree of clemency" for all "acts committed between September 1 and October 4 out of bitterness over the atrocities committed by the Poles."[18]

By May 1941, and in preparation for the invasion of the Soviet Union, Heydrich had organized four Einsatzgruppen (EG), designated A, B, C, and D. Each mobile unit was between five hundred and nine hundred men strong and was divided into several *Einsatzkommandos* (EK—task detachments) and *Sonderkommandos* (SK—special task detachments) for a total strength of three thousand men. These special task forces were considered part of the SS and carried its uniform and insignia. Each EG was assigned to an army group and was formally under the command of the army. But in practice the units operated autonomously under the direction of the RSHA, the main office of the security police headed by Heydrich. Many of the officers commanding these units came from the RSHA. Other officers were taken from the SS, the SD (Himmler's intelligence service), the Gestapo, the Waffen-SS, and the criminal police. Almost all of them were early members of the movement and committed Nazis. Not a few had been involved in the violence that characterized the political life of the 1920s. Forty-three percent are said to have been university graduates.[19] Many had advanced degrees in law, philosophy, and economics, and there was at least one former minister.[20] The lower ranks of the Einsatzgruppen were recruited from the same organizations, though their ideological commitment was more diverse. Of 990 members of EG A, 340 had been members of the Waffen-SS.[21] None of them were hoodlums or common criminals.

The task of these units was to provide security behind the advancing German armies, their most important mission being to kill Jews, political commissars, and other Communist functionaries, as well as wandering Gypsies.[22] A planning document spoke of the need to seize "unreliable elements (partisans, saboteurs, Jews, leading communists)."[23] The Einsatzgruppen were assisted by German police battalions, by units of the Wehrmacht (Germany's armed forces), the Waffen-SS, as well as by local militias. By the end of the year 1941, the Einsatzgruppen had managed to murder more than one-half million Soviet Jews,[24] and that was more than the number of Soviet soldiers killed in combat.[25] At the time of the Wannsee conference of January 20, 1942, convened to organize the Final Solution of the Jewish Question for all of Europe, some 900,000 Jews had already lost their lives in the East.[26] Reliable estimates put the total number of Jews killed by the Einsatzgruppen in the Soviet Union at 1.5 million.[27]

The mass killing began with some trial and error. The use of machine guns to mow down large numbers of Jews proved unsatisfactory because too many victims did not die immediately. Large numbers of badly wounded had to be given the *coup de grâce* one by one, which proved a traumatic experience for the killers. Hence in some instances, officers, whose job it was to finish off the merely wounded, would instead use grenades.[28] Eventually the practice evolved of lining the Jews up standing or kneeling next to a ditch, with their backs to their executioners, and using individual shooters. Soon this routine was further "improved" by making the victims enter the pit and lie down before being shot. This way of killing became known as "sardine packing," because by having the Jews lie next to and on top of each other, the pit became neatly packed like a can of sardines. "*Sardinenpackung*" apparently was invented by Friedrich Jeckeln, one of four higher SS and police leaders in Russia, who coordinated the activities of the Einsatzgruppen in their area of responsibility.[29] They have been called "pacesetters of the annihilation process."[30] Jeckeln became known as a particularly brutal and ruthless individual, but was repeatedly praised by Himmler for his dedication. Sentenced to death by a Riga court at the end of the war, Jeckeln was hanged on February 3, 1946, before some four thousand spectators, who had come to witness this act of retribution.[31]

At first, the massacres targeted only male Jews, whose murder was justified on the grounds that they were Communist functionaries or putative partisans, saboteurs, or just members of the "Judeo-Bolshevik system" threatening German rule. However, very soon reports began to mention also the shooting of Jewish women and children. The transition to such total annihilation took place in different units at different times, with Himmler acting as a catalyst.[32] In his eyes, the killing of children was necessary in order to prevent them from seeking revenge for the murder of their parents once they had reached adulthood.[33] An accounting submitted by EK 3 of EG A noted that at Rokiskis (in Lithuania) on August 15 and 16, 1941, some 3,200 women and children had been killed. From here on, statistics of murdered women and children became a regular feature of the reports, and their number often exceeded that of killed adult males because the men had already been murdered in earlier actions. Between August 18 and 22, the same EK 3 shot 466 Jewish men, 440 Jewish women, and 1,020 Jewish children; between August 29 and 31, the toll was 582 Jewish men, 1,731 Jewish women, and 1,469 Jewish children. A similar ratio prevailed at Kaunas. Here EK 3 on October 29 reported the killing of 2,007 Jewish men, 2,920 women, and 4,273 children.[34] Of 131,850 Jews murdered by EK 3 between July 4 and November 29, 67 percent were women and children.[35]

The extent to which the killing of women and children had become routine can be seen in the statement made by a member of EK 6 at a postwar trial. Walter Helfsgott testified that he had taken care that the executions be carried out humanely and without cruelty. When he was asked what that had meant, he replied, "When encountering a Jewish woman with an infant on her arm, we shot the woman first and then the infant."[36] It appears that the killer saw nothing wrong in the murder of Jewish women as long as they were spared witnessing the death of their children.

The inclusion of women and children in the program of annihilation stemmed from orders issued by Himmler and Heydrich, though the precise form of these orders is not known. The commanders of the killing units understood them to represent the intentions of their superiors, and they acted accordingly. The practical decisions, when and where to do it, on what scale, and whether to leave some working Jews and their families alive, was left to local SS commanders, in cooperation and coordination with the military and civilian administrations.[37] The commander of EG A, SS officer Walther Stahlecker, expressed regret that the German civilian administration and the Wehrmacht, who needed Jewish artisans for urgent work, prevented him from killing all the Jews.[38] Stahlecker, who had made EG A the most murderous of the four killing units, was later killed in a clash with Soviet partisans.

Some of the killings were described as "cleansing the ghetto of superfluous Jews," and this phrase explains why by September 1941 the majority of murdered Jews in Lithuania were old men, women, and children. Most of the younger men had already been killed during the preceding weeks. The inmates of the ghetto were classified according to their ability to do heavy labor, and during a time of increasing scarcity of food, Jewish women and children were considered useless eaters. Himmler also was in charge of planning the settlement of Germans in the newly conquered eastern territories. Hence, beyond satisfying his ideological predispositions, the annihilation of the Jews also served the purpose of making room for German settlers.[39]

A report from Vilnius, Lithuania, dated July 13, 1941, noted that about "500 Jews and other saboteurs" were being liquidated daily. "The work of all units has developed satisfactorily. Above all, the liquidations, which now take place on a large scale, are operating smoothly."[40] A description of these "liquidations," carried out by EK 8 (EG A), was compiled by a postwar German court:

> Villages or the Jewish quarters of towns would be surrounded. Sick persons unable to walk would be shot right in their homes. The others would be taken to a central collection point, and from there the victims were marched or driven to the place of execution, usually an abandoned tank ditch or a freshly dug pit. Here they had to surrender all items of value and strip to their underwear. Sitting half-naked on the ground, often in extremely cold weather, they would hear the shots that took the lives of their neighbors. When their turn came, they were forced to walk into the pit and lie face down on top of the freshly killed victims. Those who moved too slowly were hit with rifle butts or whips. At first each layer of dead bodies would be covered by a thin coating of earth, but this practice was soon abandoned as being too time consuming. The effect of the victims having to step and lie on the still warm and bloody corpses of their relatives or neighbors, the court noted, must have been singularly horrifying. Shooters then killed the Jews with a bullet to the head, and the mass grave was covered with earth.[41]

The officers in charge of the Einsatzgruppen knew that the almost daily practice of killing could take a heavy psychological toll on their men, and they therefore adopted various stratagems to limit the damage. The burden of murder was shared among as many individuals as possible so as to alleviate it for each one. Some officers used the model of a military firing squad shooting from a distance, which helped minimize individual responsibility.[42] The executions were carried out in shifts, and the men took turns doing the actual shooting and loading the magazines. In one unit, it was decided that two men would share the shooting, with one gunman aiming at the victim's head and the other at the chest. This practice ran counter to the need for "productivity" in carrying out the massacres, but it had the advantage of diluting the responsibility for the killing.[43]

Occasionally, and especially before large-scale massacres, commanders gave speeches justifying the killing. But that was often insufficient encouragement. Given the gruesome and bloody nature of the task of whole-scale murder, especially the killing of women and children, the practice evolved of giving the shooters large quantities of alcohol. Once intoxicated, the executioners behaved with even more cruelty than usual, often denying the death shot to the gravely wounded.[44] The offer of free alcohol did indeed help quiet the nerves of the executioners, but it also meant that the shooting became inexact. There are reports of Jews who had merely been wounded managing to work their way out of the pits. If caught, the unlucky escapees would be shot on the spot or taken back for another round at the ditch. The number of those badly hurt, unable to get out from underneath the dead victims, and therefore buried alive, will never be known. Postwar court testimony about the deeds of a different EK reported that wounded victims pleaded from the pit, "Please shoot to kill!" or "Put an end to it!"[45] At times, Jewish men were forced to dig their own grave. In one such case, while working at this task, they were taunted with warnings such as, "Hurry up Isidor! Soon you will be with your god."[46]

A report of a mass shooting comes from a German engineer, Hermann Graebe, who on October 5, 1942, witnessed such a slaughter near Dubno, the site of an old Jewish community in Ukraine. This report was introduced as evidence at the Nuremberg trial of the major war criminals in 1945. One of Graebe's assistants had told him of the shooting of several hundred Jews in three large pits:

> Moennikes and I went straight to the pits. Nobody prevented us. I heard a quick succession of shots from behind one of the mounds of earth. The people who had got off the lorries—men, women and children of all ages—had to undress upon the orders of an SS man, who carried a riding or a dog whip. They had to put their clothes on separate piles of shoes, top clothing and underclothing. I saw the heap of shoes that must have contained eight hundred pairs, great piles of clothes and undergarments. Without screaming or weeping these people

undressed, stood in family groups, kissed each other, said their farewells, and waited for a sign from another SS man who stood near the pit, also with a whip in his hand.

During the fifteen minutes that I stood near the pit, I did not hear anyone complaining or beg for mercy. I watched a family of about eight, a man and a woman, both about fifty, with their children, aged about one, eight, and ten and two grown-up daughters of about twenty to twenty-four. An old woman with snow-white hair was holding the one-year-old child in her arms, singing something to it and tickling it. The child was crowing with delight. The man and wife were looking on with tears in their eyes. The father was holding the hand of a boy about ten, speaking to him softly. The boy was fighting back his tears. The father pointed to the sky, stroked the boy's head and seemed to explain something to him.

At that moment, the SS man at the pit shouted something to his comrade, who separated off about twenty persons and ordered them to go behind the mound of earth. Among them was the family I have mentioned. I still clearly remember a dark-haired, slim girl who pointed to herself as she passed close to me and said, "Twenty-three." I walked to the other side of the mound and found myself standing before an enormous grave. The people lay so closely packed, one on top of the other, that only their heads were visible. Nearly all had blood running over their shoulders from their heads. Some of them were still moving. Some lifted an arm and turned a head to show they were still alive. The pit was already two-thirds full. I estimated that it already contained about one thousand people. I looked around for the man who had shot them. He was an SS man who was sitting on the edge of the narrow end of the pit, his legs dangling into it. He had a submachine gun across his knees and was smoking a cigarette. The people, completely naked, went down some steps which had been cut in the clay wall of the pit and climbed over the heads of those already lying there, to the place indicated by the SS man. They laid down in front of the dead or injured people. Some of them caressed those who were still alive and spoke to them softly. Then I heard a series of shots. I looked into the pit and saw that the bodies were still twitching or that their heads lay motionless on top of the bodies which lay before them. Blood was pouring from their necks.[47]

The single largest massacre of the Holocaust took place in Kiev, where SK 4 (EG C), supplemented by a Waffen-SS company, and two police regiments murdered 33,771 Jews in two days in the ravine Babi Yar. After a bomb attack in the center of Kiev, Jeckeln ordered all the Jews of the city to assemble the following day at a central location. It appears that most of the more than 30,000 who showed up on September 29, 1941, thought that they would be relocated. Fritz Höfer, a truck driver in SK 4, attested to the mass shooting that ensued:

One day I was instructed to drive my truck outside of town. I was accompanied by a Ukrainian. It must have been about 10 o'clock. On the way there we overtook Jews carrying luggage marching on foot in the same direction that we were travelling. There were whole families. The further we got out of town the denser the columns became. Piles of clothing lay in a large open field. These piles of clothing were my destination. The Ukrainian showed me how to get there.

After we had stopped in the area near the piles of clothes the truck was immediately loaded up with clothing. This was carried out by Ukrainians. I watched what happened when the Jews—men, women and children—arrived. The Ukrainians led them past a number of different places where one after the other they had to remove their luggage, then their coats, shoes and overgarments and also underwear. They also had to leave their valuables in a designated place. There was a pile for each article of clothing. It all happened very quickly, and anyone who hesitated was kicked or pushed by the Ukrainians to keep them moving. I don't think it was even a minute from the time each Jew took off his coat before he was standing completely naked. No distinction was made between men, women and children. One would have thought that the Jews that came later would have had a chance to turn back when they say the others in front of them having to undress. I still surprises me that this did not happen.

Once undressed, the Jews were led into a ravine which was about 150 meters long, 30 meters wide and a good 15 meters deep. Two or three narrow entrances led to this ravine through which the Jews were channeled. When they reached the bottom of the ravine they were seized by members of the *Schutzpolizei* (police) and made to lie down on top of Jews who had already been shot. This all happened very quickly. The corpses were literally in layers. A police marksman came along and shot each Jew in the neck with a submachine gun at the spot where he was lying. . . . There were only two marksmen carrying out the executions. One of them was working at one end of the ravine, the other on the other end. I saw these marksmen stand on top of the layers of corpses and shoot one after the other. . . . In addition to the two marksmen there was a "packer" at either entrance to the ravine. These "packers" were Schutzpolizisten, whose job it was to lay the victims on top of the other corpses so that all the marksman had to do as he passed was fire a shot. . . . A biting wind was blowing; it was very cold. The shots from the ravine could not be heard at the undressing area. This is why I think the Jews did not realize in time what lay ahead of them.[48]

Another member of SK 4a recalled "the complete terror of the Jews when they first caught sight of the bodies as they reached the top edge of the ravine. Many Jews cried out in panic. It's almost impossible to imagine what nerves of steel it took to carry out that dirty work down there. It was horrible."[49] The reaction of this man, who felt sorry for himself rather than for the victims of the massacre, was common. The German court that tried ten perpetrators of this crime in 1968 noted that many of the victims were merely wounded and some of them managed to work their way out from the layers of corpses. Those who were too badly hurt and could not get out were buried alive when a pioneer unit of the Wehrmacht detonated the banks of the ravine in order to hide the massacre.[50] When it was all over, Higher SS and Police Leader Friedrich Jeckeln organized a celebratory banquet during which alcohol flowed freely.[51]

The use of Ukrainians at Babi Yar was not unusual. The Germans recruited auxiliaries, so-called *Hiwis* (a German abbreviation of *Hilfswillige*, or voluntary assistant) as well as local militias, whom they assigned to conveying Jews to their place of execution, forcing them to undress, and similar duties. At times, in order to spare the German killers psychological stress, they also utilized local collaborators for shootings. In one case, an officer considered a group of eighteen- to twenty-year-old Waffen-SS men too young to carry out an execution of Jewish children. Many of the EK men, who were also expected to participate in this shooting, were married and themselves had children. Hence it was decided to utilize members of a Ukrainian militia.[52] This practice is said to have been quite common.[53]

The recruitment of local forces involved various ethnic groups, but the largest contingent were Ukrainians. By the end of 1942, the German authorities in Ukraine employed 238,000 local police.[54] Many of them belonged to the Ukrainian Nationalists (OUN) and shared the Germans' fervor against "Jewish Bolshevism." Jews had constituted the largest single ethnic group in the NKVD, the hated Soviet secret police. During the hasty retreat, it had proved impossible to evacuate the prisons, and the NKVD had executed some ten thousand captives, most of them political prisoners. The Jews were blamed for these murders, and in revenge the Ukrainians killed thousands of Jews in pogrom-like massacres. The locals also proved valuable in leading the German killers to Jewish households. According to one estimate, some thirty thousand to forty thousand Ukrainians participated in one way or another in the Nazi murder of the Jews, though reasons other than anti-Semitism, notably personal greed, careerism, and peer pressure, also figured in this collaboration. The Ukrainians soon developed a reputation for cruelty, a matter that continues to burden Jewish-Ukrainian relations to this day.[55]

Local elements were also recruited in the Baltic states. Three companies of Latvians served with Reserve Police Battalion 11 in Minsk.[56] A militia, formed in July 1941 and commanded by Viktor Bernhard Arajs, stood out for its eagerness to help the Germans. The German postwar court that sentenced Arajs to life imprisonment found that he had been an ardent hater of Jews, and in fact the "Kommando Arajs" played a key role in the murder of thirteen thousand Riga Jews. In other locations, the Arajs men and Germans took turns shooting Jews.[57] In Lithuania, the majority of the killings were carried out by Lithuanians.[58] On July 2, 1941, after EG A had reached Kaunas, the second-largest city in Lithuania, EK 3 formed a mobile unit (*Rollkommando*) in order to comb the Lithuanian prisons and kill "dangerous Jews and Bolsheviks" generally.[59] It was composed of eight to ten Germans and several dozen Lithuanian volunteers who did the actual shooting. The *Rollkommando* was commanded by the SS officer Joachim Hamann. A report composed in January 1942 noted that this unit had killed 139,346 persons. "The rural areas of Lithuania are free of Jews [*judenfrei*]."[60]

In most cases, before being shot, the victims had to take off their clothing and be completely naked, the last and ultimate dishonor and degradation inflicted upon the hapless sufferers. Females more often than males had to undress before their killers, who found time to take pictures of the naked women. Their clothing was shipped to Germany to be distributed to needy Germans. Human beings generally do not congregate naked. To deprive humans of their clothing is to make them like animals. After the war, some killers on trial indeed testified that these nude animal-like bodies were easier to kill.[61] Alcohol was dispensed liberally. In the evening, returning drunk to their quarters, the killers bragged about the number of Jews they had murdered.[62]

The relatively small Jewish population of Estonia was killed by local police units, with the primary pretext here being anti-Communism. As in Ukraine, the Jews were said to have been a mainstay of Soviet rule and were held responsible for the crimes committed by the Soviet occupiers. They were considered ideological enemies, but this enmity was so strong that even elderly women and children were caught up in the destruction. By aggressively pursuing their Jews, Estonian nationalists sought to ingratiate themselves to the Germans. One scholar of the subject speaks of "murder in the name of nationalism" or "murder without hatred."[63]

The Einsatzgruppen continued their homicidal activities when they became part of the German occupation forces and were converted from mobile units to stationary outposts. During the years 1942 and 1943, these posts undertook the liquidation of Jewish ghettos by shooting. Acting as a "master race" on occupied territory further corrupted attitudes and behavior, and each step in degrading and mistreating victims made the next step easier.[64] In a trial that lasted nine months, the German court that judged eight members of the outpost Tarnopol in Western Ukraine noted the "dreadful nature" of these actions, which was apparent from the testimony of witnesses:

> Before the victims made their last steps toward the pit, they had to take off all of their clothing. . . . They then had to stand, face toward the grave, before "their" executioners. Following a command, the marksmen shot at their assigned targets from close proximity into the back of the head, and a quick kick pushed the body into the pit. At times families were allowed to undertake this last walk together. Children had to walk like adults. Infants were carried by their mothers. The first shot was aimed at the mother. As soon as she fell, the shooter fired at the child. Since many shots did not result in the death of the victims, one could see twitching limbs amidst the corpses and hear groaning. Here and there such wounded would receive a coup de grâce. Otherwise these unfortunates suffocated under the bodies of the victims who followed them or later when the pits received their superficial covering. The permanent leveling of the mass graves had to wait until the ground had ceased rising. Bodies swelling from the gases of putrefaction raised the ground for several days.[65]

From the onset of the war in the East, the numerically small mobile killing units were supplemented by battalions of police. A total of some twelve thousand police, organized in twenty-four battalions, participated in the invasion of the Soviet Union and in the implementation of the Final Solution.[66] Alone or in cooperation with the Einsatzgruppen, they helped search for Jews, guarded Jews about to be killed, and participated in the actual killing. One estimate puts the number of Jews murdered by police units at one-half million.[67]

The merger of the police and SS into an organic whole was one of Himmler's early aims. By 1941, about 30 percent of policemen holding the rank of officer belonged to the black elite; among the rank and file, the percentage was about 16 percent. The police battalions were composed of policemen from the Order Police (the uniformed police force), young recruits, and police reservists conscripted for active service. Some men were volunteers. Between one-quarter and one-third were members of the Nazi party.[68] In addition to military training, they also had received intensive ideological indoctrination on how to treat the "Jewish-Bolshevik enemy." The "Jewish question" was an essential part of this instruction, in which the Jews were portrayed as parasites, defilers of the German race, and the most dangerous enemy of the German people.[69] Few other groups among the German population managed the transformation from upstanding citizen to mass murderer as quickly as the members of the police who constituted the police battalions.[70]

The best-known example of this smooth transition is Reserve Police Battalion 101, the subject of Christopher Browning's pioneering 1992 study. Within a few short weeks, most members of this unit, about two-thirds of whom Browning called "ordinary men" with a working-class background, became efficient killers of Jewish men, women, and children. The members of this unit were not necessarily avowed anti-Semites, but they simply considered the Jews outside of their circle of human obligation and responsibility. They represented the "enemy," and this helped the men become accustomed to mass murder. The most astonishing rationalization, Browning relates, was that of a thirty-five-year-old metalworker from Bremerhaven, who during the postwar interrogation explained how he had come to terms with killing children:

> It so happened that the mothers led the children by the hand. My neighbor shot the mother and I shot the child that belonged to her, because I reasoned with myself that after all without its mother the child could not live any longer. It was supposed to be, so to speak, soothing to my conscience to release children unable to live without their mothers.[71]

Yet the deeds of Reserve Police Battalion 101, dreadful as they were, were not the most horrific crime committed by the police battalions. Probably the most cold-blooded massacre of Jews by a police unit took place on June 27, 1941, in Bialystok in German-occupied Poland, carried out by Police Battalion 309. The battalion was a part of Security Division 221, which prior to the invasion of the Soviet Union had been instructed on how to deal with the armed foe as well as with the civilian population. The troops of the Red Army, they were told, were not just military but also political enemies: "In accordance with Jewish-Bolshevik teachings, they will use not only military weapons. Our forces have to take this into account, and, if necessary, take appropriate drastic and ruthless measures against the hostile civilian population."[72] These instructions fell on fertile soil. Many of the officers and noncommissioned officers of this unit, a German postwar court found, were fanatic National Socialists, and most of the rank and file, too, shared the hatred of Jews. The singing of anti-Semitic songs in the mess hall was a common practice.[73] Inasmuch as this atrocity took place on the sixth day of the campaign in the East, it cannot be explained by the brutalizing effect of war, but clearly was linked to strong anti-Jewish sentiments.

The following description of the episode is based on the verdict of the German court that tried two members of Police Battalion 309 for murder in 1973. The action was initiated by Lieutenant Heinrich Schneider, nicknamed "Pipo," who had developed a reputation for killing Jews indiscriminately. It was said that he "saw red" when someone merely mentioned the subject of Jews. In the course of the afternoon of June 27, members of the police unit, aided by local inhabitants, searched for Jews of military age and drove them to the main synagogue of the city. After several hundred Jews—estimates vary between five hundred and eight hundred—mostly men but also some women and children, had been forced into the synagogue, members of the battalion carried canisters of gasoline into the building and barred the doors. A heavy machine gun was set up outside and trained on the main portal of the synagogue. The policemen then threw hand grenades through a window, which set the synagogue on fire.

The locked-in Jews, who sensed what was afoot, began to sing a chorale-like song, but after the explosion of the hand grenades and the resulting fire, the song was overshadowed by a huge scream. Meanwhile, some strong Jewish men had managed to break open the main entrance, but when they emerged from the synagogue, many of them with burning clothing, they were mowed down by machine gun fire. Some Jewish women appeared at the windows, holding up children and shouting that the Germans should at least spare the children, but the soldiers shot both the women and children. In order not to be burned alive, some Jews climbed through the windows and intentionally exposed themselves to gunfire. One man hanged himself on a protruding column. The fire eventually spread from the synagogue to the Jewish quarter, and some one thousand additional people lost their lives in the ensuing blaze.[74] The commanders of the police battalion and the security division stood by and did not interfere. The official log of the division recorded that the synagogue had been set ablaze by gunfire after German soldiers had come under fire from partisans holed up inside.[75]

Gross atrocities like the events of June 27, 1941, in Bialystok were not the norm, but the near-daily practice of mass executions did not lag far behind in brutality. Women who refused to disrobe were set upon by dogs.[76] The German court that tried six members of Police Battalion 306 documented gruesome scenes that occurred during the liquidation of the ghetto of Stolin, a small town in Ukraine. One witness, who had accompanied a group of Jews to the pit where the Jews were being shot, recalled that a child buried under corpses began to scream. The shooters thereupon fired into the pit until the screaming stopped. An infant seen kicking under its dead mother was pulled out, thrown into the air, and blown apart by a volley from a submachine gun. The events at Stolin, beginning with the rounding up of the defenseless inmates of the ghetto and ending with their death in the pit, were described by witnesses as "repulsive, harrowing, and hideous."[77]

Another such massacre took place on October 12, 1941, in Stanislawow, Galicia, and has entered the history books as "Bloody Sunday." On that day, Police Battalion 133, reinforced by Ukrainian militia and a local police unit, shot at least ten thousand Jews. The Jews of the town were taken to the Jewish cemetery, where the Ukrainians had dug large graves and where they were shot in groups of 200 to 250. The German court, which sentenced the officer in charge of this operation, Hans Krüger, to life imprisonment, described how men and women had been driven to the place of execution in trucks like cattle to the slaughter:

> Here not only the men but also the women had to undress completely before their executioners and their helpers, thus causing them the most profound dishonor and degradation in the face of death. While the first groups were led to the pit and had to look into their own grave, the other waiting victims either had to witness the horrid scene or were forced to listen to the sound of shots as well as to the wailing and cries of woe of their fellow-sufferers. When a little later they approached the pit, they saw the bloody corpses and deformed and distorted bodies of their colleagues, acquaintances, and friends. Their horror lasted until they too were hit by numerous bullets.[78]

The shooting began at noon and lasted until darkness. One survivor described Krüger as running back and forth, exhorting his men with the words "Quicker! Quicker!"[79] At nightfall, the zealous SS officer tried to continue the execution under the headlights of trucks but finally had to stop the killing.[80]

Officers regularly provided explanations as to why the killings were necessary, but the daily routine of murder was nonetheless difficult for the police men. An order dated July 11, 1941, instructed the commanding officers of Police Battalion 307 to arrange for social evenings "so as to obliterate the impressions of the day."[81] The shooters also received special allocations of schnapps. A day after the massacre at Babi Yar, shaken members of the police battalion who had assisted in the atrocity entered a local liquor store and availed themselves of its contents until they had become completely drunk.[82] The Hiwis too usually drank heavily, and much of their conduct was so brutish that even their German fellow-killers reacted with disgust. For example, several witnesses described a mass killing of children at which the Ukrainians, already drunk before the action, tossed infants into the air and fired at them like clay pigeons.[83]

The winter of 1941–42 saw a hiatus in mass executions. The ground was frozen hard, and it proved difficult, if not impossible, to dig pits for the shootings. By the spring of 1942, many of the mobile police units had been converted into stationary posts, and they were reinforced by members of the *Gendarmerie* (policemen from rural communities in Germany) and locally recruited police. These posts assisted in the "evacuation" of Jews from the ghettos to the extermination camps and engaged in *Judenjagd*, the hunting down of Jews who had gone into hiding. The gendarmes often carried out this pursuit with great cruelty. A German engineer who had served in Ukraine described how a gendarme officer seized a small child from the arms of its mother, spun it around a few times, and then smashed the child's head against the doorpost. The officer then told his comrades, "That is the best method; one just has to learn it."[84] Based on a careful study of the files of the police in German-occupied Poland (the so-called *Generalgouvernement*), one scholar estimates that the number of Jews who fell victim to this *Judenjagd* in Poland alone was close to two hundred thousand.[85]

It has been noted that the hunting down of Jews, even more than the mass executions, in many cases would have allowed at least some men in these posts to refrain from killing.[86] But, as in the case of the Einsatzgruppen, the number who availed themselves of this option was small. The overall record of the police battalions and the stationary gendarmerie in no way differs from that of the Einsatzgruppen.[87]

The notion of the "clean Wehrmacht" was laid to rest by historical scholarship early on, but it dominated the thinking of the German public until the 1990s, when the touring exhibition "War of Extermination: Wehrmacht und Verbrechen 1941 to 1944" sparked an extensive and often-acrimonious discussion about the complicity of the armed forces in Nazi crimes. Documentary evidence now demonstrated the close cooperation between army units, the various mobile killing units, and the civilian administration in the implementation of anti-Jewish measures. This cooperation was based on a common mentality, a cluster of ideas made up of radical nationalism, anti-Semitism, anti-Bolshevism, and loyalty to Hitler. The Wehrmacht did not initiate the annihilation of the Jews, but neither did the armed forces oppose it. Indeed, without the active support of the Wehrmacht, concludes the most careful study of this issue by the German historian Johannes Hürter, the mass murder of the Jews in the East could not have proceeded so quickly and efficiently.[88]

As early as the fall of 1935, the army had prepared leaflets to be used in case of an armed conflict with the Soviet Union. These instruments of psychological warfare told soldiers of the Red Army that they were fighting not for Russia but for "the commissars and party functionaries, most of them filthy Jews." These were the real beneficiaries of the war. The country was "governed by Jews and former criminals." The leaflets encouraged Soviet soldiers to turn their bayonets against the cursed Jewish commissars and to beat them to death.[89] Similarly, an essay entitled "The Jew in German History," published in 1939 for instruction of the Wehrmacht in the National Socialist worldview, stated that world Jewry constituted a "poisonous bacillus" that had to be fought like "the plague of the nations."[90]

By the time war broke out, and increasingly thereafter, the armed forces were in a grip of a broad anti-Jewish posture.[91] Most of the soldiers were recently conscripted young men who had spent their formative years in an increasingly Nazified school system and in the militarized atmosphere of the Hitler Youth and *Arbeitsdienst* (compulsory Labor Service), which exposed them to relentless indoctrination.[92] The Wehrmacht too increasingly had taken on ideological indoctrination. Officers were expected to be proficient in National Socialist ideas, and they were assisted by National Socialist Guidance Officers (NSFO) organized in 1943.[93] Matters of race and the Jewish question stood in the center of this teaching.[94] The struggle against world Jewry, a publication of the Wehrmacht declared in 1939, was a struggle for the purity and health of the German people. The Jews were described not only as the enemy of Germany but as "a plague for all nations."[95] The army's information bulletin for the troops (*Mitteilungen für die Truppe*) declared in 1941 that the Jewish political commissars of the Red Army constituted a demonic element. It would offend animals, the article declared, to describe the appearance of these men as "beastly" (*tierisch*). In October 1942, an instruction reminded the officer corps that it must adopt a "clear and unambiguous attitude in the Jewish question" and support the "present struggle against the Jewish-Bolshevik enemy."[96] The destruction of the Jews was portrayed as the necessary precondition of achieving peace and order in the world. This teaching may not have turned all of the Wehrmacht into fanatical anti-Semites, but it created a readiness for the mass killings in which they became enmeshed. There were some exceptions to this finding, but for the most part, the record of the Wehrmacht is far from clean. The number of members of the Wehrmacht who took part in the murder of the Jews—hunting down, selecting, guarding, conveying, and actually killing Jews—is estimated in the tens of thousands.[97]

Hitler set the tone for the war of annihilation in several orders issued to the troops prior to the launch of Operation Barbarossa. A *Führererlass* (Führer decree) of March 3, 1941, spoke of the coming war as not only a clash of arms but also as a battle of ideologies. To win this war it was necessary to "eliminate the Jewish-Bolshevik intelligentsia."[98] A second decree, issued on April 6, declared that the war against Bolshevism "demands ruthless and aggressive action against Bolshevik agitators, snipers, saboteurs, and Jews and tireless elimination of any active or passive resistance."[99] Jews thus were included among those who could be shot on sight and without trial. Still another decree of May 13 laid down the rule that offenses against enemy civilians were no longer to come under the jurisdiction of the military courts. Such crimes were to be prosecuted only "if necessary for the maintenance of discipline or the security of the troops."[100] German soldiers thus were given virtually complete freedom with regard to the treatment of the civilian population. A directive of June 6, known as the *Kommissarbefehl*, provided that the political commissars who accompanied the Red Army were to be shot by the troops capturing them or be turned over for execution to the Einsatzgruppen.[101] High-ranking Wehrmacht officers at first expressed their dismay at the suspension of the law of war, which they feared would undermine discipline, but eventually they made their peace with it and fell into line.[102]

A personal message from Hitler to the armed forces on the eve of the invasion once again accused "the Jewish-Bolshevik rulers in Moscow" of having sought domination over the people of Europe.[103] Portraying the struggle against Jewish Bolshevism as a defensive measure conveniently shifted the responsibility for the murders in the East to their victims.[104] After Stalin began to speak of a "war of annihilation" in November 1941, terror against the civilian population could be justified as a defense against the ruthless Bolshevik opponent.

The final step that put Jews squarely into the crosshairs of the Wehrmacht was the equation of Jews and partisans, and Hitler was fully aware what this meant. "The war against the partisans," he declared on July 16, 1941, "has its advantages. It enables us to exterminate all those who oppose us."[105] On a visit to the newly occupied territories on July 8, Himmler is said to have declared that "every Jew is to be regarded as a partisan."[106] Even though attacks by partisans had hardly begun, the murder of the Jews was justified as a measure necessary for the security of the advancing German armies. The troops were exhorted to shoot anyone they even suspected of being an irregular fighter (Freischärler). A training course held in September 1941 in Mogilev in conjunction with EG B and SS units summed up the deadly equation: "Where there is a partisan, there is a Jew, and where there is a Jew there is a partisan."[107] An order issued by the commanding officer for German forces in Belarus on November 10, 1941, pointed out that since the Jews "continue to make common cause with communists and partisans, this foreign element has to be exterminated in its entirety."[108] The killing of Jews thus had become an integral part of waging war. The alleged danger from partisans served as a cover for genocide. Every German soldier now had a license for the murder of Jews.[109] Distraught about this development, a German officer noted in his diary, "We destroy not just the Jews who fight against us, but the aim is literally to wipe out the Jews as a people."[110]

Several orders from the highest echelons of the Wehrmacht further fanned the flames of the campaign against the "Jewish-Bolshevik system." On October 10, 1941, Field Marshal Walter von Reichenau, commander of the Sixth Army, reminded his men that they were not only soldiers but also "a carrier of a merciless racial idea and the avenger of all the bestialities that have been inflicted on the Germans and related peoples. Therefore the soldier must have complete understanding for the necessity of the harsh but justified atonement of Jewish subhumanity. It has the goal of nipping in the bud uprisings in the rear of the Wehrmacht, which, as experience shows, are always instigated by Jews."[111] A little more than a month later, on November 20, General Field Marshal Erich von Manstein, commander of the Eleventh Army, similarly exhorted his men to conduct the campaign against "Jewish Bolshevism" with "unprecedented severity" and without "compassion and weakness."[112] Probably the harshest such orders were issued by General Gustav Freiherr von Bechtolsheim, commander of the 707th Infantry Division in Belarus. On October 16, he declared, "The Jews, as the intellectual leaders and carriers of Bolshevism and of the communist idea, are our mortal enemy. They have to be annihilated."[113] And in his monthly report on the fighting for the period of October 11 to November 10, Bechtolsheim stressed, "Since the Jews continue to make common cause with Communists and partisans, the restless extirpation of this foreign element must be carried out."[114] Jews, it should be noted, are mentioned in these orders as a general category, irrespective of sex, age, or function.[115]

Given these and similar orders from above, it is not surprising that lower-ranking officers and the rank and file of the Wehrmacht quickly and effectively joined in the murder of the Jews. Since the numerically small Einsatzgruppen could not be everywhere, the first anti-Jewish measures often were initiated by army units, especially the secret military police (*Geheime Feldpolizei*).This included the registration of the local Jewish population, sequestration into ghettos, forced labor, "reprisals," and the shooting of "hostages."[116] Indeed, the cooperation between the Wehrmacht and the EGs began virtually simultaneously with the invasion of the Soviet Union. EG B reported to Berlin on July 24, 1941, that EK 8, stationed in Baranowicze, "works particularly well with the Wehrmacht." Together they had "liquidated 381 persons ... Jewish activists, functionaries and looters."[117] In Tarnopol, regular German soldiers killed about six hundred Jews and set fire to their houses.[118] EG C reported on August 20 that they continuously received reports from the Wehrmacht about the execution of "communist functionaries and Jews."[119] At the massacre of Babi Yar, it was an army pioneer unit that detonated the walls of the ravine in which the Jews had been shot. The Wehrmacht also provided some one hundred trucks to take away the clothing and valuables that the victims had left behind.[120] From the very beginning of the war against the Soviet Union, according to an agreement worked out with Heydrich in March 1941, the special units of the security police operating on Soviet territory received logistical support such as food and lodging from the army.[121] An order issued by army chief of staff Franz Halder on June 11 commanded the army to assist the SS commando units "by all means, as long as the battle situation allows."[122]

A German officer known for his brutality had organized the killing of some seventy-five Jews in a Ukrainian village on July 1942. The men had had to dig the pit for the shooting, and the officer was reported to have pushed crying women and children into the mass grave with sadistic pleasure. The officer later went on trial before a military court, probably primarily because he was also accused of rape, the mistreatment of subordinates, and theft. In his defense, the officer maintained that he had ordered the shooting of the Jews in order to prevent their making common cause with partisans. Moreover, he had sought to heed Hitler's warning that the war would mean the destruction of the Jews. The court-martial agreed that these circumstances constituted mitigating factors and sentenced the officer to one year imprisonment for homicide rather than murder. The indifference with which the military judges viewed the murder of Jewish women and children was evident in the finding of the court that "during such mass shootings it was unavoidable that women and children would cry and beg for mercy."[123]

It is reckoned that during October and November 1941, some sixty thousand Jews were murdered in Belarus with the participation of the 707th Division.[124] EG A estimated that *Heeresgruppe Mitte* (Army Group Center) by December 1941 had shot "about 19,000 partisans and criminals, that is, mostly Jews."[125] On March 20, 1942, General Karl von Roques, commander of rear area south, gave orders that all units were to support EG D "as much as possible" by providing transport, shelter, food, and cordons at shootings.[126] By the summer of 1942, "cleansing operations" conducted by Army Group South had killed twenty thousand Jews.[127] At times, it was an army unit that requested help from the Einsatzgruppen or other killing units. In July 1941, General Sixt von Arnim, commander of the 95th Infantry Division, ordered the execution of some two hundred Jews near Shitomir (Ukraine). An observer, the soldier Günter Drechsel, characterized the killing, carried out with the assistance of an SS unit, as "dreadful."[128] In September 1941, the 17th Army asked SK VIb for assistance in dealing with the Jews of Krementschug (Ukraine), because there had been three cases of sabotage. Six days later, 1,600 Jews were shot.[129] For the expected occupation of Leningrad, Army Command 17 planned to hand over "Jews of any age and sex" to the Security Police.[130]

This is not to say that every German officer or common soldier, the proverbial *Landser* or grunt, was an active participant in the killing of Jews. We know of at least one report by a general staff officer that mentions the opposition of frontline commanders to the shooting of Jews, prisoners of war, and commissars.[131] There is the story of the eighteen-year-old soldier Wolfgang Holzapfel who witnessed a massacre of Jews, including women and children, by a Sonderkommando in Shitomir and related how this experience collapsed his world. "What does the leadership of the state do with its men who want to fulfill their duty to Führer, people and fatherland in an upright and clean manner?" he wrote in a letter.[132] We do not know how many other soldiers reacted the same way to the operations of the Einsatzgruppen, but he probably was not the only disillusioned Nazi idealist. A study of the role of the Wehrmacht in Belarus found a spectrum of varied participation in the killing. This range of behavior was based on choice, for the admittedly severe system of discipline offered a surprising degree of individual agency.[133] Many orders were less than precise, and the way they were implemented depended on an individual's decision.

Certain types of military units, the tank formations for example, did not participate in the rounding up of Jews and therefore faced fewer temptations to abuse their power. Horst Fuchs Richardson has published the letters of his father, Karl Fuchs, who was a member of the 7th Panzer Division. The elder Fuchs had fully absorbed Nazi propaganda about "Jewish Bolshevism." He supported the war against "these subhuman beings," the "scum of the earth." He hoped that the Führer would save Germany from the "Bolshevik hordes" led by "Jews and criminals." It is an open question whether the good Nazi Fuchs would have acted out his hatred of Bolsheviks and Jews if the opportunity had presented itself. As it is, the elder Fuchs is not linked to any atrocity, nor are the officers who commanded his unit. Fuchs Richardson describes them as "officers of the old school, regarding ill treatment of civilians and prisoners as unsoldierly and immoral, as well as harmful to discipline and morale."[134] We do not know how unusual the 7th Panzer Division was. We have at least one report of the commanding officer of a tank unit ordering the shooting of a captured Soviet political commissar. The quick and routine manner in which this execution was carried out suggests that this was not the only violation of the law of war of its kind. The officer in question was an ardent German nationalist and anti-Communist who personally participated in the shooting of the commissar.[135]

During the early months of the war against the Soviet Union, hardly any Wehrmacht officers had expressed misgivings about the systematic annihilation of Jews, and many participated in this crime. The swift victory in the *Blitzkrieg* (lightning war) against France had created a wave of admiration for the Führer and silenced any criticism of his orders. This mood of acquiescence appears to have changed in the fall of 1941, which began with a long period of rain, changing the earth into mud, and ended with ice and snow. The result was a serious decline in morale, the consequence of the severe Russian winter for which the troops were unprepared as well as a result of the stalling of the German advance before Moscow.[136]

The change in mood is said to have affected the attitude of Wehrmacht officers toward the harsh mode of warfare ordered by Hitler. A report about an inspection of the front composed by Major Rudolf Christoph Freiherr von Gersdorff on December 9, 1941, noted, "I have gained the impression that the shooting of the Jews, prisoners of war and also of commissars is rejected by the officer corps almost everywhere. . . . The shootings are regarded as a violation of the honor of the German army."[137] On March 21, 1943, von Gersdorff attempted to assassinate Hitler by a suicide bombing at a display of captured Russian flags and arms in Berlin. The attempt failed when Hitler left earlier than expected by the military plotters. Von Gersdorff was a resolute opponent of Hitler, and it is possible that the impression of a growing alienation in the officer corps conveyed in his report of December 1941 was colored by wishful thinking. It is a matter of record that throughout the years 1942 and 1943, Wehrmacht units continued to participate in anti-Jewish actions.

Disagreements between Wehrmacht and German occupation authorities occurred here and there over the issue of holding on to skilled Jewish artisans. The SD conceded in an undated report (probably from early 1942) sent to Berlin that while the Jews represented a very cheap source of labor, they "continue to be the most reliable carrier of the Bolshevik ideology." The Wehrmacht therefore considered "an early solution of the Jewish question imperative for the maintenance of security."[138] Needless to say, this disagreement involved simply the timing of the annihilation of the Jews. Significantly, here it was the Wehrmacht that advocated a more radical course.

An agreement of October 7, 1941, between Heydrich and the High Command of the Army (OKH) provided that the commanders of prisoner-of-war camps were to allow special units of the SD to seize "unacceptable elements," a category that included communist party functionaries and intellectuals, political commissars, and Jews. The liquidation of these captives was to take place outside of the camps, and knowledge about these killings was to be kept from the other prisoners and the general population.[139] A typical order regarding the treatment of Jewish prisoners of war ran, "German soldier, always consider, where Jews still live, there is no security behind the front. Jewish civilians and partisans do not belong in the prisoner-of-war camps, they are to be shot."[140]

EG C reported a temporary dispute with regard to the treatment of Jewish prisoners of war. In a report dated November 3, 1941, the Einsatzgruppe praised the "excellent concord that existed between it and all elements of the Wehrmacht," but complained that at times they had experienced difficulties in searching the POW camps for Jewish captives. At the end of July, the OKH had ordered that Jewish prisoners be segregated, and from early on some commanding officers of POW camps had shot the Jewish prisoners. In several instances, however, the Einsatzgruppen fretted, their men had not been admitted to the POW camps. "All too often the Einsatzkommandos had been subjected to more or less hidden complaints on account of their firm attitude in the Jewish question." The report noted that a new order issued by the High Command of the Wehrmacht was expected to clarify the issue.[141]

A completely different situation was reported by SK 4a of the same Einsatzgruppe on November 12. The unit boasted that, due to its collaboration with the Sixth Army, it had been able to execute 55,432 men, "most of them Jews and a great part of these Jewish prisoners of war, who had been handed over by the Wehrmacht." For example, in a POW camp at Borispol (east of Kiev), they had shot 752 Jewish prisoners on October 10 and 357 captives on October 18, among them several commissars and 78 wounded Jewish prisoners, who had been turned over to them by the camp doctor. "The smooth completion of the action in Borispol can be attributed to the energetic support of the officers of the Wehrmacht at that location."[142] It has been estimated that the Germans shot at least 50,000 captured Red Army soldiers solely because they were Jewish.[143] Since the killing of Jewish prisoners of war began right after the invasion of the Soviet Union, captured Jewish soldiers have been called the "first *de facto* Jewish victims" and "the first victims of the Holocaust."[144]

Wehrmacht commanders were little troubled by the repudiation of well-established conventions of the international law of war contained in Hitler's orders for a new kind of warfare against the Bolshevik-Jewish enemy. However, they were concerned that the unauthorized killing of civilians could lead to a drastic decline of discipline. Hence some commanders gave orders that such kill-ings were to be regarded as insubordination and punished accordingly.[145] Yet when such prosecutions took place, the courts imposed entirely inappropri-ate light penalties. Thus Franz H. was charged with killing a Jewish woman in Swenigorodka, Russia, in November 1941 probably because the killing had taken place while he, together with several comrades, had been engaged in ransack-ing a house. When the woman sought to protect her possessions, the accused ordered her daughter to dig a large hole in the garden, made the woman stand next to this pit, and then shot her with an explosive bullet that tore away half of her head. After a military court had made sure that a prosecution was desirable, on July 24, 1942, it convicted the killer of homicide and sentenced him to six months' imprisonment.[146]

In another case of the murder of a Jew without authorization, the legal proceedings were halted because they threatened to expose the systematic annihilation of the Jewish population in the East. Karl Schu. was a senior non-commissioned officer in the Organization Todt (OT), which, among other tasks, carried out building and engineering projects for the Wehrmacht. During the serious manpower shortages that developed from 1942 on, the OT employed large numbers of foreign forced laborers and prisoners of war. A colleague of Schu., charged with murder and theft of property in Russia, alleged that Schu. had ordered the killing, and that he had also commanded the shooting of a Jewish prisoner of war. During an interrogation on March 9, 1942, Schu. admit-ted freely that he had ordered the shooting of the Jewish prisoner. He had done so, he testified, because he had come to know that "all Jews in the East have been knocked off. In all larger towns more than 10,000 Jews have been knocked off." There now arose the unwelcome possibility that, in order to excuse his mis-deed, Schu. might name names and try to provide proof of his assertion that Jews in Russia were being systematically killed. At that point the charges were dropped.[147]

The Waffen-SS, one of the most murderous branches of the Nazi war machine, was formally part of the Wehrmacht but also enjoyed considerable autonomy. From 1944 on, some army units operated under the command of Waffen-SS offi-cers and vice versa, and there developed complex linkages between Wehrmacht and Waffen-SS.[148] At first, most members of the Waffen-SS were volunteers with a strong commitment to the National Socialist ideology.[149] According to one investigation, 75 percent of a sample of Waffen-SS men were members of the Nazi party, as opposed to only 10 percent in a sample of regular soldiers.[150] During the war, the Waffen-SS greatly expanded, eventually reaching thirty-eight divisions. By the end of the year 1943, the Waffen-SS had 501,000 men.[151] Its peak strength is estimated at about 600,000 men,[152] and in 1945 it included about 200,000 foreign volunteers.[153] This growth somewhat diluted the ideolog-ical homogeneity of the Waffen-SS, but its units remained at all times a willing instrument and participant in the destruction of the Jews. One of the first explicit orders for the killing of all Jews was issued by the commanding officer of the 1st SS Cavalry Regiment on July 29, 1941: "No male Jew is to remain alive, and no [Jewish] family is to remain in any location." Thus instructed, on August 2 the SS unit murdered about 2,000 men, women, and children in the Belarus town of Chomsk.[154] On July 31, Himmler directed a similar order to the 22nd Cavalry Brigade of the Waffen-SS before its sweep of the Pripet marshes on the border between Belarus and Ukraine: "All Jews must be shot. Drive the female Jews into the swamp."[155] As far as is known, not a single member of the Waffen-SS ever declined to participate in the killing of Jews.[156]

3

Portraits of Killers

The men who carried out the mass shootings of Jews came from different parts of German society, and not all of them were Germans. There was no typical perpetrator. The shooters were much like the personnel of the concentration camps: there were sadistic types motivated by the basest instincts, committed Nazis who regarded the murder of the Jews as an ideological imperative, opportunists who hoped to better their status, "ordinary men" who followed orders or killed so as to not break ranks with their comrades, and finally those who for a variety of reasons sought to avoid this unpleasant assignment.[1] It is impossible to determine the exact proportion of these different groups. According to one estimate, the number of "excess perpetrators," men who acted on their own impulse rather than simply following orders, was about 50 percent.[2] Another author believes that no more than 20 percent fit this category and considers 60 percent to have been *Befehlstäter* (perpetrators) who acted pursuant to orders.[3] Christopher Browning found that between 10 and 20 percent of the members of Police Battalion 101 sought to escape participation in the killing.[4]

The fact that not a few individuals were able to evade participation in the massacres shows that there was some room for maneuver and choice. The perpetrators were not at the mercy of irresistible pressures to obey. The excuse of having to follow orders or risk one's own life is invalid both legally and morally. Finally, the diversity of perpetrators belies Daniel Goldhagen's argument that the Holocaust was the result of a German demonological anti-Semitism.[5] There is ample evidence of a wide spectrum of attitudes toward the Jews that existed during the entire Nazi era, a factor that resulted in a range of behaviors even during the killing operations in the East.[6] The participation of Ukrainians, Romanians, and citizens of the Baltic states in the murder of the Jews, many of whom exceeded their German counterparts in their cruelty, further undermines Goldhagen's thesis.

The number of sadistic guards in the concentration camps who actually enjoyed the brutal treatment of the inmates was small, and the same can be said about the killers who carried out the mass shootings. The horror of these episodes was the result of the very essence of these executions, and was not caused by particularly brutal individuals. Yet such sadists did exist. Many of these men had engaged in plenty of violence before becoming Nazis, and killing Jews was merely a continuation of a long career of brutality. Whether their hatred of Jews was genuine or merely a pretext, such individuals could now indulge in bloody rampages. They were given absolute power over the Jews and they relished it.

The SS officer Johann Demant, for example, was known as an individual who mistreated Jews whenever he could. Most of the Jews of Hrubieszow in southeastern Poland had been sent to the extermination camp Sobibor in June 1942, but several hundred had been held back for forced labor. At Demant's trial in 1968, witnesses testified that inmates of the ghetto hid whenever they heard his steps to escape his sadistic cruelty. Demant personally supervised the murder of the remaining Jews in October 1941. Some two hundred of them were lined up next to a ditch and shot, but several victims were merely wounded. Nevertheless, Demant ordered a work detail to cover the ditch with earth, burying the wounded alive. The German court sentenced Demant to life imprisonment.[7]

Born in 1895, Oskar Dirlewanger, a PhD in economics, was an early member of the Nazi party and notorious for sexual escapades and alcoholic orgies. Repeatedly jailed for various offenses, Dirlewanger was given the chance to redeem himself in May 1940 by serving at the head of the newly formed *SS-Sonderformation Dirlewanger* (SS Special Unit Dirlewanger), attached to the Waffen-SS. The unit was originally composed of poachers and other petty offenders but eventually included all kinds of violent criminals, including convicted murderers. Dirlewanger set the tone for his unit. Assigned to fight against partisans in Poland and later in Belarus, the Dirlewanger unit became known for its gang rapes and the torturing of captives, including women and children. Detailed to the suppression of the Warsaw uprising in the summer of 1944, Dirlewanger's men did what they were good at—massacres, rapes, and plundering. After the collapse of the Warsaw uprising, Dirlewanger received the Knight's Cross, the highest award in Nazi Germany for extreme battlefield bravery and outstanding military leadership. The unit went on to fight in Slovakia in October 1944. At war's end, Dirlewanger was taken prisoner and killed by his guards.[8]

Karl Schultz was second in command of a post of policemen in the Mir region of Belarus. He too was well known as a beast in the form of a man. Oswald Rufeisen, who served the policemen as an interpreter, regarded Schultz as "a brutal man, a sadist, [who] took great pleasure in torturing people in general, and Jews in particular. For example, when faced with two prospective victims, a mother and a child, he would kill the child in front of the mother and only after a day or two execute the mother." He was a heavy drinker, and drinking "only increased his cruelty."[9]

A sizable percentage of the killers were devoted Nazis who murdered out of ideological conviction. Their zeal was not the result of sadistic inclinations but was based on their strong commitment to the Nazi ideology. Many of these men had developed their radical right-wing ideas during the 1920s. A large number were *alte Kämpfer* (literally "old fighters," longtime members of the Nazi party) who had been socialized into a climate of violence—brawls at political meetings, streetfights with political opponents, and political assassinations.[10] A high proportion were well educated. One recent author speaks of an "anti-Semitism of reason."[11] They harbored no hatred toward Jews as individuals, though they considered them distinctly inferior. The Jewish issue had to be solved to satisfy the needs of the German people for *Lebensraum* and to build the Thousand-Year Reich. From this perspective, it was but a small step to the readiness to commit mass murder once the opportunity presented itself and their higher-ups had let it be known that the time for the *final* solution of the Jewish problem had arrived. In many of the Einsatzgruppen, officers were required to participate in at least one shooting, but this was not generally a problem.

A good example of these technocrats of terror was Otto Ohlendorf, the head of Einsatzgruppe D. Born in 1907, Ohlendorf studied economics and law and achieved the degree of doctor of jurisprudence. He became known as a highly gifted National Socialist academic. Ohlendorf joined the Nazi party in 1925 and the SS in 1926, and he eventually advanced to heading the domestic operations of the SD, the intelligence arm of the SS. He viewed his service as the commander of an Einsatzgruppe as another way of proving his readiness to serve the Nazi state in any matter deemed necessary. Ohlendorf served in the East for a full year, longer than any other leader of an Einsatzgruppe. As he told the military tribunal trying the Einsatzgruppen case in 1946, he had carried out his duties in the Soviet Union "to the best of his ability and with a clear conscience."[12] In practice this meant that between June 1941 and March 1942 his unit in southern Ukraine and the Crimea killed more than ninety thousand people, the great majority of them Jews. Ohlendorf personally supervised at least two mass executions.

At his trial, Ohlendorf tried to minimize his anti-Semitic views, but he acknowledged that he had regarded the extermination of the Jews, including children, as a necessary measure. From being a desk-perpetrator, the gifted Nazi had become an active participant in mass murder.[13] Ohlendorf told the Nuremberg prison psychiatrist Leon Goldensohn that, in his view, the bombing of German cities with phosphorus had been "at least as bad as the shooting of those Jews." Moreover, he had merely followed orders coming from Berlin.[14] After lengthy appeals, Ohlendorf was executed by hanging at Landsberg prison on June 7, 1951.

Ernst Biberstein was another SS officer convicted at the Einsatzgruppen trial. Born in 1899, Biberstein had for a time been a Protestant minister. He joined the Nazi party in 1929 and eventually renounced the church and his ecclesiastical garb. A committed National Socialist, Biberstein joined the Reich Ministry for Church Affairs in August 1935, served in the Wehrmacht for several months in 1940, and became head of the Gestapo in Oppeln (Silesia) in June 1941. He was made head of EK 6 of Einsatzgruppe C in July 1942. He admitted having been present for at least two mass killings, one of which he described as follows:

> I personally superintended an execution in Rostow which was performed by means of a gas truck. The persons destined for death—after their money and valuables (sometimes the clothes too) had been taken from them—were loaded into the gas truck which held between 50 and 60 people. The truck was then driven to a place outside the town where members of my Kommando had already dug a mass grave. I have seen myself the unloading of the dead bodies, their faces were in no way distorted; death came to these people without any outside signs of spasm.[15]

Biberstein showed no regret for what he had done. At his postwar trial, the former theologian declared in his closing statement, "As to the charge of the prosecution, I do not feel guilty before God and my conscience." Biberstein was condemned to death, but his sentence was commuted to life imprisonment. As with many other convicted Nazi criminals, Biberstein was a free man by 1958.[16]

General Gustav Freiherr von Bechtolsheim, commander of the 707th Infantry Division in Belarus, is representative of an army officer whose vehement anti-Semitic convictions made him into an ardent pursuer of the Jews. Bechtolsheim viewed the Jews as dangerous Communists who had to be destroyed. He is considered responsible for the death of more than twenty thousand Jews. Born in 1889, Bechtolsheim served in the First World War and later in the Freikorps Epp, one of several right-wing paramilitary groups that arose at the end of the war and fought the newly formed Weimar Republic. In 1919, Bechtolsheim participated in suppressing the abortive *Räterepublik* (Soviet Republic) in Munich. An assessment of his political outlook by his superiors in 1939 rated him as having "a positive disposition toward the national socialist state." In an early 1942 report, he wrote, "Without exception, Jews are identical with the partisans." His conduct as a murderer of Jews in the East fully confirmed this appraisal. He has been called one of "many Holocaust perpetrators in military garb."[17]

Correspondence from the eastern front shows us how successful Nazi propaganda had been in spreading anti-Semitic teaching. Most of the writers of these surviving letters were lower-ranking officers or common soldiers who expressed their loathing of Jews in simple but graphic language. These sentiments undoubtedly were genuinely felt rather than produced on demand. Nazi censorship was concerned with incidents of criticism, not with the absence of Nazi phraseology. The letters reflected the conviction that the Jews represented a dangerous subhuman lot, and this demonization legitimized their murder. The missives also reveal the great faith most of these men had in the Führer as the savior of Germany.[18] There is no way of knowing how many other German soldiers shared these ideas. However, given the large number of such letters, it is not unreasonable to assume that such sentiments were widely held.[19]

Many of the letters spoke of Germany as being under assault from the "Jewish-Bolshevik conspiracy." The great task of the struggle against Bolshevism "lies in the destruction of eternal Judaism." In Russia, observed Corporal H. K., "the Eastern Jew now reveals himself in all his brutality."[20] The Jews, wrote another noncommissioned officer, "are swine in human form," and we will "free mankind from this pest." You can be sure, one soldier assured his family, "that the Jews are being sent to the right place, where they can no longer oppress any people."[21] An NCO called the Jews the "parasites of the human race," who, like other parasites, "have to be extirpated."[22] They "ooze filth," wrote another, and looking at them, one can only conclude "that they have no right to live on God's earth." As of now, bragged one writer, "we have sent 1,000 Jews to kingdom come, but that is much too little for what they have done." Still another informed *Der Stürmer*, the viciously anti-Semitic tabloid-style newspaper published by Julius Streicher, that after more than two years in the East, he and his comrades had come to fully appreciate the danger presented by the Jews. "Extirpation and annihilation are the only appropriate remedy, and we hope that the hour is not far when the last [Jew] will have dug his own grave." During a supper conversation, reported one writer, "much to my surprise, we were unanimous in our conviction that the Jews have to be removed from this world."[23]

The diary of a soldier assigned to the Minsk ghetto shows the same vehement anti-Jewish sentiments:

> It is now 3 P.M. For the last hour all Jews still living here, 962 persons—women, old men, and children—are being shot. Finally. A detachment of twenty policemen carries out the operation. Two men take turns in shooting. The Jews pass in single file through two huts (near the pit). In the first they hand over their valuables, in the second their head coverings, their furs and their boots. . . . Heartrending cries are being heard. Those who try to escape are shot on the spot. First it is the turn of the children, then the old men and women. . . . Those who refuse to comply are worked over with rubber truncheons. Children who have been hidden are discovered. . . . Tomorrow the operation will be concluded. In the nearby town of Tscherwen, the same detachment will finish off 1,200 Jews. In this way the pest is being eradicated. From the window of my place of work the ghetto is 500 meters away, and I can hear well the cries and the shooting. Too bad that I am not there.[24]

Soldiers at times volunteered for the shooting of Jews. A thirty-six-year-old police officer from Vienna, the father of two infants, happily reported such an

opportunity to his wife: "For tomorrow I have volunteered for a special operation. . . . For the first time I will have the opportunity to use my pistol. I will take
28 bullets. Most likely that will not be enough. . . . What is the importance of
2,200 Jews, who once again are too numerous in a town and have to be finished
off?" Three days later he described what it had been like: "With the first truck [of
victims] my hand shook a bit while shooting, but one gets used to it. By the tenth
truck I calmly took aim and shot comfortably at the many women, children and
infants. . . . Infants were flying in big sweeps through the air and we blew them
away while they were still flying and before they hit the pit and the water. Away
with this brood, who have plunged all of Europe into war and now even stir up
America."[25] Another police officer recalled that at a certain operation so many
men volunteered that there was no need to assign shooters.[26] The same situation
appears to have existed in Police Battalion 322. An officer reported that it was
never a problem to form shooting detachments, since there were always enough
volunteers, and it was usually the same men who stepped forward. He surmised
that some of these men did so for the opportunity to "organize" something, that
is, to get hold of some of the valuables the victims had to hand over.[27]

Standing orders forbade members of the Wehrmacht to participate voluntarily
in executions carried out by the Einsatzgruppen, but several soldiers stated that
they had asked for and received permission to do just that.[28] Peer pressure may
have been a factor when men volunteered for a shooting detachment in their
own unit. However, this element would not explain why Wehrmacht soldiers
went out of their way to join executions carried out by the mobile killing squads.
Soldiers and occupation officials, and occasionally also their wives, were at times
spectators at the killings. The phenomenon became known as *Hinrichtungs-
Tourismus* (execution-tourism).[29]

Christopher Browning has posited that genocidal anti-Semitic killers constituted a small minority and that the majority of those engaged in the murder of the Jews were passively complicit—they were indifferent to the fate of
the Jews.[30] The court verdicts and other materials I have examined support
this view. The largest group of killers was made up of individuals who carried
out this unspeakable work because they had been ordered to do so. That these
orders constituted a crime by ordinary standards of morality mattered less than
the fact that these actions had been commanded by their superiors. Obeying
orders and doing one's duty was part of their patriotic credo. Members of the
Wehrmacht had sworn to render "unconditional obedience" to Hitler, their
"supreme commander." After the end of the war, a high-ranking officer invoked
this oath as the explanation why he had participated in the massacres. "At the
time I took it for granted that orders issued by the government of the day had to
be obeyed."[31] A good German soldier respected the oath he had taken. As a company commander of Police Battalion 322 declared before shooting Jews in Pinsk,
"Comrades, today we have to fulfill a task, which is unpleasant for a German

soldier. However, orders are orders, and we are used to obeying. Others, not we, carry the responsibility."[32]

For many officers and rank-and-file soldiers, obeying and carrying out the unpleasant assignment they had received was made easier by the fact that the victims were Jews, whom they had been taught to despise. Still, the reaction of the police officer quoted above was not unusual. For many of these men, the killing of defenseless men, women, and children did not come easily. And yet it was a job that had to be done. We read in a typical letter, "Murdering is not what we like, but when we realize that this is necessary for the survival of the German people, we carry out even this task with pride and conscientiousness— everybody doing their assigned task."[33] In a time of war, one had to support the fatherland, no matter what, and this attitude led to a suspension, or at least a weakening, of a critical stance toward the massacres they were asked to carry out. To maintain their psychological equilibrium, they convinced themselves that the killings were righteous. In postwar testimony, many of the defendants used words like *Schweinerei* (swinish mess) for what they had experienced. Yet with the passage of time, the killing became routine and begat a new normality. Some may still have felt sorry for themselves, but they no longer felt guilty.[34]

The defendant R., formerly a member of a police battalion attached to EG B, had participated in the mass shooting of Jews in Mogilev (Belarus) in October 1941. At his trial in 1963, he testified that because at the time the killings had been ordered by a legitimate authority, his superiors, he had not considered them wrong. A conflict between what is ordered by the state and what is right (between *Gesetz* and *Recht*) he had considered impossible by definition.[35] This kind of attitude was widespread and allowed these men to quash whatever hesitations to kill they may have had. Paul Johannes Zapp had been the commanding officer of SK 11a and was convicted of murder in 13,449 cases in 1970. Zapp, the court found, had fully known that taking the life of men, women, and children merely because they belonged to an allegedly inferior racial group was wrong. However, he had believed that these measures were based on an order of the Führer, and that he was obliged to carry out this order with "unconditional obedience."[36]

Albert Rapp, the head of another Sonderkommando, was convicted of multiple murders in 1965. He had recognized, he stated at trial, that the mass killings he had participated in were "contrary to the accepted principles of European ethics and morality." However, he had believed that these maxims had to yield to the "national socialist political and racial ideology."[37] Kurt Dre had been a lieutenant in a reserve battalion and in 1972 was found guilty of having been an accessory to the murder of 1,800 Jews. The court concluded that the officer had played down "the clear requirements of right and wrong" in order to carry out the murderous commands he had received. He had considered it his duty to conduct himself "in accordance with the demands of his superiors."[38]

As Germany's military campaign against the Soviet Union got bogged down, leading Nazis sought to galvanize the fighting spirit of the troops by talking of the horrors that the German people would suffer from the Jewish arch-enemy in case of a German defeat. In such a case, Göring declared in a speech delivered on October 5, 1942, the Jew would achieve his hateful goal of annihilating Germany. The victims thus had become the potential perpetrators against whom Germany had to protect itself. By making the destruction of the Jews appear as a defensive measure, made necessary by the alleged Jewish aim to destroy Germany, Nazi propaganda probably helped make the task of the killers somewhat easier.[39]

And yet, despite the different rationalizations employed to facilitate the routine of killing, the psychological toll was heavy. Himmler was aware of this problem and gave orders to organize evening get-togethers that would divert and entertain the troops. At these gatherings, comrades would "eat together in the best German familial style and listen to music, lectures in order to be introduced to the beautiful subject of German intellectual and emotional life."[40] These gatherings took place, accompanied by plenty of alcohol, but they failed to alleviate the problem of stress. There were nervous breakdowns, men running amok, and other manifestations of a deep-seated unease. Hence Himmler, himself not unaffected by the sight of dead bodies, encouraged the pursuit of a mode of killing that would be easier on his men. The employment of explosives did not work out, but the use of gas turned out to be promising.

Clad in striped camp uniforms, prisoners stand at roll call in the Buchenwald concentration camp. Exhausted from work and regardless of the weather, inmates at times had to stand in formation for hours. *United States Holocaust Memorial Museum, courtesy of Robert A. Schmuhl, 10105*

An SS officer at Buchenwald presides as prisoners are hung from their wrists. Most of the inmates undergoing this torturous punishment incurred permanent injuries, and not a few died. *United States Holocaust Memorial Museum, courtesy of Nederlands Instituut voor Oorlogsdocumentatie, 48063*

Women survivors lie on stretchers in the liberated concentration camp Bergen-Belsen in April 1945. Some thirteen thousand of the freed inmates died during the days after liberation despite medical efforts to restore their health. *United States Holocaust Memorial Museum, courtesy of Ulla Knowles, 33767*

When it was liberated, Bergen-Belsen held thousands of naked and unburied corpses in various stages of decomposition. A correspondent for the *London Times* called the scene "something beyond the imagination." *United States Holocaust Memorial Museum, courtesy of Hadassah Bimko Rosensaft, 78259*

The door of the gas chamber in the Dachau concentration camp was marked, in large black letters, *Brausebad* (shower bath). Although Dachau was not an extermination camp like Auschwitz, the gas chamber may have been used for medical experiments on inmates and for executions. *United States Holocaust Memorial Museum, courtesy of National Archives and Records Administration, College Park, 00276*

This map of Jewish executions carried out by Einsatzgruppe A in the Baltic states was part of a report sent by the killing unit's commander, SS brigadier Walther Stahlnecker, to Berlin. The report documented the killing of more than 220,000 Jews between June 22 and October 15, 1941. *United States Holocaust Memorial Museum, courtesy of Thomas Wartenberg, 80190*

During a mass execution in occupied Soviet Union, the victims kneel by the side of a mass grave. Others are seen lying dead in the pit. Some of the soldiers stand on the side, for the shooters took turns in carrying out the killing. *United States Holocaust Memorial Museum, courtesy of National Archives and Records Administration, College Park, 89063*

Jewish women from the Mizocz ghetto stand in line before their execution by Ukrainian auxiliary police. Prior to being shot, victims usually had to take off their clothing, and these garments were sent to Germany. Their killers found time to take pictures of the naked women. *United States Holocaust Memorial Museum, courtesy of Instytut Pamieci Narodowej, 17877*

German soldiers look on as a member of an Einsatzgruppe prepares to shoot a
Ukrainian Jew. Previously killed Jews lie in the pit that served as a mass grave. *United
States Holocaust Memorial Museum, courtesy of Sharon Paquette, 64407*

A German police officer shoots Jewish women from the ghetto of Mzocz who were still alive after a mass execution. The coup de grâce was not always administered, however, and there were reports of wounded victims pleading to be put to death. *United States Holocaust Memorial Museum, courtesy of Instytut Pamieci Narodowej, 17878*

The SS rounds up a group of Jewish men in Plonsk, Poland, for deportation. About twelve thousand Jews from Plonsk and its vicinity were sent to the Auschwitz death camp between November 1 and December 5, 1942. *United States Holocaust Memorial Museum, courtesy of Instytut Pamieci Narodowej, 18772*

SS officers perform the infamous process of selection on the ramp at Auschwitz-Birkenau. It is estimated that some 74 percent of the Jews who arrived there—women, children, and the old and infirm—were sent to the gas chambers, while the rest were kept alive to perform forced labor. As a result of abuse and inadequate nourishment, the average life span for those selected for work was three to four months. *United States Holocaust Memorial Museum, courtesy of Yad Vashem, 77234*

Smiling female auxiliaries of the SS pose with the adjutant of Auschwitz, Karl Hoecker, at a retreat near Auschwitz. Some of the female guards became known for their extreme cruelty. Irma Grese, for example, was called the "Beast of Bergen-Belsen." *United States Holocaust Memorial Museum, courtesy of anonymous donor, 34762*

4

Serving in a Death Factory

On August 15, 1941, Himmler witnessed a mass shooting in Minsk. All but two of the victims were men. After the shooting, which left Himmler visibly moved, SS-Obergruppenführer Erich von dem Bach-Zelewski, one of the three senior SS and police officers in charge of the killing operations in the newly occupied Soviet territories, told Himmler that these mass executions were a terrible psychological burden on the men doing the shooting. Himmler thereupon suggested to Arthur Nebe, the head of EG B who had arranged the "demonstration," that other "more humane" killing methods be found—that is, methods that were easier on the executioners. A bit later, Nebe arranged for a killing with explosives. Twenty-four mental patients were put into a wooden bunker, but the explosion failed to kill the patients. Several of them emerged from the bunker covered with blood and screaming loudly. That left the use of carbon monoxide, a gas that already had been used extensively during the so-called euthanasia program, which involved the murder of the handicapped and mentally disabled. A room on the ground floor of the insane asylum of Mogilev was bricked up, and the exhaust of a passenger car and a truck was directed into the room. Five patients who had been brought into the room were dead after about fifteen minutes. Finally, it seemed, the Nazis had found a more bloodless method of mass killing.[1]

This promising new means of murder was employed in several killing centers in the East. The sole purpose of these camps was annihilation; they were factories of death. A small number of victims were kept alive to help operate the camps, but all other inmates were killed immediately upon arrival. Some of the camps also murdered Soviet prisoners of war and Gypsies. The first such site was in Chelmno, northwest of Lodz. Beginning on December 8, 1941, an SS unit under the command of Herbert Lange employed a gas van, a mobile gas chamber disguised as a truck. Since early 1940, Lange had led a *Sonderkommando* (Special Detachment) to carry out euthanasia killings of mental patients in East Prussia and nearby sites by means of shooting and a gas van. In the face of popular unrest, Hitler "officially" had had to end the euthanasia program on August 24, 1941, though it in fact continued on a reduced scale. The expertise of Lange and his men was now employed to kill Jews. The victims were led to believe that they would be resettled. Instead, they were asphyxiated by the exhaust of the gas van. One estimate puts the number of Jews murdered in this way at Chelmno between 1941 and 1943 at 225,000.[2]

It had been expected that the use of gas vans would spare the nerves of the executioners, but this turned out to be wrong. The victims took longer to die, and their cries of despair could be heard before the vans gradually turned quiet. Even though much of the dirty work of unloading and burying the corpses and cleaning out the van was done by "work Jews," the view of the soiled and entangled bodies and the distorted faces of the hapless victims once again traumatized the killers.[3] The driver of a Sonderkommando stated that the "the use of the gas vans was the most horrible thing I have ever seen." The bodies, when unloaded, "were covered with vomit and excrement. It was a terrible sight."[4] A member of EG D in the Crimea, which also for a time employed a gas van, related that "the men who took part in such actions said they would rather have shot those people than be on duty during the use and emptying of the van."[5]

In each of the death camps of Belzec, Sobibor, and Treblinka, no more than twenty to thirty-five Germans supervised some 700 to 1,000 Jewish inmates and 90 to 130 Ukrainians.[6] The fact that much of the work in the extermination factories was done by others served as an excuse by German defendants at postwar trials. For example, Gustav Münzberger, deputy commandant at Treblinka, who was in charge of moving the victims into the gas chambers, maintained that he had not played any significant role. "There really was nothing much for us to do. We simply had to be there. That was all." The court did not accept this plea and sentenced him to twelve years imprisonment as an accomplice to murder.[7]

Jewish labor was highly organized. There was the platform detail that removed the bodies of those who had died on the way and cleaned the railroad cars, the sorting team that collected the victims' luggage and clothing and prepared the booty for shipment, the hair cutters who cut the hair of the women to be used for insulation, the "gold Jews" who collected the valuables from the undressing area and also carried out body searches of women, including in their genitalia (this operation always attracted onlookers from the SS), the gas chamber disposal team that had to take away the dead bodies for burning, the forest team that cut wood for heating and cooking in the camp as well as for the burning of corpses, and many others. The groups of "work Jews" were themselves liquidated periodically and replaced by new arrivals.[8]

The death camp of Belzec began operating on March 17, 1942, when the deportation of the Jews of Lublin began. This action was part of the larger plan of killing the more than two million Jews packed into crowded ghettos in the "General Government," the part of Poland not incorporated into the Reich. Already back in September 1941, Hans Frank, the governor of this territory, had talked of the need to destroy the Jews under his rule, whom he called "exceptionally harmful gluttons" to whom one should show no pity.[9] The killing operation, code-named Operation Reinhard, got underway in the spring of 1942. It was commanded by the SS and Police Leader Odilo Globocnik, the former Gauleiter of Vienna, who acted on verbal orders given to him by Himmler. Goebbels noted in his diary on March 27, "Beginning with Lublin, the Jews in the General Government are now being evacuated eastward. The procedure is a pretty barbaric one and [is] not to be described here more [accurately].... Not much will remain of the Jews."[10] The victims themselves for the most part had no idea what awaited them. Even when ominous rumors trickled back to the ghettos, people were reluctant to believe them.

Secrecy and deception were the cornerstones of this "evacuation." When a train carrying the Jews stopped, they believed that they had arrived at a transit camp. The gas chamber resembled an ordinary bath. At the entrance were large pots of flowers. Men entered first and women and children followed. Then the doors were shut, the engine that supplied the gas was started, and after a few minutes everyone was dead from asphyxiation. After the chamber had been ventilated, a group of Jewish workers entered and removed the bodies. Then the corpses were taken to the place of burning. Here the "burning detail" arranged the bodies in layers. One member of this group remembers that the SS expert on body burning instructed them to put fat women on the first layer. Sometimes as many as three thousand bodies would be piled up on the roaster, which then was ignited. Another survivor recalls that from a distance the fire looked like a volcanic eruption. The stench and heat were unbearable.[11]

In addition to Jewish work details, much of the physical work in the Nazi extermination camps was done by so-called Trawniki, an auxiliary force recruited primarily from Red Army prisoners of war. Their name was derived from the village of Trawniki near Lublin where they were trained. The Germans employed Trawniki primarily for those tasks that required close contact with their victims, such as unloading and cleaning the trains, and driving the Jews toward the gas chamber.[12] But, of course, there also was a German staff. There were the SS men and doctors who manned the ramps of the railroad stations and selected a few of the arriving Jews for work while the majority (sometimes all) were sent to the gas chambers. Others supervised the undressing of the victims, packed them into the "shower rooms," and handled the gas. There were those responsible for overseeing the different Jewish Sonderkommandos and the inmates who sorted the looted property, and finally a commandant and his administrative staff.

The normal routine of death by asphyxiation in the gas chamber was bad enough, but at times there were problems with the machinery that prolonged the agony of the victims. Kurt Gerstein was a mining engineer and a member of the Confessing Church who volunteered for the SS in order to find out about the destruction of the Jews and alert the outside world. He witnessed one such snafu at Belzec:

Heckenholt was the driver of the diesel truck whose exhaust gases were to be used to kill these unfortunates. S.S. sergeant Heckenholt was making great efforts to get the engine running, but it refused to start. Captain Wirth came up. He was obviously frightened because I was watching a disaster. Yes, I saw it all and waited. Fifty minutes, seventy minutes ticked away on my stop watch, but the diesel would not work. Inside the gas chambers the people waited, waited in vain. . . . Furious at the delay, Captain Wirth lashed out with his whip at the Ukrainian assisting Heckenholt. It was two hours and forty-nine minutes—all recorded by stopwatch—before the diesel started. Right up to that moment, the people had been shut up alive in those four crowded chambers, four times 750 people in four times 159 cubic feet of space! Another twenty minutes dragged by. Many of those inside were already dead. They could be seen through the small window when an electric lamp inside went on for a few moments and lit up the chamber. Finally, at the end of thirty-two minutes, all were dead.[13]

During eleven months of 1942, the Belzec death factory gassed between 600,000 and nearly 1 million Jewish victims.[14] At Sobibor, which began operation in June of 1942, at least 250,000 were murdered.[15] The most efficient camp was Treblinka, some six miles from Warsaw, which had eight gas chambers and where close to 1 million were killed. Given the large number of Jews to be killed, the use of gas vans with their limited capacity would not have worked.

Some Jews never made it to the death camps. The railroad cars transporting the Jews were overcrowded, it often was hot, and there was no water. Many died from heat exhaustion or suffocation. One survivor recalls that those who managed to reach an opening to breathe and stuck out their heads were shot dead by the guards accompanying the train.[16] Richard Glazar, who was selected for the "work Jews" and spent ten months in Treblinka, mentions that some committed suicide upon arrival.[17]

Chil Rajchman, who worked as a barber and later in the removal of bodies, describes the state of the victims after the doors of the gas chambers had been opened:

There was a difference in the appearance of the dead from the small and from the larger gas chambers. In the small chambers death was easier and quicker. The faces often looked as if the people had fallen asleep, their eyes closed. Only the mouths of some of the gassed victims were distorted with a bloody foam visible on their lips. The bodies were covered in sweat. Before dying, people had urinated and defecated. The corpses in the larger gas chambers, where death took longer, were horribly deformed, their faces all black as if burned, the bodies swollen and blue, the teeth so tightly clenched that it was literally impossible to open them, and to get to the gold crowns we had sometimes to pull out the natural teeth—otherwise the mouth would not open.[18]

By late 1943 Operation Reinhard had run its course. About 1.7 million Jews had been gassed to death, and in the General Government few Jews were still alive. Sobibor, which had experienced an uprising of its courageous inmates in October 1943, was the last of the three Operation Reinhard death camps to be closed down. But this was not the end of the killing of Jews in the German-occupied East. During the fall of 1943, Himmler decided to liquidate all Jews still kept alive for forced labor, an action codenamed *Aktion Erntefest* (Operation Harvest Festival). As part of that action, on November 3–4, 1943, some 17,000 Jews were shot at Majdanek on the outskirts of Lublin, at first a concentration camp but from 1943 on also an extermination camp. The total number of Jews who lost their lives in Majdanek is estimated at 90,000.[19]

The second camp that had the double function of serving as both a concentration camp and a death factory was Auschwitz, near Cracow. In time, this site became the largest killing facility, and the name "Auschwitz" more than anything else has come to symbolize Nazi depravity. Auschwitz has been called not only the scene of unparalleled, factory-style mass murder, but also a break with Western civilization itself.[20]

In the summer of 1940, a concentration camp for Poles was established on the grounds of a former army camp outside the town of Oswiecim (Auschwitz). In anticipation of the German attack on the Soviet Union and the expectation of large numbers of prisoners of war, the camp was expanded. In October 1941, construction started at Birkenau, less than two miles away, of a large camp for 100,000 prisoners of war that was named Auschwitz II. Wooden structures originally built as stables for fifty-two horses became living quarters for more than 400 prisoners. It was at Birkenau in early 1942 that the first gas chambers were constructed. About 2,000 victims could be squeezed into them at any one time. By March 1943, four gas chambers and crematoria specifically designed and built for mass murder were in operation. At their top capacity, they could "process" 4,416 victims in twenty-four hours.[21]

Trainloads of Jews arrived in Auschwitz from all over Europe—the Netherlands, Belgium, France, Slovakia, Norway, and as far away as the islands of Crete and Rhodes. The high point was reached during the summer and fall of 1944, when some 426,000 Hungarian Jews, previously outside the clutches of Eichmann, were deported to Auschwitz. During this peak period, some 24,000 people were killed every day. At a time when the German war effort suffered from a serious shortage of rail stock, two to three cargo trains filled with Hungarian Jews reached Auschwitz daily. The last train, with Jews from Theresienstadt, a transit camp in Czechoslovakia, arrived on October 30, 1944. Poles, Soviet prisoners of war, and Gypsies also were killed at Auschwitz, but Jews made up about 90 percent of the victims. Incomplete sources make it impossible to establish with any precision the total number of Jews murdered. But according to the best calculations, at least 1.1 million Jews were killed or died in Auschwitz.[22]

On arrival, the deportees were told to leave their luggage on the ramp and line up in rows of five—men on one side and women and children on the other. The two formations stood only a few yards apart, but anyone who tried to leave his or her place was hit by SS guards and returned to the appropriate column. According to the recollection of one of the SS men on the ramp, "there were heart-breaking scenes of adieus. Husbands were separated from their wives, mothers were for the last time waving good-bye to their sons."[23] SS doctors then began to select those fit to work. Muscular men up the age of forty had the best chance of being chosen for slave labor. Mothers with babies were unfit as a rule, and the same held for those appearing to be weak and sickly. A former guard recalls that in November 1942 "a crying baby was found amid trash discarded by arriving prisoners. The baby's mother had evidently abandoned it in hopes that she would then be chosen for a work crew and not sent to the gas chamber. A fellow SS member, angered by the cries, beat the infant to death."[24]

Those selected to be gassed often were loaded on trucks; those fit for work were marched to the camp for men or for women, where they were tattooed with a number.[25] From here on, they were not human beings, but a commodity to be used. At regular intervals those no longer able to work would be killed by an injection or sent to the gas chambers. The selection quotas on the ramp varied from month to month. Sometimes entire transports were sent straight to the gas chambers. The majority of women and practically all children were selected to be killed. On the basis of 329 transports whose numbers can be reconstructed, one scholar calculates that on the average 74 percent of the arriving Jews were sent to be gassed, while about 26 percent were kept alive for forced labor in industrial enterprises such as IG Farben.[26] Their life span, too, was short. It is estimated that after three to four months, most of those selected for work were dead, having perished as a result of hunger, exhaustion, or abuse.[27]

We have the testimony of surviving members of the Jewish Sonderkommando as well as of SS men who worked in the gas chambers and crematoria about what happened next. The victims selected to be gassed were taken to a large undressing room. Here they were told in a friendly voice that they would now bathe and be disinfected to prevent epidemics in the camp. After that, they would be taken to their barracks and be given hot soup. Members of the Jewish Sonderkommando instructed them to hang their clothing and to remember the number of the hook so that they would find their clothing after they came out of the shower. The Jewish "helpers" rationalized their forced cooperation in the machinery of destruction with the argument that they spared the victims unnecessary fear and suffering. Women, children, and the old and sick undressed first, and they also were the first to be led to the room, which had the name "Shower Room" written in several languages on a large sign. The shower room could hold up to two thousand people. The men followed, and then the thick door was shut. Those inside heard the heavy bolts being secured. It was at that point, with naked men and women squeezed closely together, that the hapless victims must have realized that something was not quite right. There were screams and beatings on the door. Several victims usually noticed that covers had been removed from vents in the ceiling. Into these holes SS men with gas masks emptied the content of cans of Zyklon B. The granules of this pesticide, prussic acid usually used for fumigation, dissolved into gas and did their deadly work.[28]

Zyklon B was supposed to work more quickly and with greater certainty than carbon monoxide. It had been tried out on Soviet prisoners of war and had shown itself to be effective. Moreover, to accomplish the mass killing taking place in Auschwitz, the use of exhaust from internal combustion engines was hardly feasible. Rudolf Höss, the commandant of Auschwitz, is supposed to have expressed the view that the use of Zyklon B resulted in a practically instant and painless death.[29] However, in his memoir Höss writes that only those very close to the vents through which the poison was thrown, about one-third, "died straight away. The remainder staggered about and began to scream and struggle for air. . . . Those who screamed and those who were old or sick or weak, or the small children, died quicker than those who were healthy or young."[30]

The reports of witnesses are similar. A Jewish Sonderkommando member who worked on removing the bodies relates that "you could see on their faces the pain that the asphyxiation [had] caused."[31] Another "work Jew" described the terrible sight when the Sonderkommando opened the door: "You could find people whose eyes hung out of their sockets because of the struggles the organism had undergone. Others were bleeding from everywhere, or were soiled by their own excrement, or that of other people. . . . Some bodies were all red, others very pale, as everyone reacted differently. But they had all suffered in death."[32] Miklos Nyiszli, a Jewish physician who attended to the personnel of the crematorium, also viewed the scene after the door had been opened. "I felt it my duty to my people and to the entire world to be able to give an accurate account of what I had seen if ever, by some miraculous whim of fate, I should escape." Dr. Nyiszli reported that bodies were lying on top of each other. The gas first inundated the lowest layers of air, and that made the victims trample on one another in order to get a few feet higher and try to escape the gas. "What struggle for life it must have been!" he wrote.[33]

Other Jewish detachments took over at this point. The "dentists" pried open the mouths of the dead to extract or break off any gold teeth or gold bridgework. Together with the other valuables like necklaces and wedding rings, they collected some eighteen to twenty pounds of gold daily. Next the "barbers" cut off the hair of the women and bundled it into sacks. Finally the incineration detail loaded the bodies on metal pushcarts and pushed these into the ovens of the crematoria. Eventually there were four crematoria, each with several ovens. This meant that several thousand corpses could be cremated each day. It took twenty to thirty minutes to incinerate the bodies. The ashes were loaded on trucks and used for fertilizer or dumped into the Vistula River and nearby ponds.[34]

During the summer and fall of 1944, the annihilation of several hundred thousand Hungarian Jews overloaded the system. It was hindered by a shortage of Zyklon B, and the crematoria could not cope with the huge number of corpses. Hence several open-air pyres were set up to burn bodies. According to the survivor Hermann Langbein, who served as clerk and became a key witness at the Auschwitz trial in 1963–1965, there was at least one instance in 1944 when Jewish children were thrown alive into the huge fires. Another witness testified to having seen several trucks with about five hundred children driving up and dumping the children into the burning pit. There were screams and then silence.[35] The Jewish inmate Dr. Ella Lingens also saw how small children were thrown alive into the pyre.[36] The order for this "time and gas-saving measure" is said to have been given by camp commandant Höss.[37]

After Höss once again had taken command of Auschwitz in 1944, he made the entire camp personnel sign the following declaration:

1. I am aware of the fact that I will receive the death penalty if I appropriate any Jewish property.
2. I will maintain strict secrecy with regard to the measures necessary for the evacuation of the Jews, even with my comrades.
3. I will enlist my entire person and my ability to work for the quick and smooth carrying out of these measures.[38]

During the course of postwar trials, most of the Auschwitz defendants claimed not to have known of the wholesale murder of the Jews at Auschwitz. This declaration is one of many pieces of evidence that this claim was false.

Medical experiments on prisoners, treating them like guinea pigs, were carried out in many concentration camps, but those that took place in Auschwitz have received special notoriety because of the participation of the infamous Josef Mengele. Holding doctorates in both anthropology and medicine, Mengele had a special interest in identical twins, and he used his experiments to try to prove the genetic origins of racial and social differences. In May 1943, Mengele was posted to Auschwitz and became chief physician to the Gypsy family camp.[39] In addition to these duties, Mengele had plenty of time to follow his research interests. He had measurements made of about 250 pairs of twins and also conducted morphological and X-ray examinations. Many of the subjects were then killed by injections of phenol to the heart, and their bodies were dissected. Another of Mengele's research projects involved the study of hereditary factors in eye color. Miklos Nyiszli, a Hungarian pathologist who worked in the crematorium but also had to assist Mengele in his experiments, recalls that in one instance an entire family of eight was killed so that their heterochromatic eyes could be sent to the Kaiser Wilhelm Institute for Anthropology in Berlin for further study.[40]

Mengele, who held the rank of an SS Hauptsturmführer, was a typical Nazi scientist, a man with no moral scruples. Mengele's willingness to kill subjects in order to gain access to their organs is in line with his reputation as one of the most fanatical and ruthless SS doctors doing duty on the selection ramp. Paradoxically, Mengele also could show kindness, in particular to Gypsy children. He established an elaborately equipped kindergarten and personally brought them toys and sweets. A German Gypsy survivor testified at a legal proceeding in 1973 that Mengele had arranged special rations for some patients with diphtheria and thus saved their lives. Several other inmates gave similar testimony at the Auschwitz trial.[41] Other Nazi killers are said to have displayed the same mixture of cruelty to most of their victims and kindness to a chosen few. Compassion and brutality, it appears, could coexist in the same individual. Tzvetan Todorov calls this kind of "behavioral inconsistency" a trait common to all guards.[42]

Rudolf Höss served in the Dachau and Sachsenhausen concentration camps before assuming his post as commander of Auschwitz in May 1940. He stayed in Auschwitz until November 1943, and after several months of work at the SS Economic-Administrative Main Office in Berlin, Höss resumed command in mid-1944. In his autobiography, written in 1947 in a Polish prison, Höss described growing up in a family with a deeply religious atmosphere. His father was a devout Catholic who raised his son on strict military principles. He was taught to be "obedient to all grown-up people," and from early on fought any "sign of tenderness." After serving as a soldier in World War I, Höss joined one of the Freikorps, paramilitary units who fought the Communists in the Baltic region, the Ruhr, and Upper Silesia. "I found a home again, and a sense of security in the comradeship of my fellows." Höss was also involved in the killing of a "traitor" within the ranks, as a result of which he was sentenced to a prison sentence of ten years in 1924. As a member of the Nazi party since 1922, Höss enlisted in the SS in 1934 and soon thereafter was posted to Dachau. "To me it was just a question of being an active soldier once again, of resuming my military career." And from there his career took off.[43]

Höss was not a sadist, his biographer Joachim Fest stresses. "Among his most outstanding characteristics were strict attention to duty ... and finally a marked hankering after morality, an abnormal tendency to submit himself to strict imperatives and to feel authority over him.... It was this moral longing, as powerful as it was undirected, that made Rudolf Höss suitable material for the demands of the totalitarian ethic, because it contained everything he was seeking: simple formulas, an uncomplicated schema of good and evil, a hierarchy of normal standards oriented according to military categories, and a utopia."

At first it was difficult for him to be harsh or watch executions. However it was through a "continual process of hardening that he became the type of passionless fundamentally disinterested murderer to whom, beyond the given objective purposes, murder meant nothing." In 1944, he told a comrade, he had long since ceased to have any human feeling.[44]

Höss managed to separate being in charge of mass murder from his private life. He was devoted to his family, especially his children. The psychiatrist Robert Jay Lifton speaks of the existence of two selves or a "doubling" personality in such situations. There was the Auschwitz self, which enabled people like Höss to function psychologically in an environment so different from the values of their upbringing, and secondly the prior self he needed in order to continue to see himself as a humane husband and father.[45] "Doubling" thus served as a guilt-avoidance mechanism. It is likely that the continual alternation between his off-duty emotions and the vexations of daily routine, between the idyll of the quiet evening at home and the executioner's trade, was not possible without occasional complications. Occasionally his subconscious mind may have rebelled against the imposed split in his personality.[46] But on the whole, he managed this split existence quite well.

When the prison psychiatrist Goldensohn asked Höss whether putting so many persons to death did not upset him, he answered, "I thought I was doing the right thing.... I don't know what you mean by being upset about these things because I didn't personally murder anybody." To the question of whether the gassings and burning of corpses did not haunt him, Höss replied, "No, I have no such fantasies."[47] When in the summer of 1941 he was ordered by Himmler to prepare the installations for mass executions, Höss recalled, "the reasons behind the extermination programme seemed to me right. I did not reflect on it at the time: I had been given an order, and I had to carry it out. Whether this mass extermination of the Jews was necessary or not was something on which I could not allow myself to form an opinion, for I lacked the necessary breadth of view." The "basic orders" received from Himmler and issued in the name of the Führer were sacred. "They brooked no consideration, no argument, no interpretation.... What the Führer, or in our case his second-in-command, the Reichsleiter SS, ordered was always right."[48]

Höss took pride in running his death factory with efficiency. With the satisfaction of the successful planner, he pointed out that the gas chambers of his own camp had a capacity ten times greater than those of Treblinka.[49] Höss was an able engineer of death. He regarded the Jews as "enemies of our people," but, as he emphasized, "I have never personally hated the Jews." He looked with disgust on the sensationalism of Streicher's hateful rag, *Der Stürmer*. "This paper caused a lot of damage and, far from serving serious anti-Semitism, it did a great deal of mischief."[50] Indifferent to the fate of the hundreds of thousands who were put to death during his watch, Höss felt sorry for himself having to bear the stress of being the chief executioner. He had to look at death itself through a peephole of the gas chamber. "Believe me, it wasn't always a pleasure to see those mountains of corpses and smell the perpetual burning."[51] This kind of sentimentalism did not save him from the gallows. Tried by the Poles, Höss was hanged at Auschwitz, the scene of his crimes, on April 16, 1947. His body was cremated and the ashes scattered into the Sola River adjacent to the camp.[52]

Höss's adjutant, Robert Mulka, was a man of a more robust nature, who appears to have had no qualms about doing his job in the Auschwitz death factory. He had volunteered for the Waffen-SS in 1941, at the age of forty-six. The German court that tried him concluded that Mulka had served as a reliable member of the Auschwitz team. On four occasions Mulka had done service on the ramp, and he therefore was found guilty of being an accessory to the murder of at least three thousand people. Once, when Mulka was in charge of the ramp operations, it was reported to him that "this pig," a member of the Jewish "ramp detachment" (who handled the luggage of the new victims), had spoken to the arriving Jews. Mulka thereupon gave the order, "Finish him off, it is late." Two SS men then bludgeoned the inmate with their truncheons until he was dead. Mulka was given a prison sentence of fourteen years.[53]

Franz Stangl served as commandant of Treblinka during Operation Reinhard in 1942 and 1943. Born in Austria in 1908, Stangl became a police official and a secret member of the illegal Austrian Nazi party. Stangl was a conscientious and efficient organizer of mass murder. In an interview with the journalist Gitta Sereny in 1971, he claimed to have been upset by the killing, but he acknowledged that he had been dedicated to his work. "I had to do as well as I could. That is how I am."[54] In 1943, Himmler ordered the promotion of those camp officers who had "contributed significantly to the success of Operation Reinhard," and Stangl was among those whose performance was considered especially praiseworthy.[55] After the war, Stangl escaped to Brazil, but he was tracked down by Nazi-hunter Simon Wiesenthal and extradited to Germany. The postwar court that sentenced him to life imprisonment on December 22, 1970, held him responsible for the murder of at least four hundred thousand Jews. Stangl died of heart failure in prison in June 1971.

Kurt Franz, the deputy commandant of Treblinka, was by all accounts an exceptionally violent man. A member of the SS, Franz worked early on in the euthanasia program. He volunteered to be a guard in the camps and served in Buchenwald, Belzec, and finally for almost fourteen months at Treblinka. He vilified the Jews working in the camp by referring to them as "assholes," "filth," and "shit." Franz showed himself to be a sadist who always found an opportunity to abuse and torture. He killed Jews upon impulse and had his dog tear inmates to pieces. Franz ordered inmates to be whipped and personally carried out this brutal punishment. At his trial, witnesses related that in early 1943 Franz saw how an SS man killed a Jewish infant by repeatedly hitting his head against the wall of the barracks. Franz exclaimed that he could do this much better. He seized another infant and banged his head against the wall with such force that the infant died instantly.

When Franz was arrested in 1959, police searching his home found an album of photographs, including photos taken at Treblinka. The album had the inscription "*Schöne Zeiten*" (Good Times).[56] At his postwar trial Franz was found guilty of the murder of 35 people and of being an accessory to the murder of 139 additional individuals. "A large part of the streams of blood and tears that flowed in Treblinka," the court concluded, "was due to his role." Franz's cruelty and the reign of terror that he imposed on the camp, the court ruled, showed that he pursued the destruction of Jewish life with zeal and conviction.[57]

Otto Moll supervised the burning of the corpses at Auschwitz. Filip Müller, who served in the burning detachment under Moll, described him as "cruel, brutal and unscrupulous. For him Jews were subhuman creatures, and he treated them accordingly. He gloated over the suffering to which he submitted his victims and constantly thought of new torments and novel methods of torture. His sadism, his callousness, his bloodthirstiness and his lust to kill knew no bounds."[58] Other witnesses confirm this appraisal. He was "half-crazy, a sadist." Moll killed for the flimsiest of pretexts or for no reason at all. "For him, murder was a children's game."[59] Moll, concludes one historian, was no "ordinary man."[60]

Heinrich Arthur Matthes was responsible for the Jewish work crews at Treblinka between August 1942 and September 1943. He also supervised driving the new arrivals into the gas chambers, gave the command for closing the doors of the "shower," and was in charge of disposing of the corpses of the victims. The court trying him for murder noted that he worked efficiently, ensuring that the entire process proceeded with dispatch so as to accommodate the next shipment. Matthes was found guilty of the murder of four inmates and being an accessory in the murder of at least one hundred thousand Jews.[61] Also on trial in the Treblinka case was Willi Mentz, who came to Treblinka in the summer of 1942 and stayed there until November 1943. His main assignment was overseeing the camp hospital, which actually functioned as another execution site. Arriving sick Jews who could not walk were taken there because they would have impeded the smooth flow of the victims into the gas chamber. Ill Jews assigned to work crews were also killed there. The victims were forced to line up naked at the rim of a pit dug for the burning of corpses, and Mentz killed them with a shot in the back of the neck. The court noted that Mentz made no effort to ascertain whether those shot were really dead. "The fact that he omitted such checks and allowed the merely wounded to be burned alive indicates the cruel and ruthless attitude of the defendant toward his victims."[62]

Josef Erber joined the SS in 1939 and came to Auschwitz in late 1940. He served in various capacities there, including in the Political Department (the Gestapo), until the evacuation of the camp in January 1945. Erber participated in at least fifty selections on the ramp and also decided on the gassing of female work Jews who were no longer able to work. In one instance, he made women inmates jump over a ditch. Those who fell in were sent to the gas chamber. A German court established that Erber was responsible for the death of at least 261 female inmates, and it sentenced him to life imprisonment.[63] When Ebbo Demant interviewed Erber for his film *Lagerstrasse* (Camp Street) *Auschwitz*, he claimed to have been unjustly convicted. He had, after all, experienced "very difficult times." High officials had visited Auschwitz at regular intervals, but none of them, he said, had ever pointed out to him that what was happening there was wrong.[64]

Ernst Zierke was of a similar type. He participated in the euthanasia program and from June 1942 until March 1943 served in the Belzec extermination camp. Zierke supervised the undressing of the victims before they were led to the gas chamber. According to the testimony of one of his comrades, he was not a brutal man and, like many others in this position, simply did his duty at the post he was assigned. Moreover, working in a death factory was relatively lucrative. There were supplements in pay, good food, plentiful allocations of liquor, and regular home leave in addition to the right to receive visitors. Many of these men found opportunities to appropriate gold or other valuables that had belonged to the victims. Doing one's duty in such a place was certainly safer than serving as a combat soldier.[65]

A Jewish survivor of Auschwitz described Johann Gorges in a similar manner. "Although he carried out his orders obediently he never did more than he had been bidden, neither did he indulge in sadistic tortures. No doubt he would have led a normal and uneventful life, had not fate taken him to Auschwitz as a member of the SS."[66] The Auschwitz survivor Ella Lingens calls such persons "drab little people who would never have been conspicuous if no occasion for extraordinary behaviour had been offered to them."[67]

According to the veteran prosecutor Adalbert Rückerl, "Hardly any of [those serving in the Polish extermination camps] would have turned criminal in a constitutional state."[68] Yitzhak Arad, who researched the background of the personnel of the Operation Reinhard death camps, has noted that the great majority of the SS personnel who ran the camps and supervised the extermination activities were absolutely ordinary people. "Under the regime of Nazi Germany, these perfectly 'ordinary' people were turned into something extraordinarily inhuman."[69] Most of these men were opportunists who followed the path of least resistance, and the very same opportunism that had induced these men to turn criminal within the moral vacuum of Third Reich Germany enabled them to reconvert without much difficulty to their role as law-abiding citizens once this vacuum was refilled with the ethical guidelines of the postwar democratic state.[70]

It appears that most of the subordinate camp staff shared their superiors' hostility toward the Jews. While the SS men in the concentration camps varied somewhat in the way they handled inmates, those who manned the extermination machinery for the most part carried out their deadly assignment conscientiously and often eagerly. Their treatment of the Jewish work details employed in the camps was often cruel. Some of these men were sadistically inclined. Others probably became brutalized by the routine of serving in a death factory. Brutalization, Raul Hilberg has suggested, often was an expression of impatience. "Guards standing in front of gas chamber doors would use whips or bayonets to drive the victims inside."[71] One German witness puts it thus: "One could react like a normal human being in Auschwitz only for the first few hours. In that camp everyone was sullied. You were caught and had to go along."[72]

Few SS men were able to elude the brutalizing effect of the death factories, but Jewish survivors recalled two such men in Treblinka who not only did not mistreat inmates but at times helped them. Erwin Herman Lambert was in charge of a building detachment. He treated his Jewish workers well and at times brought them food from the German staff kitchen. Karl Ludwig also treated Jewish prisoners humanely and helped save the lives of several inmates. For a time, Ludwig served at Sobibor, where he brought bread to the Jewish detail repairing shoes. Another SS man in Sobibor, J. Klehr, provided bread to work Jews as well.[73] Unfortunately, such good SS men were the exception.

A very large share of the personnel in the death camps of Operation Reinhard were veterans of the euthanasia program known under the code name Aktion T 4. The gassing facilities of the camps were built and inspected by experts from T 4.[74] The number of SS personnel directly involved with the machinery of extermination was relatively small, and our knowledge of them is limited. It is reasonable to assume that many of them were similar to those involved in the mass shootings, that is, killers out of a sense of duty. Many had dealt with dead bodies during the euthanasia program, and they were accustomed to mass murder. Even those who initially were shaken by the mass murder eventually fell into line. After his first selection on the ramp, the young SS physician Hans Delmotte is reported to have experienced a nervous breakdown. But with some encouragement from his colleagues, Delmotte soon settled into his job.[75]

Dick de Mildt, a professor of law at the University of Amsterdam, has suggested that for "these men no additional incentives or preparations beyond their marching orders were needed to turn them from 'mercy killers' into the fieldworkers of the 'Final Solution.'" They would not have acted differently if they had been ordered to kill as enemies of the Reich all those having blond hair or wearing spectacles.[76] I regard this inference as speculative and probably incorrect. Although they were not ideologically obsessed, all of these men had been exposed to anti-Semitic agitation, and most of them had come to regard the Jews as outliers about whose fate nobody cared. Alf Lüdtke has coined the term *Alltag-Rassismus* (everyday racism) for this attitude.[77] Their willingness to follow orders probably would not have been sufficient to make them kill the blond-haired and bespectacled. Indeed, as the postwar Einsatzgruppen trial would demonstrate, even the officers of these murder units were unwilling to carry out just any orders to kill.

Plunder was an integral part of Nazi policy toward the Jews. The Reich confiscated economic enterprises, and as Jews were deported, the state took over their apartments and buildings. By early 1943, the proceeds from auctioning these possessions amounted to 7.2 million Reichsmarks.[78] The final plundering phase took place in the killing centers.[79] Here even body parts were taken and processed for industrial use. The factories of death not only snuffed out the lives of about three million Jews but also created a rich source of booty for the Nazi state and the murderers. It was common knowledge that all echelons of the killing machinery appropriated whatever valuables they could get hold of. Himmler regarded such unauthorized enrichment as irreconcilable with the "decency" he expected from his men and repeatedly tried to end the widespread corruption. This endeavor failed, and the killers continued to seize Jewish gold, fur coats, and other valuables for their personal gain.

Yet enough was left for the national treasury and the German people. Guidelines issued in 1942 listed the goods that should be seized. The list included blankets, umbrellas, baby carriages, pants, women's underwear, shaving utensils, pocket knives, scissors, fountain pens, and the like.[80] On January 5, 1944, Odilo Globocnik reported to Himmler that Operation Reinhard had yielded the equivalent of 180 million Reichsmarks ($72 million) consisting of currency, gold jewelry, diamonds, clocks, and other valuables. A total of 1,901 train cars, loaded with clothing, towels, tablecloths, and textiles, had arrived in Germany.[81] These effects were distributed to needy Germans or sold at auctions for the benefit of the state. In Auschwitz, in the summer of 1944 and at the peak of the extermination process, as many as 1,600 male and female prisoners worked in two shifts to dispose of the possessions of the killed. According to Höss, twenty train cars per day were loaded with confiscated property. The facilities where the loot was stored and sorted became known as "Canada," a country that symbolized riches. When Soviet troops liberated Auschwitz in January 1945, they discovered 293 sacks of human hair weighing a total of seven tons. There were also piles of shoes, spectacles, and much more.

The murder of the Jews at Auschwitz yielded six tons of dental gold, most of which was deposited at the Reichsbank.[82] Oswald Pohl, the head of the SS Economic and Administrative Office, through whose hands much of the gold was channeled, was asked by the prison psychiatrist Goldensohn whether it ever had occurred to him that this gold had human blood on it. He replied that he "never brought the gold articles to the Reichsbank personally." He knew that "it came from the exterminated Jews.... But I didn't touch it."[83] After the war, Pohl went into hiding, disguised as a farmhand. He was found eventually, tried, and hanged at Landsberg prison.

5

Evading Participation and Opposing the Killing

On December 12, 1941, Himmler issued directives regarding the importance of providing entertainment for the units carrying out the Final Solution of the Jewish Question. The order spoke of the "difficult task" and the "difficult duty" with which the killing detachments were charged. It was imperative, Himmler went on to say, that those members of the SS and the police who felt unable to carry out this assignment be relieved "in a timely fashion" and sent on leave or transferred to a different type of duty.[1] This directive may not have been the first such instruction, for the principle that weak-natured individuals could be excused from the killing was adhered to by practically all units from the start of the invasion of the Soviet Union in June 1941. We know that not a single person who asked to be relieved on grounds of psychological difficulties was tried by a military court and severely punished. The first careful study confirming this fact was carried out by Hans Buchheim of the Institute for Contemporary History in Munich for the Auschwitz trial in 1964.[2] Herbert Jäger, professor of criminology at the University of Frankfurt, undertook an even more comprehensive examination of the subject in 1967 and came to the same conclusion. Among 103 cases of individuals who asked to be excused from participation in the mass killings, not one suffered a harsh punishment for making this request.[3] Himmler and his subordinates did not want to rely on "weak natures" for carrying out the "difficult task." Moreover, the fact that the trial of such a person would have required a court to confront the killing innocent men, women, and children was undoubtedly one of the reasons why such trials never took place.

Other sources convey the same message. Shortly before the beginning of the war against the Soviet Union, Heydrich is said to have told a group of SS and Gestapo officers that they could expect "difficult orders." Those who believed that they could not follow such orders were to say so, and they would be assigned to other duties. At postwar trials, SS officers who had served in the killing units confirmed the possibility of being reassigned and freed from further participation in the killing. Franz Six, the commanding officer of Vorkommando Moscow

(EG B), testified at the Eichmann trial that several SD officers successfully applied to the RSHA for transfer. Another officer told the Einsatzgruppen trial that the head of Einsatzgruppe B had allowed the transfer of those too weak to carry out the mass killings. All witnesses mentioned that such men usually were shifted to front-line duty or similar assignments.[4]

One of the first Nazi leaders to mention the psychological burden of participating in mass executions was Hans Frank, the governor of the *Generalgouvernement* (German-occupied Poland). The occasion was a meeting on May 30, 1940, convened to discuss Hitler's order to murder the Polish intelligentsia. "Gentlemen," Frank declared, "we are not murderers. For the police official or SS-Mann who is required to carry out the execution as part of his official duties, this is a terrible task. It is easy to sign hundreds of sentences of death, but carrying them out is a terrible burden for German men, decent German soldiers and comrades."[5]

The campaign against the Jews during the war against the Soviet Union greatly increased the psychological burden described by Frank. We know that there exists an inverse relationship between distance and killing: taking life is easier as the distance between perpetrators and their victims increases.[6] This relationship was observed in a follow-up to the study on obedience carried out by the psychologist Stanley Milgram in the early 1970s, and it is evidenced in real warfare.[7] Dropping bombs from a high-flying plane is less taxing on one's psyche than thrusting a bayonet into an enemy combatant. The way in which the annihilation of the Jews was carried out during the first year of the war involved precisely the kind of close contact between killer and victim that is known to be difficult. Hence it is not surprising that the practice of wholesale murder exacted a heavy emotional toll. One study of the subject estimates that about 20 percent of the members of the Einsatzgruppen had major psychological difficulties.[8]

The majority of those who requested reassignment from this nasty job were not necessarily morally opposed to the murder of the Jews, but were simply unable to take part in it themselves. The massacres made them physically or emotionally sick, and the killing of women and children was especially trying. Participants experienced nervous breakdowns, and there were suicides and episodes of men running amok. Robert Lifton interviewed a German psychiatrist who had treated members of the Einsatzgruppen. He reported having encountered severe anxiety, nightmares, tremors, and numerous bodily complaints in his patients.[9] Today we call these reactions post-traumatic stress disorder.

The highest-ranking SS officer to suffer a nervous collapse as a result of his role in the mass killings was the Higher SS and Police Leader Erich von dem Bach-Zelewski, who was in charge of EG B and other units engaged in antipartisan warfare and the murder of Jews in central Russia. Von dem Bach attended mass executions and on at least one occasion participated in the shooting.[10] He had developed the reputation of being an enthusiastic Nazi and tough street fighter during the 1920s, and once in Russia he continued to pursue the elimination of all ideological opponents with efficiency, brutality, and zeal.[11] Yet in March 1942 Bach had to be hospitalized with a serious intestinal disorder and a nervous breakdown. Ernst-Robert Grawitz, the chief medical officer of the SS, reported to Himmler that Bach suffered from nervous exhaustion and from "hallucinations concerning the shootings of Jews he had overseen and other grave events in the East."[12]

Bach himself refused to acknowledge that he had shown weakness. He accused his doctors of having "poisoned him emotionally" and talking him into a nervous collapse. "As your veteran fighter," he wrote Himmler, "whose energy is improving daily, I reject such a distortion of the facts." He went on to say that he would prove within the year that "your old warhorse will not let himself be kept down by such matters."[13] Bach was as good as his word, and a few months later he was back at the job of killing Jews and conducting antipartisan operations. In August 1944, Bach was given command of all troops fighting the Warsaw uprising, and he again distinguished himself by his brutality. In exchange for his testimony at the Nuremberg trial of his former superiors, Bach was never accused of any war crimes. But in 1961 he was convicted of the murder of several German Communists in the early thirties, and he died in a Munich prison on March 8, 1972.

The case of Alfred Filbert, an SS officer in charge of an Einsatzkommando, confirmed that being an ardent Nazi and hater of Jews proved to be no protection against nervous collapse. The jurist Filbert led EK 9 of EG A and distinguished himself in exterminating the Jewish community of Vilnius. In 1962, a German court sentenced him to life imprisonment for being an accessory to the murder of at least 6,800 people. In his defense, Filbert argued that he had asked to be transferred to another duty in Berlin, but the court concluded that he had not done so for reasons of conscience. Quite the contrary, Filbert had ordered the shooting of as many Jews as he could seize and had conducted himself toward his victims in a most "inhuman" manner. Filbert, the court determined, had requested to be relieved because of the "nervous strain" that resulted from leading EK 9.[14] The record showed that Filbert was sent to Berlin because he suffered from a nervous disorder and severe depression after doing killing duty for four months. One can infer from this failure of nerve that the traditional moral condemnation of killing the innocent persisted to some degree in the minds of even the most fanatical Nazis. Despite their belief that the Jews represented an inferior species, their old values and conscience had not died completely.[15]

A considerable number of soldiers and others involved in the killing of Jews experienced similar psychological problems. At a shooting of some two thousand Jews in Belarus, a member of a police unit suffered a nervous breakdown and had to be removed from the scene screaming. The experience was so shattering for another member of this unit that he deserted.[16] Others experienced less severe symptoms of psychological stress. Some of these men overcame their problem and adjusted to the routine of murder; others asked to be relieved, and most of their requests were granted.

A member of EG C recalled that at the first execution "I only managed to shoot about five times. I began to feel unwell, I felt as though I was in a dream. . . . I went and stood about fifty meters away from the firing squad. It was obvious that I was in no state to continue shooting. The nervous strain was too great for me."[17] Testimony at the postwar trial of members of EK Tilsit revealed that a number of members of the unit, then eighteen and nineteen years old, became sick and vomited at the shooting of several Jewish teenagers. Some of the victims had been only wounded, and there were cries from the pit to end their suffering. Two of the young shooters were in such bad shape that they had to be relieved, and the commanding officer had to take their place.[18] A member of another such unit described the scene at the shooting of nearly four hundred Jewish men, women, and children: "There was chaos at the place of execution. Several men felt sick. The victims fell into the ditch and some of them were still alive. . . . I felt sick when I saw the bloody mass moving in the ditch and I turned round, with my stomach heaving. I eventually drank a lot of schnapps."[19] Another shooter who became ill after he had killed two women and two children confessed, "I could not eat or work for two days. On the first day, I stayed in bed."[20] A participant in a massacre at Mogilev recounted, "After this event I could neither sleep nor eat. The others reacted the same way."[21] Many more such occurrences are recorded.[22]

As a rule, men who experienced these and other kinds of psychological problems were excused by their superiors from participation in the killing. Those known to have "weak natures" were often given escort or cordoning duties. We also know of cases when officers announced ahead of an action that those not up to the task could be exempted. Major Wilhelm Trapp made this offer to the men of Reserve Police Battalion 101 in July 1942, and some ten to twelve men availed themselves of it. Several months later, Lieutenant Heinz Buchmann excused four men in his company.[23] The same policy prevailed in Police Battalion 320[24] and in EG D, where the men were informed of the possibility of being excused at a training session.[25] Many of these arrangements were made discreetly. Christopher Browning points out that "evasion was easily tolerated but protest and obstruction most emphatically were not." He estimates that the share of those in the police units who sought to evade the killing was about 10 to 20 percent.[26] The practice of accommodating these requests was in line with Himmler's thinking, as he wanted the important task of annihilating the Jews be carried out by men of strong conviction. Moreover, the officers in charge of carrying out the killing operations were no doubt interested in minimizing complications and preferred to rely on volunteers, who were usually available.[27]

Many of the men who asked to be exempted from the killing hated the Jews for making them participate in the odious assignment of killing them. Paul Blobel, the commander of EK 4a (EG C), was one of many who after the war expressed self-pity because of what they had had to do. "The nervous strain was far heavier in the case of our men who carried out the executions than in that of their victims. From the psychological point of view they had a terrible time."[28] A forty-three-year-old noncommissioned Wehrmacht officer likewise blamed the victims. He called the executions a *Schweinerei* (swinish mess) and added, "We were the ones who had to suffer."[29]

We know of eighty-five cases of members of the Wehrmacht who actually refused orders to execute civilians or prisoners of war.[30] We can assume that the majority of these refusals were motivated by the desire not to have to kill defenseless human beings. Here are some examples: A member of the auxiliary unit told his superior, "I did not come to Russia to shoot women and children. I myself have a wife and children at home." The officer did not insist on his participation in the shootings.[31] A German forestry official who was detailed to a ghetto-clearing operation objected to this assignment and complained to his superior that "it cannot be my task as head of the forestry office to shoot Jews dead."[32] A driver in a Sonderkommando was reproached for not having participated in any of the shootings. He replied that he was a "good Catholic" and could not reconcile executions with his conscience. Word about this refusal spread, and the man was transferred to duty in the Netherlands in order not to undermine unit discipline.[33] A member of Police Battalion 322 had managed to evade the shooting of Jews. When his acts were discovered and his superiors asked him why he had failed to do his part, he replied that he "did not want to shoot defenseless, innocent human beings." In this instance the soldier thereupon was ordered to take part in the killing of five young Jews and a Jewish couple, and the commanding officer gave orders to make sure that the outlier did indeed hit his target.[34]

In some cases, men seeking to avoid their assignment to murder pretended to be sick. In October 1941, a member of an Einsatzkommando feigned being mentally ill and was sent to a hospital in Germany. According to testimony at a postwar trial, he was visited there by Ohlendorf, the head of EG D, who reproached him for his weakness. The recovering "mental patient" replied that he had been raised as a Catholic and could not shoot defenseless human beings.[35]

Rudolf Lorenz had volunteered for a parachute unit but ended up in Russia killing Jews. After a while, he refused further participation on the grounds that his nerves were shot. The episode that brought him to this point was the shooting of fifteen fifteen- to eighteen-year-old Jewish boys and girls, who were made to dig their own grave and then were executed. He was sent to a hospital, received electric shocks and other treatments, and was sent back to Russia. He tried to lodge a complaint with the commanding general of his unit but was unable to get through to him. After a second round of treatments in a psychiatric hospital, Lorenz, together with four other soldiers, tried to desert, but they were caught. All five were condemned to death for their attempt. Lorenz survived because his mother, who had been a classmate of Hitler's sister Paula, persuaded her to forward to Hitler a plea to pardon her son. The war ended before this process had run its course.[36]

Klaus Hornig was a first lieutenant in the police, and in October 1941 was sent to join Police Battalion 306 in Lublin. Hornig was a believing Catholic who had refused to join the SS. At the end of October, he was ordered to shoot 780 prisoners of war who were political commissars and Jews, but he told his commanding officer that he could not carry out this order because it violated both international law and Article 47 of the German military code. That article states that the person giving an order generally is responsible if an order violates a legal provision. The subordinate carrying out the order would also be punished as an accomplice if he knew that the order in question involved an illegal act. Hornig further stated that only "SS-Lümmel" (SS louts) would use brutal methods such as driving civilians from their homes. Hornig was transferred to Frankfurt and charged with undermining morale, because he had told his men of the illegality of shooting prisoners of war. His trial before an SS and Police court took place in May 1943, and he was sentenced to two and a half years' imprisonment. Hornig appealed this conviction, but he was subsequently charged with having listened to a foreign radio station in July 1944. For this offense, he was sent to the Buchenwald concentration camp. Here he was tried again for undermining military morale and sentenced to a jail term of five years and seven months as well as continued imprisonment in the concentration camp. Hornig was ultimately freed when Allied troops liberated Buchenwald on April 11, 1945.[37]

Even in the Auschwitz death camp, it was possible to be relieved of objectionable duty or be transferred out. Alexandre Lasik found several such occurrences in his research on the Auschwitz personnel for the period of 1940–1942.[38] Kurt Jurasek, an SS officer initially assigned to the camp pharmacy, was ordered to supervise the Jewish inmates who had to remove gold teeth from the dead victims. Passing the crematorium on the way, he decided that he would have no part in this process. Jurasek was exempted. His request to be transferred out of Auschwitz was granted, and within three weeks he was sent back to Germany.[39] There is also the case of Hans Wilhelm Münch, a bacteriologist who was drafted into the Waffen-SS and sent to the Auschwitz branch of the Hygienic Institute of the Waffen-SS. Münch refused to serve on the ramp to select victims for the gas chambers. When his superior insisted, Münch traveled to Berlin and obtained exemption from this duty from the head of the Hygienic Institute.[40] After the war, Münch was tried by a Polish court in Cracow, but he was acquitted on the basis of the testimony of former camp inmates whom he had protected.

Several Jewish survivors report that at times soldiers and policemen guarding a column of Jews being led to the place of execution failed to shoot at those trying to escape or shot without aiming.[41] In a few cases, soldiers and officers not only refused to participate in the murder of Jews but also actively tried to prevent it. In July 1942, First Lieutenant Albert Battell, the commander of a local Wehrmacht garrison in Przemysl (in southeastern Poland), was informed that the remaining Jewish workers in the town would be *ausgesiedelt*, that is, liquidated. Thereupon Battel, who had gained the reputation of being a friend of the Jews, used armed men to block the bridge leading into the town. After the intervention of higher echelons, Battel had to give up the blockade, and he was reprimanded. On October 3, Himmler wrote to Bormann that after the end of the war he would give orders to arrest the rebellious officer.[42] Trying the officer during the war might have burdened smooth relations between Wehrmacht and SS. Such a trial also inevitably would have provided undesirable publicity to the killing operations. For these reasons, Battell emerged from this episode unscathed. The German postwar court that dealt with this incident noted that this dispute between the Wehrmacht and the police unit tasked to carry out the liquidation attracted considerable attention. And in fact, Yad Vashem in Jerusalem named Battell posthumously as one of the "Just of the Nations."[43]

The *Feldwebel* (deputy platoon leader) Anton Schmid was a devout Catholic who considered it his Christian duty to save as many Jews as possible. Schmid ran a workshop in Vilnius where he employed 150 Jews, even though there was work for only 50. Members of the Jewish resistance were allowed to meet in his apartment. The Germans began to liquidate the Riga ghetto on November 29, 1941, and shortly thereafter Schmid transported one of the leaders of the resistance, Mordechai Tenenbaum, to Riga in order to save the famous Jewish historian Simon Dubnow. Unfortunately the attempted rescue came too late. Dubnow had already been shot. Schmid also issued false identity cards to endangered Jews and used his truck to convey them from the ghetto. He is said to have saved the life of about 350 persons in this way. Eventually the courageous German soldier was caught. He was tried by court martial and executed on April 13, 1942. He too was made one of the "Just of the Nations."[44]

Officer Wilm Hosenfeld, also a Catholic, joined the Nazi party in 1935 but became disillusioned as a result of his experiences in occupied Poland. In a letter to his wife dated July 23, 1942, Hosenfeld expressed his disgust and his depressed state as a result of the mass murder of Jews he was witnessing. "Is this what German soldiers die for at the front? Hardly anything like this has ever occurred in recorded history. Perhaps primitive men ate each other, but the slaughter of an entire people—men, women and children—in the twentieth century is such a terrible burden of guilt ... that one wants to bow one's head in shame." Hosenfeld went on to say that he could not believe that Hitler wanted such "abominations" to take place.[45] The officer who thus dissociated himself from the "enormities" of the regime did more than use strong words. Stationed in Warsaw in September 1939, Hosenfeld issued false identity cards and provided employment for those endangered by the SS. As he declared in another letter, "I try to save everyone who can be saved." It was Hosenfeld who helped the well-known Jewish pianist Wladyslaw Szpilman, who had taken refuge in a bombed-out house, in an act of bravery recreated in the film *The Pianist*. After the Germans had crushed the uprising in the Warsaw ghetto, Hosenfeld recorded in his diary that "we are all cowardly and did not risk enough." The German people would have to pay for the horrible things that took place there.[46] Hosenfeld was captured by the Red Army in January 1945 and died in a Soviet prison in 1952. On November 25, 2008, in part as a result of the efforts of Wladyslaw Szpilman, Hosenfeld was also chosen as one of the "Just of the Nations" by Yad Vashem.[47] Altogether, Yad Vashem recognized about forty-five Wehrmacht soldiers as saviors of Jews. The actual number of such men may have been even higher.[48]

On May 3, 1944, a German soldier whose name is not preserved made an attempt to save thirteen Hungarian Jews by smuggling them to Romania hidden in a Wehrmacht truck. At a border checkpoint, the Jews were discovered hidden between barrels. Six days later, the soldier was tried before a military court for treason in wartime, specifically for attempted "Jew smuggling," and was sentenced to death. The general in command of all German army units in Romania ordered that the execution of the soldier be made known to his troops. The order mentioned that the smuggling had taken place in return for a payment of money but leaves open the question of whether humanitarian sentiments may also have played a role.[49]

Trying to save Jews was dangerous. After the start of the deportations of German Jews to the East in the fall of 1941, all contact with the Jewish population was declared to be a punishable offense. An RSHA decree of October 24 of that year threatened imprisonment in a concentration camp for any display of sympathy for the Jews. As the fortunes of war turned against Germany, discipline in the Wehrmacht became deadly. During the first year of the war, military courts handed down 29 death sentences every month; by November 1944, that number had increased to 526.[50] Hence the freedom of action of soldiers seeking to help Jews was strictly limited, and such actions carried a high personal risk.[51]

Help for Jews at times came from unexpected quarters. A former *Gauleiter* and the head of the civilian occupation of Belarus, Generalkommissar Wilhelm Kube, was involved in a series of morally ambiguous events. Hilberg has referred to it as "one of the strangest episodes in the history of the Nazi regime."[52] Kube was an early member of the Nazi movement, and his anti-Semitic credentials were impeccable. In an article published in 1934, he declared the Jews to be as dangerous for white people as "the plague, consumption and syphilis are for the human race. . . . The carrier of the plague must be eradicated and isolated." He had no objection to the murder of the Jews of Belarus, and in one instance even requested such a killing. Yet he was troubled by taking the lives of the German Jews whom he had earlier vilified. Observing that some of them carried medals for outstanding service in World War I, he concluded that these people after all were part of "our cultural heritage" and should not be treated like the "debased eastern Jews."[53]

Kube also took exception to the manner in which the policy of annihilation was carried out. One of his subordinates reported to him about a 1941 operation conducted by Police Battalion 11 in the town of Slutsk that "bordered on sadism. During the action the city itself presented a horrible picture. With indescribable brutality by the German policemen as well but especially by the Lithuanians, the Jews were dragged out of their lodgings and driven together. There was shooting everywhere in the city, and bodies of Jews who had been shot piled up in the streets. . . . Altogether the entire scene was more than ghastly." Moreover, the men of the police battalion had plundered "in an outrageous way," taking with them "anything useful, such as boots, leather, textiles, gold, and other valuables." Watches and rings were torn from the Jews "in the most brutal way."[54] When Kube conveyed this information to his superior, Reichskommissar Hinrich Lohse, he mentioned as an example of completely unacceptable methods the fact that wounded Jews had been buried alive and eventually had worked their way out of the mass grave. Such occurrences represented *eine bodenlose Schweinerei* (a fathomless swinish mess) that should be reported to the Führer and Reichsmarschall Göring.[55]

The tension between Kube and the SS engaged in implementing the Final Solution continued for the next two years. In addition to intervening on behalf of individual Jews, Kube tried to protect some four thousand German Jews by employing them in ghetto factories. These endeavors drew an angry response from Eduard Strauch, the SS officer in charge of the Security Police and the SD in Belarus. In a memo dated July 20, 1943, Strauch summarized a telephone conversation he had had with Kube earlier that day. This conversation took place after Strauch had arrested seventy Jews employed by Kube's office and had taken them away for *Sonderbehandlung* (special treatment):

> I stressed my lack of understanding of the fact that Germans would make an issue over a few Jews. Time and again my men have been accused of barbarism and sadism, while I am simply doing my duty. Even the fact that Jews selected for *Sonderbehandlung* have had their gold crowns removed by dentists has been made the subject of conversations. Kube replied that this kind of conduct was unworthy of a German and of the Germany of Kant and Goethe. It would be our responsibility if our conduct sullied the reputation of Germany all over the world. Men were allegedly slobbering all over. I protested energetically against this description and expressed my regret that in addition to performing this disgusting work we were also were being made the target of mudslinging.[56]

Strauch sent this memo to Berlin, but Kube remained in his position. He was killed on September 22, 1943, by a bomb planted in his bedroom by a Russian woman. Strauch was sentenced to death by two postwar courts and died in prison while awaiting execution.

Kube's conflicted attitude toward the destruction of the Jews was not unique. We know of others in the East who objected to the manner in which the killings took place, even though they did not deny the rightness of annihilating the Jews. After the men of SK 10b and the attached Police Reserve Battalion 9 had executed one hundred Jews in Czernowitz, they discussed the operation in their quarters. Several of the men described the way in which the Jews had been shot as a *Sauerei* (mess), but they did not question the deed itself.[57] A Protestant minister wrote his wife in 1941 that the Latvians' killing of Jews with spades had caused "general disgust." Everyone was agreeable to lining up the Jews up against the wall, but not to such "disorderly knocking down."[58] Nechama Tec writes of a police officer in a town in Belarus who opposed what he regarded as "chaotic and haphazard executions." He called it a *Schweinerei* and insisted that the Jews be shot in an "orderly fashion." The same officer refused to participate in the hunting down of Jews who had gone into hiding.[59]

Even the manner in which the Jews of Berlin were deported inspired criticism. The editorial office of *Das Schwarze Korps*, the official publication of the SS, happened to be situated next to the location where Jews were assembled prior to being deported. The editor of the paper complained to Rudolf Brandt on Himmler's personal staff that both his employees and foreign visitors had been subjected to what he called a "degrading and shameful" sight—Jews being brutally lashed by a Gestapo official in the course of deportation. Such treatment was termed intolerable and sheer madness. The writer stressed that his complaint had nothing to do with humanitarian feelings but with his sincere conviction that things had to be done in a properly German manner. "After all, we do not want to look like frenzied sadists."[60]

Another morally ambiguous event arose in the early days of the invasion of the Soviet Union. At the beginning of August 1941, a German division occupied Bjelaja Zerkow, south of Kiev, and its commander asked the SK 4a (EG C) to kill the the town's Jews. Within ten days, a company of Waffen-SS attached to the Sonderkommando shot some 850 Jews, but it left a group of 90 children under the age of five alive, abandoned without food or water. The screams of the children caused Wehrmacht soldiers to call in two military chaplains, who found them half naked, covered with flies, and lying in their own excrement. All this was reported to the first staff officer of the division, Lieutenant Colonel Helmuth Groscurth. After Groscurth had been told that the Waffen-SS unit intended to kill the children, he used armed men to block the departure of a truck filled with children. He also contacted his superiors to try to postpone the killing. The issue was discussed at several echelons of command, and

Field Marshal Reichenau, the commander of the Sixth Army, personally decided that the operation "had to be completed in a suitable way."[61] That left open the question who was going to undertake the disagreeable assignment. August Häffner, an officer of the Sonderkommando, pointed out that the men of the Waffen-SS unit, eighteen to twenty years old, were too young, and the men of the Sonderkommando were married men who had their own children and thus were equally unsuitable. Hence the murder of the ninety children was carried out by a group of Ukrainian auxiliaries. At his postwar trial, Häffner described how the children were lined up at the edge of a pit and then shot. "The wailing was indescribable."[62]

The above facts are uncontested, but Groscurth's role in this episode remains equivocal. In a letter to his wife dated November 21, 1939, he wrote that the actions of the SS in Warsaw left him "ashamed to be a German."[63] He also had links to the resistance group around Admiral Wilhelm Canaris, the head of military intelligence. A deeply religious Protestant, Groscurth in his diary testifies to his strong anti-Nazi feelings. He did indeed try to prevent, or at least postpone, the killing of children. In a report on the affair, he wrote, "Measures against women and children were undertaken which in no way differed from atrocities carried out by the enemy about whom the troops are continually being informed." And yet, as Saul Friedländer argues, it appears that his actions with regard to the Jewish children were motivated less by humanitarian sentiments than by concern for the reaction of his men. "The execution," Groscurth wrote, "could have been carried out without any uproar if the field and local headquarters had taken the necessary steps to keep the troops away.... Both infants and children should have been eliminated immediately in order to avoid this inhuman agony."[64] On the other hand, the historian Nicholas Stargardt has suggested that Groscurth had no choice but to couch his argument against killing the children in terms acceptable to his superiors.[65]

All of these cases involved individuals who to varying degrees and for different reasons managed to avoid participation in the murder of Jews or who even attempted to prevent it. Others voiced criticism, sometimes even in public. After the invasion of Poland in 1939, General Johannes Blaskowitz, commander of the Eastern Territories, condemned the conduct of the SS and the slaughter of Jews and Poles. He also took exception to "illegal executions," a complaint that Hitler dismissed as "childish."[66] In a memo dated November 27, 1939, he noted "the tremendous brutalization and moral depravity which is spreading rapidly." High-ranking SS and police officers "demand and openly praise acts of violence and brutality."[67] This attitude, Blaskowitz argued, constituted an "unbearable burden" for the Wehrmacht.[68] Hitler was outraged by this characterization, and Blaskowitz learned his lesson. In a presentation made on February 6, 1940, the general labeled Poles and Jews as "our archenemies in the East" and pleaded for a more systematic strategy against them.[69]

In the summer of 1943, the military physician Christian Schöne mentioned the killing of the Jews in a chain letter to the next of kin of missing soldiers and demanded an end to the massacres "for reasons of morality and honor." The good doctor was court-martialed, but he got away with a prison sentence of one year.[70] Those responsible for ordering the Final Solution knew that there would be negative reactions here and there, but they were determined to disregard them. After a meeting with Hitler on June 19, 1943, Himmler noted in a memo that the "evacuation" of the Jews would be carried through with iron determination despite the "restiveness" (Unruhe) that was to be expected.[71]

The overall number of German soldiers and officers who demurred at murdering Jews was small, and the share of those who did so on moral grounds was smaller still. David Kitterman analyzed eighty-five cases of unwillingness to kill in Russia and found that about one quarter of these were based on reasons of conscience as opposed to weakness.[72] Kitterman's findings are not the last word on the subject, but the overall picture is probably correct. It appears that not a few of those who objected to the murder of the Jews and actively tried to help them were believing Christians, but we know that being a Christian did not prevent numerous others from participating in the killing. Virtually all Nazis were the baptized children of Christians, and the continued adherence of the great majority of the German people to the Christian faith did not constitute an effective bulwark to the relentless process of destruction. Almost eighteen thousand Catholic priests, theology students, and lay brothers served in the Wehrmacht as military chaplains, but not one of them voiced dissent from the policy of annihilation.[73] The record of Protestant military chaplains has not yet been examined in detail, but it appears not to be any different.[74] For all these men, dedication to the fatherland and promoting the salvation of Christian souls was more important than challenging the genocidal practices of the Nazi regime. These policies were antithetical to everything their faith stood for, but this theoretical conflict failed to prevent their deportment of accommodation and compromise.

The fact that there were men willing to opt out shows that acquiescence to the Nazis' goals was not the only possible course of action.[75] Even if not everyone was prepared to face the risks involved in outright refusals, it was possible to be excused for having a weak nature. As von dem Bach-Zelewski testified at Nuremberg, at issue was "not life and death but the willingness to incur damage to one's career."[76] The often-invoked imperative of absolute obedience turned out in practice to be less than categorical.

‖ 6 ‖

The Perpetrators on Trial: Flawed Justice

The historian who seeks an answer to the question "Why did they do it?" can find valuable assistance in the legal proceedings against Nazi criminals. In order to impose an appropriate punishment for these individuals, German courts had to establish the circumstances surrounding the crimes of the Nazi regime and to probe the motives of the perpetrators. The cumulative record of these investigations has thus contributed important historical knowledge. Moreover, what appear to be mere legal issues also assist inquiry into the role played by individual killers and the reasons for their readiness to engage in mass murder. The way in which the courts handled the distinction between perpetrator and accomplice or the concept of superior orders, for example, helps us understand the dilemmas faced by participants in the program of murder.

At the same time, it must be acknowledged that this process of retribution often failed to serve the ends of justice. The courts applied a crude version of the concept of totalitarianism, according to which only Hitler, Himmler, and Heydrich and their immediate entourage were the real perpetrators of the Holocaust, while most others were judged, at worst, to be accessories to murder.[1]

In many ways, Germany's record in facing up to its Nazi past has been exemplary. It stands in sharp contrast to the disappointing way in which countries such as Japan have dealt with their unsavory record in World War II. The horrors committed by the Nazi regime between 1933 and 1945 have been fully acknowledged, large sums of money have been paid to its victims, almost two thousand informative memorials have been established at the sites of former concentration camps and other war-related venues, and scholars continue to conduct significant research on why and how these crimes could occur. A generation of younger historians, in particular, has dedicated itself to the task of making sure that these terrible events will not be forgotten and that their lessons will be learned. On the other hand, the legal accounting by German courts for the unprecedented violations of human decency and morality by the Nazi state has drawn criticism both inside and outside Germany. The German Jewish survivor and highly regarded public intellectual Ralph Giordano has spoken of this flawed record as a "second guilt."[2]

The failure of the German judiciary to provide for timely and just retribution for Nazi crimes has been recognized at the highest levels of the German government. On June 10, 2013, the German Ministry of Justice released the text of a symposium organized to investigate the role that the retention of former Nazi judges after 1945 may have played in the adjudication of Nazi crimes.[3] One of the featured speakers on that occasion was Giordano, who argued that in spite of sincere efforts at many levels of the legal profession for more than fifty years, "the great German effort to bring Nazi perpetrators to the bar of justice remains a farce."[4] The fact that these strong words could be uttered at an official gathering of government officials indicates how seriously the issue of punishing Nazi criminals is taken in today's Germany.

One can begin the discussion of this subject by looking at some key statistics. The number of personnel serving in the concentration camps by early 1945 had reached about forty thousand men and women. Some six thousand men rotated through the Einsatzgruppen, and they were assisted by an estimated fifteen thousand men in police battalions and twenty-five thousand Waffen-SS troops. The number of members of the Wehrmacht involved in Nazi crimes can only be guessed. In all, then, we reach a figure of at least one hundred thousand men and women potentially implicated in various offenses, especially the Holocaust. Through 2005, West German authorities had investigated 172,294 individuals, but brought charges against only 16,740 alleged wrongdoers—fewer than 10 percent of all suspects. The death of some defendants and several amnesties eliminated 2,045 of the accused, and 13,952 defendants were brought to trial. 6,656 of these individuals, about 48 percent, were convicted.[5]

This less-than-impressive record gets worse when we consider the kinds of offenses involved in these convictions. The largest number involved crimes against political opponents during the early days of the Nazi regime, malicious denunciations, and the events of Kristallnacht. Only 9 percent comprised crimes committed in the concentration camps, and a mere 7 percent related to the Holocaust, the most heinous of Nazi crimes. Only 981 of the convictions were for acts of killing.[6] Obtaining convictions against defendants implicated in the murder of the Jews in the East undoubtedly was fraught with many difficulties. When survivors, traumatized by the horrific experiences they had gone through, testified at these trials, they often found it difficult to recall events with the precision demanded by the courts. SS members for the most part refused to testify against their former comrades. But the small number of defendants tried and found guilty for involvement in the Holocaust remains striking.

Still more surprising, in view of the serious nature of these offenses, are the light sentences imposed. Most of those directly involved with the murder of the Jews—more than two thirds of the members of the Einsatzgruppen— were convicted merely of being accomplices to murder.[7] Before the death penalty was abolished by the Basic Law of 1949 (the German constitution), the courts imposed sixteen sentences of death. Thereafter, only 166 defendants were sentenced to life imprisonment, the most severe punishment possible for those convicted of murder.[8] In other words, of the 981 individuals accused of killing, only 182 individuals, or fewer than 20 percent, received the maximum penalty allowed under German law for these crimes. According to one study, of a sample of 1,770 former members of the Einsatzgruppen, only 136, or 7.5 percent, were successfully prosecuted, and only 8 of these received the maximum penalty of life imprisonment. Moreover, not a single Wehrmacht officer was convicted for crimes against Jews.[9]

It is no doubt true that to try some 100,000 suspected Nazi criminals would have constituted an enormously difficult undertaking. At the end of the war, the legal apparatus for such an endeavor simply did not exist. It has also been suggested that an important part of the problem was the difficulty of finding the perpetrators after 1945. One researcher has demonstrated this arduousness with the example of a police battalion involved in the mass murder of Jews. Of 889 former members of this battalion whose names could be ascertained, some 400 had been killed in the course of the war, had been declared missing and dead, or had died between the end of the war and the beginning of such trials in the 1960s. Thirty held Austrian citizenship and were therefore immune from German prosecution, and another 271 could not be located. Some of them had probably fled abroad. Since 130 men, as investigators established, had had no share in the massacres, this left 58 who could be tried, but by the time attempts were made to bring them to justice, many of them were no longer fit to stand trial.[10]

And yet this line of argument is less than convincing. The number of possible defendants may not always have been as small as in the above example. For instance, in the 1965 proceedings against members of Police Battalion 303, which was involved in the murder of about 50,000 Jews, it was possible to interrogate 376 men out of a total strength of 883 soldiers.[11] Moreover, we know that many of those who submitted medical certificates of incapacitating illness had obtained these attestations fraudulently from doctors who sympathized with the former Nazis. This way of avoiding punishment came to be called "biological amnesty," and many judges readily accepted these certificates even when their bogus character was obvious.[12] Finally, the number of those who escaped trial by death or being too old and ill would have been far smaller if the trials of members of the killing units had started soon after the end of the war rather than in the 1960s. The far more serious impediment than locating the criminals was the fact that many of the judges trying these cases found ways to minimize the terrible wrongdoing of which these men stood accused. It was not that the postwar judiciary *could* not achieve appropriate retribution for these crimes but that many of the judges taking on this task *would* not do what justice required. This failure is brought into focus when we compare the record of the German courts with that of the Allied tribunals.

After Germany's defeat in 1945, many of the leading figures of the Nazi regime committed suicide. Besides Hitler, this list included Himmler, Joseph Goebbels, Philip Bouhler, Bernhard Rust, and Otto Thierack. Goering killed himself shortly before he was to be executed. The International Military Tribunal at Nuremberg (October 20, 1945–October 1, 1946) tried twenty-four defendants and condemned twelve of them to death, three to life imprisonment, and four to prison terms ranging from ten to twenty years. All of these men were "desk murderers," that is, they were deeply involved in organizing the murder of millions but did not themselves soil their hands with the actual killing.

We have no reliable figures for trials of Nazi criminals in the Russian zone of occupation. The East German Communist regime, known as the German Democratic Republic, tried 1,642 defendants. Of these, 216 individuals received the death penalty or a term of life imprisonment, while the remainder were given lengthy prison terms.[13] The extent to which these defendants were tried with due process of law remains the subject of controversy. In the three Western zones of occupied Germany, some 35,000 defendants were found guilty by military tribunals, and about 6,500 sentences of death were carried out.[14] Many of these trials involved the kind of criminals with which we are dealing in this book.

Between August 17 and November 17, 1945, a British military court tried forty-five men and women who had served in the Bergen-Belsen concentration camp, including its commandant, Josef Kramer. Eleven of the accused were given the death penalty, and fourteen were acquitted. Significantly, and in contrast to the trials of Nazi criminals by German courts in subsequent years, the defendants were charged not only with specific acts of abusing and killing inmates but also with being part of a conspiracy to ill-treat the persons who were under their care. They were part of a body of people who acted like a lynch mob, members of an organization engaged in "common action."[15]

It was at the Dachau trial of 1945 that this doctrine of common action was fully developed. On November 15, 1945, forty men who had served in the Dachau concentration camp faced an American military court that tried them for killing, mistreating, and starving individuals incarcerated there. The precise number of inmates subjected to inhuman treatment could not be determined, but it amounted to many thousands. William Denton, the young American lawyer who prosecuted the case, noted at the outset that the defendants were not charged with killing, beating, and torturing inmates but with "participating in a common design to kill, to beat, to torture and to subject these subjects to starvation." The operation of such a camp required that a number of individuals act together. Irrespective of a defendant's specific position in the camp, each of the accused "constituted a cog in this wheel, or machine of extermination." Hence a "prima-facie case of guilt" arose once it was shown that an individual had served at Dachau and consequently had participated in the common design. It was the very system of the concentration camp with its attendant practices of killing and mistreating inmates that was criminal.[16]

The doctrine of common design was derived from American criminal law and is similar to the concept of conspiracy. Unlike the case of conspiracy, however, the doctrine of common design does not require the joint planning of the criminal conduct. It merely provides that all participants in an unlawful act are to be considered principals. If A and B go out to rob a bank, and, in the course of the robbery, A kills an employee of the bank, both A and B are responsible for the murder even if B acted only as a lookout. When applied to the situation of the concentration camp, this meant that it was not necessary for each defendant to have committed all of the crimes that the prosecution had shown to have taken place. The individual defendant's guilt was proven by his membership in the staff of the camp and by his knowledge of the common design. Such knowledge of the deadly purposes of the camp was established by the actions performed by individuals in the camp. Each was an essential part, great or small. Many had volunteered for their grim employment, and none had made any serious effort to abandon it. Most of them had acted with zeal, and this fact eliminated the excuse of having been constrained by superior orders. Only in cases where a guard had acted in a more humane manner did the doctrine of superior orders provide for mitigation of punishment, and indeed twelve of the defendants received prison terms rather than the death penalty.[17]

American military courts continued to apply the legal concept of common design at subsequent trials of Nazi criminals. The trial of sixty-one SS personnel of the Mauthausen concentration camp began on March 29, 1946. The court concluded that the running of this camp, the second-largest concentration camp, was a criminal undertaking, and that it would have been impossible for anyone serving on the staff there not to recognize this fact. Whether a member of the general SS or the Waffen-SS, a guard, or a civilian employee engaged in the operation of Mauthausen or its subcamps, all were guilty of having violated the laws and customs of civilized nations by shooting, gassing, hanging, starving, and variously killing innocent human beings. The exact names and numbers of the victims remain unknown, but they reached many thousands. Fifty-eight of the defendants were condemned to death, and the remaining three were sentenced to life imprisonment. On review, nine of the death sentences were commuted to life imprisonment; the remaining forty-nine were carried out.[18]

The Mauthausen trial was followed by 121 other American trials of Nazi criminals, with some 500 defendants. In all of these proceedings, the courts concluded that "the mass atrocity was criminal in nature and that the participants therein, acting in a common design, . . . subject to being rebutted by appropriate evidence, . . . knew of the criminal nature thereof." The only issue in these trials therefore was to determine the manner and degree of participation of each defendant. It would require "appropriate evidence" to rebut the presumed guilt of the accused.[19]

On September 29, 1947, an Allied military court began the trial of Einsatzgruppen officers. The principal charge was crimes against humanity committed by being part of an organization that murdered thousands of innocent civilians. There was no attempt to charge individual crimes.[20] As chief prosecutor Telford Taylor put it in his closing statement, "Any member who assisted in enabling these units to function, knowing what was afoot, is guilty of the crimes committed by the units." The defendants indeed had known exactly what was expected of them. They were not peasants drafted into the Wehrmacht but educated men who fully understood "the sinister program they embarked upon." The trial resulted in guilty verdicts against twenty-two defendants. Fourteen received the death penalty.[21]

When the defendants pleaded that they had merely followed superior orders, Judge Michael Musmanno asked Willy Seibert, who was eventually condemned to be hanged, whether Seibert, if ordered to do so, would shoot his parents. Seibert was unwilling to answer this question, and Musmanno refused to allow the trial to proceed until he did. The court recessed until the following day. The next morning, Seibert looked exhausted and worn out, and the judge, after giving the defendant a moment to compose himself, repeated the question: Would you kill your parents if ordered to do so? After another agonizing silence, Seibert replied, "Mr. President, I would not do so." Next came the following exchange:

MUSMANNO: Then there are some orders which are issued by the chief [sic] of state which may be disobeyed?

SEIBERT: It is inhuman—to ask a son to shoot his parents. . . . I would not have obeyed such an order.

MUSMANNO: Now suppose the order came down for you to shoot the parents of someone else, let us say, a Jew and his wife. . . . It is established beyond any doubt that [they] have not committed any crime. . . . The only thing that is established is that they are Jews and you have this order. . . . Would you shoot the parents?

SEIBERT: Your honor, I would not shoot these parents.

MUSMANNO: Yes, so therefore, this order issued by the Führer to kill all Jews indiscriminately did not have to be obeyed by the German soldiers in your estimation.

Musmanno asked each defendant the same question. Some, like Seibert, acknowledged that they would have refused such an order—a response in conflict with how they had actually conducted themselves while serving with the Einsatzgruppen. Others refused to answer. Nevertheless, Musmanno had established that obedience to orders has its limits. The defendants could not hide behind the concept of superior orders.[22]

The Einsatzgruppen trial was able to deduce the huge number of victims from the reports sent by the various killing units on a regular basis to Berlin. We have 195 such daily *Ereignismeldungen* (event reports) and, after May 1, 1942, a total of 55 weekly *Meldungen aus den besetzten Ostgebieten* (reports from the occupied eastern territories). The defense tried to call into question the accuracy of these reports, but this attempted exculpation failed. Here and there mistakes may have occurred in the tabulation of the victims. There were also instances where a unit claimed the dead Jews of another unit in order to enlarge its contribution to the task of wholesale murder. However, the well-known German concern for accuracy militated against any significant distortion of the number of reported victims. The editors of the definitive edition of these reports have concluded that "there can be no doubt about the basic trustworthiness and significance of the EM [Event Reports] as a source."[23]

Some of the early trials of Nazi criminals carried out by German courts were rigorous. Of thirty former stormtroopers who in 1933–34 had terrorized inmates of the Kemna concentration camp, the Landgericht Wuppertal in 1948 sentenced five defendants to death, and the others received lengthy prison terms.[24] Until 1950, more than 40 percent of those tried for Nazi crimes by German courts were sentenced to life imprisonment.[25] In several decisions that involved service in death camps such as Chelmno and Sobibor, the courts used the concept of the common design as developed by Allied military tribunals. Josef Hirtenreiter had served in Treblinka, a camp that, as a court noted in 1951, had the sole purpose of murdering Jews. He had several times personally killed Jews and was known among the work Jews as one of the most brutal guards. However, his guilt did not depend on these murders. It did not matter, the court ruled, whether a member of the Treblinka staff supervised the undressing of the Jewish victims, led others to the "hospital," or worked in the kitchen of the camp. It was decisive that all these activities guaranteed the smooth operation of Treblinka as a death factory. Hirtenreiter was found to have been the perpetrator of murder and sentenced to life imprisonment.[26]

The *Bundesgerichtshof* (BGH), Germany's highest court, in a decision handed down on November 25, 1964, ruled that guards in the Chelmno extermination camp were guilty of being accessories to murder simply "by virtue of their service in a Sonderkommando" tasked with the annihilation of the Jewish population of Poland. "The kind of assignment given them for the implementation of these actions is without significance in this regard."[27] Even a bookkeeper in Sobibor was convicted of being an accessory to murder in 1966 and given four years in prison. The SS officer Alfred Ittner had been sent to Sobibor in April 1942 and was in charge of keeping accounts, including those of the valuables seized from the arriving Jews. His willingness to assist in these murders, the court declared, showed an "unfeeling outlook." He had not killed a single person, but by "virtue of his position in the administration of the death factory Sobibor, [he] had made possible the mass murders of the Jews."[28] The BGH upheld this conviction. It was not necessary, the High Court ruled, to prove a direct causal role on the part of the defendant. It was enough to show that he had "supported and facilitated the actions of the main perpetrator."[29]

German public opinion, however, sympathized with the perpetrators, and legal proceedings soon began to reflect a social climate in which Nazi crimes were often seen as mere "mistakes." Not coincidentally, 1950 was also the year when German courts began again to use lay judges (Schöffen), individuals drawn from the community and close to the public pulse. When Martin Bormann Jr., a moral theologian and the son of Martin Bormann, Hitler's powerful chief of staff, was interviewed about how he judged the role of his father, he replied that his father had not necessarily been brutal or without conscience. "Human beings are prone to error. This kind of error can happen to anyone."[30] Prosecutors had neither the interest nor the resources to initiate and pursue lengthy investigations of crimes in distant places. It is noteworthy that the valuable collection of German court cases involving Nazi defendants who had committed acts of killing, Justiz und NS-Verbrechen, had to be published in the Netherlands because no German publisher was willing to bring out this compendium of Nazi crimes.[31]

"The German people," declared Cardinal Joseph Frings of Cologne in August 1945, "were far more victims than perpetrators of [Nazi] crimes." And this affirmation of victimhood continued for several years. After suffering under the Nazis, the Germans felt that they were now being persecuted and deprived of their rights by the victorious Allies.[32] For many Germans after 1945, the Allied trials of Nazi criminals constituted "victor's justice." The horrors of the Nazi regime were held to have been committed by a small clique of culprits. "Until the end of the war and until the occupation authorities informed them," a German court ruled in 1953, "the overwhelming majority of the German people did not know of these events,"[33] a claim discredited and disproven by a large body of scholarship. Information about the mass murder of the Jews was widely known in the German population.[34]

The denazification program carried out by the occupation authorities was highly unpopular. Since most Germans had something in their past that they preferred to forget, all but a small minority of intellectuals and journalists were opposed to stirring up old events. The wholesale vetting of some five million Germans was soon denounced not only by those directly affected but also by the government of the new Germany, the Federal Republic of Germany (FRG), which was composed of the former three Western zones of occupation and came into being on May 23, 1949. Denazification, declared Chancellor Konrad Adenauer on September 20, 1949, had caused "much harm and much mischief," and it was now time to let bygones be bygones.

Adenauer also promised to plead with the Allies for an amnesty for those convicted by the military tribunals.[35] When, on June 7, 1951, after a lengthy legal review process, the Allies carried out the last death sentences against Nazi defendants found guilty in the killing of tens of thousands of innocent persons, there erupted a storm of public indignation. The vice-chancellor of the FRG and a member of the liberal Free Democratic party, Franz Blücher, filed an official protest against this act of "injustice." There prevailed a deeply rooted unwillingness among the German population to face up to the vilest aspects of a political system they had so enthusiastically supported. Only very few Germans had any appetite for confronting the question of the responsibility of German society as a whole for what had taken place during twelve long years of Nazi rule.[36]

The start of the Cold War following Soviet expansion into Eastern Europe created a changed political landscape, both in Germany and in the United States. In the eyes of many Germans, the Cold War confirmed what they had known all along, that is, that Germany had always been on the right side, though the Western allies had not realized it. The new focus on the Communist enemy also led to a new Allied policy toward the defeated Germany, which now was seen as an important ally. The Adenauer government supported German rearmament. Indeed, already back in 1946, in a letter to a friend in the United States, Adenauer had sounded the alarm about the threat of Communism: "The danger is grave. Asia stands on the river Elbe." Only a healthy Europe, under the guidance of England and France and joined by the free part of Germany, could stop the "advancement of Asian ideology and power."[37] In the eyes of many Germans, it was unacceptable for them to serve on the side of the Allies as long as German soldiers who had valiantly fought against Soviet Communism were still held in prison by these same Allied governments. Hence in return for German political and military support against the Soviet Union, the Western Allies gradually ended their pursuit of Nazi criminals. They also reduced sentences and released others in successive amnesties. For example, of twenty-one sentences of death pronounced at the Buchenwald trial, seventeen were changed in amnesty proceedings. By 1951, all but four of the convicted Einsatzgruppen defendants had been released from prison; the last defendants convicted by Allied tribunals obtained their freedom in 1958.[38]

It was the 1958 Ulm trial of members of Einsatzkommando Tilsit that revealed the extent of crimes committed in the East and helped bring about a change in the German attitude toward Nazi crimes. As a result, in November 1958, the ministers of justice of the German *Länder* (states) now established a central investigative office, the *Zentrale Stelle der Landesjustizverwaltungen zur Aufklärung nationalsozialistischer Verbrechen* (Central Office of the State Administrations of Justice for the Investigation of National Socialist Crimes), to speed up legal redress for these offenses. Located in Ludwigsburg, near Stuttgart, the Central Office at first was forced to operate with a limited number of personnel. But by 1965, it had about fifty judges and prosecutors and was able to pursue the investigation of Nazi crimes vigorously. The Central Office did not have the right to indict, but its recommendations led to an increasing number of prosecutions in the German states during the following years.[39]

The military tribunals of the Western allies had made use of "Crimes against Humanity," a new formula for an old concept. International law (as for example in the Preamble to Hague Convention No. IV of 1907) had long acknowledged that even in the absence of specific provisions, civilians and belligerents remain under the protection of "the principles of the law of nations, as they result from the usages established among civilized peoples, from the laws of humanity, and the dictates of the public conscience." The Allied military courts included among crimes against humanity atrocities, enslavement, torture, rape, or other inhumane acts against any civilian population irrespective of whether these acts violated the domestic law of the country where perpetrated. The German judges objected to the use of this legal standard on the grounds that it violated the principles of the German *Rechtsstaat* (a state under the rule of law), especially ex post facto (retroactive) law, which was forbidden by Article 103 of the Basic Law. For the same reason, German prosecutors did not make use of the concept of genocide, even after the FRG on August 9, 1954, had incorporated the Genocide Convention of 1948 in the Criminal Code (Art. 220a).

None of these decisions on the part of the German judiciary is persuasive or compelling. Both crimes against humanity and the crime of genocide have long been part of international law. The Genocide Convention recognized this fact when it declared in its preamble that "at all periods of history genocide has inflicted great losses on humanity." These crimes were not specifically codified before 1945 because the kind of mass murder that took place during the Nazi era had been unimaginable. Thus the crimes of the Nazi regime could and should have been punishable according to prevailing international law. Applying this law violated neither the principle of *"nullum crimen sine lege"* (no crime without law) nor the concept of ex post facto law.[40]

The Western Allies did not appreciate what seemed to them to be legalistic technicalities, but they yielded in 1951 and allowed the German courts to rely on German law. This meant that Nazi criminals accused of killing could be convicted only if they had violated the regular provisions of the German penal code. According to this law, the statute of limitations for crimes with possible sentences of fifteen years or less was fifteen years after the crime had been committed, so no charges for manslaughter could be brought after 1960. After lengthy debates in the *Bundestag*, the parliament, in 1964–1965, 1968–1969, and 1978–1979, the statute of limitations for murder was repeatedly extended, although these extensions were far from popular. During one of these emotion-laden discussions, Günther Diehl, the government's press secretary, referred to the men who had murdered under orders as "victims of the Nazi system."[41] It was not until

January 1979, when the American film *Holocaust* was shown in Germany, that a majority of Germans came to understand and accept the scope and brutality of the Nazi era. The film had an impact far beyond what documentaries and other teaching on the murder of the Jews had been able to achieve, and on July 3, 1979, the Bundestag finally abolished the statute of limitations for murder altogether.[42] Theoretically, prosecutions of Nazi murderers could now take place as long as these men or women were still alive and could be located.

Article 211 of the Criminal Code of the FRG (a reformulation of the 1871 version) defined murder as the killing of a human person "out of thirst for blood, for the satisfaction of sexual desires, for greed or other base motives, in a cunning or cruel manner." The penalty for murder was initially death. After the abolition of the death penalty by the Basic Law of 1949, the maximum penalty became imprisonment for life. The mass murder of the Jews certainly constituted killing for reprehensible motives, and it was carried out in an inhumane manner, though proof of base motives on the part of individuals was often difficult. The motives of the killers varied and were not always base. More fundamentally, though, this definition of murder did not fit the realities of the Holocaust. The Final Solution of the Jewish Question was not the result of a series of personal criminal actions. It constituted instead state-sponsored mass murder. It was legal according to the jurisprudence of the Nazi state.

The attempt to punish these crimes according to the standards of individual wrongdoing was bound to fail. The Holocaust was a crime that could be apprehended only in its totality. The Allied military tribunals had recognized this fundamental truth and had applied the principle of a common design encompassing both systematic state-organized collective action and individual responsibility. Differentiating the perpetrators of the Holocaust on the basis of presumed motivation meant fragmenting the Holocaust into a series of distinct, often disconnected offenses, none of which begins to add up to the whole crime of genocide. This led to absurd consequences, such as punishing more lightly the SS man who, as part of his official duties in a factory of death, killed tens of thousands by throwing the gas pellets into the gas chamber than the guard who on his own initiative killed one inmate. It also meant that, as in proceedings involving ordinary cases of homicide, the courts applied the distinction between perpetrators and accomplices, a differentiation completely unsuitable for the factories of death and a distinction that quite literally allowed some defendants to get away with murder.

American courts establish the crime of murder on the basis of objective circumstances. The reasons *why* a murderer killed his victim—the psychological makeup and personal peculiarities of the defendant—are largely irrelevant. Moreover, all the participants in an act of killing are guilty of the crime, whether they fired the lethal bullet or merely acted as lookout.[43] German jurisprudence, by contrast, applies what is called the "subjective theory": a person who wills a criminal deed is a perpetrator. If this will is absent or if he carries out the act on behalf of another, the individual in question is a mere accomplice.[44] The Military Criminal Code of October 10, 1940 (which applied not only to the armed forces but also to members of the SS and police units serving in Russia) followed similar legal principles. Article 47 provided that the responsibility for the execution of an order that violates the criminal law is borne by the officer who issued the order. The subordinate obeying the order is subject to punishment only if he willfully went beyond the order or if he knew that it involved a criminal act.[45]

And yet the line between a perpetrator and an accomplice is often difficult to draw. It involves complex issues of motivation and intent. The inner disposition of an accused is not easily ascertained.[46] The question whether a person acted on the basis of his own will or merely in support of another individual generally is difficult to resolve. Hence the subjective theory often leaves the finding of the line of demarcation between perpetrator and accomplice dependent upon the discretion of judges who themselves are subject to the political and social environment in which they live. The subjective theory leads to a jurisprudence of feeling on the part of judges that lacks an objective standard. It undermines the rule of law.

The distinction between perpetrator and accomplice has been used by German courts to avoid pronouncing a harsh sentence. For example, in the so-called *Badewannenfall* (Bathtub case) of 1940, the highest German court had to deal with the mother of an illegitimate child who, right after the birth, had prevailed upon her sister to drown the newborn baby in a bathtub. The Landgericht Trier had convicted the sister of murder, which would have meant a sentence of death, but the Reichsgericht reversed this judgment. Feeling sympathy for the sister and reasoning that the real culprit was the mother, the High Court ruled that the sister, while the agent of the killing, had not carried out the deed in her own interest but rather in support of the will of another. She thus had lacked *Täterwille* (the will of a perpetrator) and therefore was a mere accomplice to be punished with a lesser sentence.[47]

This ruling was not universally accepted, and in 1956 the Bundesgerichtshof, the highest court of appeal for civil and criminal cases, explicitly repudiated it. "The person who with his own hands kills another individual is to be considered a perpetrator even if he carries out the deed in the presence of or in the interest of another."[48] However, in the Staschynskij case of October 19, 1962, the BGH once again affirmed the subjective theory, and it has reigned ever since.

Bodan Staschynskij was an agent of the Soviet secret service who, on orders of his superiors, had killed two Russian emigrants living in the Bundesrepublik. Even though Staschynskij had killed with his own hands, the BGH ruled that he should be treated as an accomplice, and he was sentenced to eight years' imprisonment. The court found that Staschynskij had spent years under Soviet rule and had been "incessantly indoctrinated" in the communist way of thinking. He had had no interest in the death of his victims and had not committed the murders "as his own" but merely as a "tool" of his superiors. A person who accepts the criminal designs of a lawless state, shows zeal in putting them into practice, and silences his conscience, the court stated, is a perpetrator. However, under certain circumstances, criminal orders issued by a state can lead to a mitigation of punishment. In the view of the court, those who oppose such orders and "carry them out because they are weak and unable to stand up to the superior strength of the state or those who lack the courage to resist and do not have the intelligence to find a way out of this predicament" are in a different situation. Even if they make use of political slogans in order at least temporarily to silence their conscience, they are to be regarded as accomplices. It was wrong to equate such individuals with those who planned these killings or with those who carried them out willingly. In a totalitarian state, the court suggested, the average person cannot be expected to resist criminal orders. Indeed, the court explicitly referred to "Germany under National Socialism" when it described how certain modern states planned political murders and other mass killings.[49]

It is no coincidence that this formulation of the role of an accomplice reads like a description of the alleged dilemma of Nazi criminals, whom the courts had come to see as pawns of their superiors, and who therefore were entitled to indulgence and a relatively milder sentence. One will not go wrong in assuming that the BGH was well aware of the usefulness of this decision, and knew that the decision would work in favor of Nazi criminals facing the charge of murder.[50] Indeed, in subsequent cases, trial courts as well as the BGH regularly invoked the reasoning of the Staschynskij case. Adalbert Rückerl, the longtime head of the Ludwigsburg investigative office, puts it thus: "There can be no doubt that the propensity of the courts to consider all but excess perpetrators [dedicated killers] accomplices rather than perpetrators is the result of the fact that in cases of a conviction as a perpetrator of murder, the courts are required to impose life imprisonment."[51] Or, as one author has derisively characterized this process, "German jurisprudence lies firmly in the Staschynskij bathtub and creates perpetrator types, artificial Nazis, that defy all reality."[52] The case affirmed the great power of judges, on whose determination the differentiation between perpetrator and accomplice depends, but the BGH did not consider this a problem and indeed stressed the right of the courts freely to exercise this judgment.[53]

According to the Staschynskij decisions, a defendant could be convicted as a perpetrator only if he or she had an interest in the successful outcome of the deed. In the case of an ordinary murder, this stake is easy to establish, for such crimes are usually committed for reasons of personal vengeance or enrichment. However, such proof is difficult in the case of the wholesale murders of the Nazi state, which often were carried out by large groups of individuals. This resulted in an absurd outcome: the killing of one inmate in a concentration camp led to the maximum penalty for murder, while the killing of thousands of victims in organized mass shootings was judged to be merely aiding and abetting the crime of murder. The consequence was paradoxical—the greater the number of victims, the lesser the punishment.[54] When Otto Bradfisch, the head of an Einsatzkommando, was tried for murder, he testified that he heard from Himmler that the order for the annihilation of the Jews had come from Hitler personally. If so, even Himmler might have to be considered a mere accomplice. Applied to the Holocaust, the reasoning of the Staschynskij case came close to assuming that there had been only one real perpetrator, Adolf Hitler, who had reigned over the will of sixty million accomplices.[55]

The punishment of accomplices became even more difficult in 1968 when the legislature adopted a replacement for Paragraph 50 of the criminal code. According to the old version of Articles 49 and 50 (now Articles 27 and 28), the imposition of a lighter punishment for an accomplice was optional. Ostensibly to prevent excessively harsh penalties for minor offenses such as traffic violations, the imposition of an easier sentence for accomplices was made mandatory unless there were special aggravating factors. This meant that crimes of violence by accomplices could no longer receive the penalty of life imprisonment unless it could be proved that the defendant had shared the base motives of the perpetrator. The absence of such motives changed the charge of abetting murder to abetting manslaughter, and the statute of limitations on manslaughter had expired by that time. For these reasons, prosecutions for being an accessory to murder now could be started only if the person had acted with eagerness, zeal, or other special factors.[56] The authors of this change in the criminal code asserted that they sought merely to provide redress for an unintended gap in the law and did not aim at Nazi crimes. Others, however, pointed out that the main impetus for this revision had come from Eduard Dreher, a former judge of a *Sondergericht* (special Nazi courts that operated outside the regular judiciary and imposed the death penalty for the slightest offenses). Regardless of the reasons for the change, it had the effect of making the prosecution and meaningful punishment of violent Nazi crimes more difficult.[57]

Fritz Bauer, the prosecutor who played a leading role in bringing about the Auschwitz trial, urged the German courts to adopt an approach similar to the concept of the common design. In an extermination camp, he insisted, everyone, whatever his or her position, was part of the killing machine, because everyone knew the purpose of the camp.[58] Hence all these individuals had to be considered active participants in the Final Solution and be judged accordingly.[59] By dissolving the organized mass murder of the Jews into separate deeds, the courts distorted the reality of the Holocaust, which was not merely the sum of discrete individual events.[60] However, the Auschwitz court did not accept this reasoning, and the Bundesgerichtshof explicitly rejected it. In defending the acquittal of the SS dentist Willi Schatz, the High Court maintained that being a dentist for SS personnel of Auschwitz did not support the camp's machinery of destruction and therefore did not make Schatz an accomplice to murder. Even the fact that Schatz had regularly collected the gold melted down from the teeth of gassed victims did not constitute a punishable offense, since, as Schatz maintained, he had lacked awareness that this action supported the criminal lethal design of the SS leadership.[61] In the following years, and until the Demjanjuk case of 2011, which involved a guard in a death factory, other prosecutors and courts followed this reasoning and likewise insisted on making a conviction dependent on a defendant's specific causal role in the killing process.[62]

From the 1950s on, most of the courts dealing with murder in the East used formulaic language that resulted in the overwhelming majority of defendants' being judged mere accomplices. The difference between perpetrator and accomplice, stated a court in 1968, does not depend on the objective circumstances of the deed but rather on a defendant's "inner disposition. He who commits the action as his own is a perpetrator. He who participates merely as a tool or accessory to the deed of another is an accomplice."[63] The policy of killing the Jews, the Final Solution, was held to have been devised by Hitler, Himmler, Heydrich, and their immediate entourage. These men therefore had been the perpetrators of the mass killings, had acted cruelly and out of base motives, and they were to be regarded as murderers even though they were no longer alive. A small number of members of the killing units who had initiated acts beyond their orders and had acted with zeal were likewise seen as murderers. They were called "excess perpetrators." In the trials of members of the Einsatzgruppen, 92 percent were convicted merely as accessories to murder.[64] Even the commanders of these units were often held to have been accomplices, mere cogs in a machine steered by others. They had followed orders and had acted not with the will of a perpetrator but with the obeisance of an accomplice. They had merely aided and abetted deeds planned and ordered by the Nazi state, and were therefore punished at most as accessories to murder. Instead of being sentenced to mandatory life imprisonment for murder, they received relatively short prison terms as accomplices.

The courts were correct in locating the origin of the Final Solution with Hitler, Himmler, and their close associates. But they were mistaken in assuming that most of those involved in implementing the annihilation of the Jews were merely following orders. Especially the officers who organized the killing operations had considerable freedom of action, and many of them carried out their duties with enthusiasm. They hunted down their victims and were the ultimate judges of who would be killed. The same held true for those doing selections of Jews arriving on the ramps at extermination camps. The notion that they were mere accomplices in actions ordered by their superiors—tools rather than independent actors—was seriously flawed.

Equally unfortunate was the emphasis on the inner disposition of the defendants. Apart from the difficulty of ascertaining this frame of mind with any kind of certainty, the approach facilitated the denial of personal responsibility. It made it possible for an accused person to argue that while carrying out certain crimes his essential inner self had remained decent. The moral bifurcation inherent in this conception was made explicit by the well-known words of Himmler, who praised his men for having carried out the destruction of the Jews while having preserved their decency.[65]

The claim that the defendants had not really willed the deeds of which they were accused was often in conflict with the description of the horrible events, which the courts laid out accurately and in great detail in the early part of the verdicts, but which they ignored a few pages later during the legal assessment of these deeds. Here are some examples.

Victor Capesius, for example, was an SS officer and camp physician in Auschwitz from the end of 1943 until Christmas of 1944. His duties included service on the ramp. According to the verdict of the Auschwitz trial, Capesius knew "that he had to determine the ability of Jewish men and women to work, that only those he selected for the work camp would remain alive, and that those he sent to the other side were killed by Zyklon B in the gas chambers." His presence on the ramp was confirmed for at least four arriving transports, and his decisions led to the death of at least two thousand people. For about three months in 1944, Dr. Capesius was also in charge of the camp pharmacy, and the court acknowledged that during this time he had done service at the gas chambers by supervising the delivery of Zyklon B. On several occasions, the court found, Capesius had appropriated property of Jewish victims, including entire suitcases filled with suits and valuables such as watches. He also obtained melted-down gold from the teeth of murdered Jews. However, the court ruled that since Capesius viewed these items as already belonging to the German state, these seizures did not establish that the SS doctor had sought the death of the Jewish owners. The court concluded that Capesius had carried out his duties on the ramp with conviction and deceit, as was indicated by his telling the arriving Jews that they would be taken to a good place. Yet despite these serious offenses, Capesius was found guilty only of being an accessory to murder, and on August 20, 1965, he was sentenced to nine years' imprisonment. He was a free man by January 1968.[66]

Willi Frank was a dentist and an early member of the Nazi party. Frank joined the SS in 1935 and volunteered for the Waffen-SS in 1940. After falling sick in Russia, he saw service as a camp dentist in Dachau and later in Auschwitz. The Auschwitz court considered it as proven that Frank had carried out selections on the ramp on at least five occasions, and that he was therefore responsible for the death of at least six thousand Jews. On at least one occasion, Frank had also served as supervisor of a gassing, personally giving the signal to drop the gas pellets, and had watched the effect of the gas through an observation window. After assuring himself that everyone was dead, he had given the signal to open the door of the gas chamber and remove the bodies. But the court noted that Frank had not distinguished himself by special zeal. It also could not be proven that he had had "a personal interest in the death of the transports." Hence Frank was found guilty only as an accomplice to murder and sentenced to seven years in prison. He was released from custody in 1970.[67]

Otto Bradfisch studied political economy and law. In January 1931, he became a member of the Nazi party, and in 1937 he joined the Gestapo. In the spring of 1941, he was appointed head of Einsatzkommando 8 (EG B), and he served in this capacity until April 1942. The Landgericht Munich I established that in this role Bradfisch had organized and carried out a large number of mass shootings. He had explained to his subordinates that, following an order by Hitler, Russia had to be made *Judenfrei* (free of Jews) and that other racially inferior elements as well as communist functionaries had to be liquidated.

The court noted that Bradfisch was known as a reliable and efficient officer who showed initiative in finding his victims. In at least two instances, he personally participated in the shooting by providing the coup de grâce to Jews lying wounded in the pit. There was no evidence, the court noted, that Bradfisch had made any attempt to escape this assignment. "His conduct was that of a faithful follower of Hitler. The will of the Führer for him was law irrespective of its content."[68] At an execution in Minsk, a member of his unit testified, Bradfisch had pointed out that "the Jews were not to be regarded as human."[69] And yet, in 1961 Bradfisch was convicted merely for being an accessory to murder, having caused the death of at least fifteen thousand people, and sentenced to ten years' imprisonment.

Ignoring Bradfisch's career in the Nazi state and his declared commitment to destroy the nonhuman Jews, the court concluded that Bradfisch had not acted with the will of a perpetrator but had been merely a "tool" of his superiors. He had carried out the orders to kill because he had been a convinced National Socialist. Even the fact that he had personally fired shots did not establish that he had acted in any other way than to loyally follow Hitler's orders. In the words of the court, "There is no indication that he expressed a hostile attitude or hostile remarks regarding the Jewish question."[70] The court did not explain how one could be at one and the same time a "convinced National Socialist" and an efficient killer of Jews and not have "a hostile attitude" toward the Jews. One author concludes that this decision stretches the legal definition of the accomplice "ad absurdum."[71]

Hans Graalfs had joined the SS in November 1933 and became a platoon leader of Einsatzkommando 8 (EG B) in 1941. In 1964, the Landgericht Kiel charged him with having been in charge of at least three shootings of Jews in which 760 lost their lives under the most horrible circumstances. Graalfs had made sure that the victims lay down "in an orderly fashion" by personally jumping into the ditch and using kicks with his boots to force the wretched Jews into the correct position. He personally shot any people who changed their position. On one occasion, when his men had difficulty in shooting children, Graalfs himself undertook the killing.

Members of his unit testified that it was possible to avoid participation in the killings by feigning nervous strain or emotional upset, but Graalfs had made no attempt to escape his deadly assignment. Ignoring this evidence, the court convicted him as being a mere accomplice to murder and sentenced him to three years' imprisonment. Graalfs told the court that he had had a half-Jewish acquaintance, that he had once allowed a Jewish woman to enter an air raid shelter, and that his wife had worked for many years in a Jewish household. On the basis of this information, the court accepted his claim that he had harbored no hostile feelings against Jews and had merely acted in fulfillment of a duty. During the Third Reich, the court noted, "the national socialist rulers, relying on the power of the state, had their numerous crimes carried out by subordinates, bound to them by military or similar obedience, and used these persons like tools. For this reason, the attitude of the subordinates to these deeds cannot as a rule be regarded as the will of a perpetrator."[72]

Rolf-Joachim Buchs was a police lieutenant who joined the SS in 1938. He had done so, he later explained, in order to further his career. Because Himmler at the time sought to unite the police and the SS, taking up membership in the SS was common. The court that tried Buchs in 1973 noted that the young officer had not been a fanatical National Socialist, and even had had a Jewish woman as a friend. On the other hand, his conduct as company commander of Police Battalion 309 had not reflected this lack of anti-Jewish sentiments. On June 27, 1941, six days into the campaign in the East, Police Battalion 309 had carried out large-scale killings in Bialystok and finally had locked about seven hundred Jews into the synagogue, where they were burned alive. Buchs heard the cries of the hapless victims for about half an hour but had personally admonished his men to shoot anyone trying to escape from the burning building. In this way, Buchs had strengthened the willingness of his subordinates to kill. He had ordered an end to the shooting only after the building no longer exhibited any sign of life. At the same time, the court concluded, Buchs had not acted from base motives like racial hatred but because of a "weakness of character" and the desire not to suffer damage to his career. Hence he was convicted merely as an accomplice and sentenced to four years' imprisonment. In justifying this sentence, the court relied upon the 1968 revision of Article 50 of the criminal code, which in the absence of base motives on the part of an accomplice during a killing required a reduced punishment.[73]

Gustav Münzberger was an SS official in the Treblinka death factory. Aided by Ukrainian helpers, Münzberger was in charge of pressing as many people as possible into the gas chamber. He screamed at them and used a whip in order to get his victims to stand as closely together as possible. It was said that he packed the gas chamber like a bulging piece of luggage. At times Münzberger shot Jews for whom there was no more room in the gas chamber, for the rules forbade the use of the gas chamber for just a few individuals. The court saw it as established that Münzberger had participated in the killing of at least three hundred thousand Jews but convicted him only as an accomplice. He had been merely "a cog in the cruel machinery of extermination," and it could not be proved that Münzberger had internalized the intended mass annihilation of the Jews. He received a sentence of twelve years' imprisonment and was a free man after six years, released for good behavior.[74]

In a few cases the Bundesgerichtshof felt obliged to grant the appeal of the prosecutors and changed the status of the defendants from accomplice to perpetrator. The SS officers Werner Scheu and Karl Struve had selected hundreds of Lithuanian Jews for execution, had commanded the operations, and had themselves participated in the shooting. Both men, the High Court ruled, had acted well beyond their orders, and therefore had to be considered co-perpetrators rather than accomplices. As the court reasoned, those who are in charge of such actions are perpetrators even if they themselves are subordinated to a higher authority. Their punishment was changed, on appeal, from ten and nine years in prison to life imprisonment.[75] But in the great majority of cases, even defendants guilty of a large number of killings were convicted merely as accomplices. Responsibility for the wholesale murders was attributed to a small group of high-level leaders who had used their subordinates as tools. This approach was in line with the widely prevailing view that the German people had been victims, forced by Hitler, Himmler, and other Nazi leaders to do bad things. Between 1959 and 1965, for example, prosecutors charged defendants as perpetrators in 70 percent of the cases brought for Nazi crimes, but the courts convicted only 25 percent of them. In the case of members of the Einsatzgruppen, the ratio was 90 percent accomplices and 10 percent perpetrators.[76]

All this would change in 2009, when a German prosecutor in Munich charged John Demjanjuk with being an accomplice to murder for having served in the death camp Sobibor. The case of the former Ukrainian guard had occupied the legal authorities of three countries for several decades. Demjanjuk had been conscripted into the Soviet army and was captured by the Germans in May 1942. Like several thousand other Soviet POWs, Demjanjuk was trained to be a concentration camp guard at the Trawniki camp in the General Government. From March to September 1943, Demjanjuk served in Sobibor and later in the concentration camp Flossenburg.

Demjanjuk immigrated to the United States in 1952 and became an American citizen in 1958, but based on information obtained in the 1970s, he was stripped of his citizenship because he had concealed his wartime service for the Nazis. He was subsequently extradited to Israel, where he was tried for crimes against humanity in 1987. Testimony from survivors had identified him as "Ivan the Terrible" from the Treblinka extermination camp, and on April 25, 1988, Demjanjuk was found guilty and sentenced to death. As his appeal moved on to the Israeli Supreme Court, the Soviet Union collapsed and new evidence became available from former Soviet archives that placed the former Trawniki in Sobibor rather than in Treblinka. On July 29, 1993, the Israeli High Court overturned his conviction, and Demjanjuk was allowed to return to the United States. His American citizenship was restored in 1998, after five years of litigation, but he lost it again in 2002 when the US Department of Justice concluded that he had been a concentration camp guard from 1942 to 1945. After more appeals, Demjanjuk was extradited to Germany in May 2009.[77]

The Central Office for the Investigation of Nazi crimes at Ludwigsburg had been looking into the Demjanjuk case since 1993, but had been unable to come up with evidence that the Ukrainian Trawniki had killed anyone at Sobibor, the burden of proof at that time. The former judge Thomas Walther, a member of the Ludwigsburg staff, was part of a new generation of prosecutors—known as the "grandchildren generation"—who were resolved to hold Nazi criminals accountable for their horrible deeds. He was assisted by Kirsten Goetz, who framed the legal theory for a new approach to Nazi crimes. Walther, in collaboration with the Munich court, brought charges against Demjanjuk without evidence of a specific offense. In essence, the indictment harkened back to the doctrine of common design developed by Allied military tribunals, which the German courts had not used for more than six decades. Demjanjuk, the Munich court charged, had been a guard at Sobibor from March 27 until the middle of September 1943. During this time, fifteen transports of Jews had arrived from Holland, some including German Jews. Two of the transports had consisted of some 1,300 children between the ages of one and sixteen. Hence Demjanjuk was accused of being linked to the death of at least 28,060 people. The only purpose of Sobibor was the murder of Jews, and everyone serving in this factory of death, irrespective of his specific function, knew it. Demjanjuk, the court ruled, had been part of the organization guarding the camp and in this way had made "a concrete sustaining contribution to the death of the deportees." On December 5, 2011, he was convicted of being an accomplice to murder and sentenced to five years' imprisonment. The short jail term was deemed to be justified by the fact that Demjanjuk was ninety-one years old.[78] Released following a successful appeal, Demjanjuk died on March 17, 2012, and because of his death his case became moot.[79]

The significance of the Demjanjuk case was considerable. The Ukrainian Trawniki had been convicted of being an accomplice to murder without proof of involvement in a specific killing. Rather, he was found to have been part of a common murderous design, and this fact was held to be sufficient. This ruling was aided by the fact that Sobibor was an extermination camp par excellence, but the Ludwigsburg prosecutor Thilo Kurz argued in March 2013 that at the very least it was applicable also to the death factory of Auschwitz-Birkenau.[80] The following month, the Ludwigsburg office announced that it was preparing charges against thirty-seven former Auschwitz guards.[81] On May 7, authorities arrested the Auschwitz cook Hans Lipschis, during whose service more than ten thousand Jews had been killed. Using digital technology, the prosecution built a model that showed what camp personnel could have seen from a specific vantage point. This proved that the smoking chimneys of the crematoria were visible from the kitchen. But the wonders of modern technology could not overcome the human frailty of old age. Lipschis was ninety-three years old, and he was found unfit to stand trial on grounds of dementia.[82]

In April 2015, the ninety-three-year-old Oskar Gröning, known as the "Auschwitz accountant," went on trial before a court in Lüneburg. During his two-year service in the death factory of Auschwitz, some three hundred thousand Jews had been murdered. The former SS man freely admitted that he had been responsible for collecting the cash of arriving Jews. "It is beyond question," he told the judge after the charges had been read, "that I am morally complicit. This moral guilt I acknowledge here, before the victims, with regret and humility." Gröning added, "As concerns guilt before the law, you must decide."[83] Groening had not personally killed anyone, but, based on the Demjanjuk precedent, he was found guilty of having been an accomplice to murder and was sentenced to four years' imprisonment on July 15, 2015.[84] The contrite SS man appealed his conviction, but the Bundesgericht rejected the appeal.

On September 21, 2015, the prosecutor of the state of Schleswig-Holstein charged a ninety-one-year-old woman with being an accessory to murder in 260,000 cases. The woman (under German privacy law, her name was not revealed) had served as a radio operator for the commandant of Auschwitz from April to July 1944. However, in July 2016, the woman was held to be unfit to stand trial.[85] The former SS man Reinhold Hanning went on trial in the city of Detmold early in 2016. Hanning served as a guard in Auschwitz from 1943 to 1944. He met Jews arriving by train and escorted them to the gas chambers. Hanning was accused of being an accessory to murder of at least 170,000 people. He surprised survivors and others attending the trial when, from his wheelchair, he declared on April 29 that he "deeply regretted" what he had done. "I am ashamed that I witnessed injustice and allowed it to continue without taking any actions against it."[86] The Detmold court pronounced a verdict of guilty on June 17, 2016, and sentenced the ninety-four-year-old to five years' imprisonment.

The number of such prosecutions in the future is likely to be limited. The youngest of the suspects are now well into their eighties or nineties, and few of them will be found fit for trial. In the eyes of some, by going after cooks and accountants, the new proceedings are scratching bottom. Others insist that all those involved in the machinery of destruction deserve to be punished. They see this as a debt owed to the victims.

According to Article 47 of the German Military Penal Code (*Militärstrafgesetzbuch* or MStGB) in force during World War II, a subordinate had to carry out the criminal order of a superior unless he knew that the order involved a common or military offense.[87] An authoritative commentary on the MStGB explained that the duty of obedience ended only if the subordinate was fully aware that the order *sought* the commission of a crime. Knowing that fulfilling the order would result in a crime was not sufficient.[88] Indeed, in the interest of strengthening the duty of obedience, the soldier was held to have no duty to question the rightfulness of an order.[89] Moreover, Articles 52 and 54 of the Civilian Penal Code in force during the Third Reich (now Articles 34 and 35) provided that a person who commits a criminal act in order to prevent a "danger to life, limb, or liberty" to himself or those close to him is innocent. Not surprisingly, a large number of accused Nazi criminals invoked these provisions of an alleged *Befehlsnotstand* (a crisis created as a result of following orders) in postwar trials in order to support their claim of innocence. By disobeying the orders for the murder of Jews, they argued, they would have risked their own lives. The claim that their participation in the killings had been coerced also helped these defendants still their guilty consciences.

German law and legal practice restrict the existence of a *Befehlsnotstand* by several limiting conditions. It is not available unless the danger to one's life resulting from the refusal to obey is immediate rather than just highly probable. The possibility of incurring a mere disadvantage, like the fear of demotion or damage to one's career, is deemed insufficient to invoke the defense. Furthermore, as applied to the Holocaust, the claim fails if the person in question has voluntarily joined a killing unit or if his political career and conduct in the field showed that he was not opposed to the murder of innocents, or if he had made no effort to escape from the brutal environment of Nazi warfare. The more serious the crime involved in the order, the Bundesgerichtshof ruled, the more strenuously an individual had to seek ways to escape the criminal act.[90] To justify the plea of superior orders, it was necessary that the will of the perpetrator be "bent by his fear of danger to life and limb." The law, a court declared in 1966, does not demand "heroic self-sacrifice," but it expects that the individual will recognize the conflict of conscience in which the criminal order has placed him. The law will excuse those, and only those, who, finding themselves under unusually strong external pressure, yielded to weakness and committed a criminal act while being in conscience opposed to it.[91]

A subordinate, another court ruled in 1970, did not have to investigate the rightfulness of every command. However, there existed a duty to question those orders that, if carried out, "violated well-known principles of human social life and generally recognized ideas of right and wrong." This statement invoked the view of the German legal philosopher Gustav Radbruch, who, in an oft-quoted 1946 essay, had branded the Nazi state an *Unrechtsstaat* (a state founded on injustice). According to Radbruch, where "there is not even an attempt at justice, where equality, the core of justice, is deliberately betrayed in the issuance of positive law, then the statute is not merely 'flawed law,' it lacks completely the very nature of law." When the conflict between statute and justice reaches an intolerable degree, there arises a "duty to disobey."[92] In the face of this obligation, the Landgericht Wuppertal court declared, it was not enough for a defendant to argue that he had been educated to obey orders. The law of superior orders would not protect those who decided to subordinate their will to that of another, to obey their Führer unconditionally, and thereby suspended their consciences. Moreover, the court ruled, "nobody can invoke the decline of respect for human life, caused by the rampages of the national socialist rulers, in order to excuse a decline in his own awareness of what is right."[93]

The factual findings of the courts revealed that many of the defendants had killed with abandon. Behind the alleged *Führerbefehl* (order of the Führer) emerged the initiative of men who often acted without detailed orders from above and with unseemly zeal. As Hannah Arendt pointed out in connection with the Auschwitz trial, no one in a high position had ever "issued orders that infants should be thrown into the air as shooting targets, or hurled into the fire alive, or have their heads smashed against walls; there had been no orders that people should be trampled to death, or become the objects of the murderous 'sport,' including that of killing with one blow of the head."[94]

The plea of superior orders as such was seldom accepted by the courts. It was the unanimous finding of all experts who testified at these trials that they had failed to find a single case where the endeavor to avoid the killing or even the disregard of superior orders to kill had led to serious harm. In view of these facts, the courts could have rejected the plea of superior orders out of hand. They did not do so because, as many judges saw it, they could not disprove the claim of defendants that they had genuinely feared for their life or liberty. Given the principle of *in dubio pro reo* ("when in doubt, in favor of the accused"), any doubt about guilt has to be resolved in favor of the defendant. Hence the courts rather freely granted the existence of a *putative* or "assumed to exist" *Befehlsnotstand*— a sincere, if mistaken, belief in the serious harm that would follow the disregard of orders to kill. The difficulty of disproving a putative crisis is one of the reasons why prosecutors generally indicted only those members of a killing unit whose hateful conduct made it easy to refute their plea of having obeyed superior orders.[95]

Not surprisingly, this situation led to miscarriages of justice. Judges who regarded Nazi perpetrators as victims of a repressive regime found it easy to believe that the accused before them had killed not out of conviction but rather as the result of a fear of deadly consequences.

The case of ten members of Police Battalion 316, accused of having participated in mass shootings of Russian Jews, is one of the crassest examples of such an unfortunate result. At the time of these massacres, the men ranged in age between twenty-four and thirty-six. Expert testimony established that it was possible to escape the killing routine by volunteering for special training or similar assignments, but none of the defendants had taken advantage of this possibility. Two of the defendants had refused to shoot women and children, and nothing was known of any subsequent punishment. There also was no evidence that the accused had carried out the shootings under threat of harm. One of the accused had attended a SS Junkerschule, a training school for officers in the Waffen-SS. To be accepted by such an institution, candidates had to undergo a stringent check on their political reliability, and indoctrination in Nazi ideology was an important part of the curriculum. Yet even such a background, the court ruled, did not prove that the person in question had agreed with the mass murder of the Jews. After a trial that lasted from December 1966 until June 6, 1968, all of the defendants were acquitted pursuant to an unrefuted defense of putative superior orders.[96]

An SS doctor who had participated in at least four selections on the ramp at Auschwitz also benefited from the doctrine of putative superior orders. At the Auschwitz trial of 1963–1965, Franz Lucas had been convicted for aiding and abetting the murder of at least one thousand people and was sentenced to three years and three months' imprisonment. The court questioned Lucas's claim that he had carried out the selections because he had been forced to do so by the commandant of Birkenau, and to escape severe punishment, Lucas, the court concluded, had been too weak to oppose his participation in the selections for the gas chambers and had taken the easy way out.[97] On appeal, the Bundesgericht rejected this reasoning and ordered a new trial. It ruled that the Auschwitz trial court had ignored evidence that pointed to a case of putative superior orders, especially testimony about Lucas's friendly disposition to inmates.[98]

When Lucas was retried, the Landgericht Frankfurt/Main ruled that it was impossible to disprove Lucas's claim that he had believed his life to be in danger and had carried out the selections for this reason only. The facts made it probable that this was a case of putative Befehlsnotstand. Hence Lucas was acquitted.[99]

Some of those involved with the Final Solution may indeed have acted out of a mistaken belief that their life was in danger. We do know that officers at times uttered such threats. It is impossible to know or even estimate the actual number of such occurrences because prosecutors generally did not charge individuals who argued a credible defense of superior orders.[100] In cases where defendants made this claim, the Deutsche Juristentag of 1966 (the biennial convention of German lawyers) found that "there are indications that courts have accepted it hitherto too freely." For this and other reasons, the lawyers expressed the hope "that at least in the future Nazi crimes of violence be adjudicated in a manner that does justice to the seriousness of the crimes."[101]

According to the German penal code, in determining the sentence of a guilty defendant, judges must weigh aggravating and mitigating circumstances. This calculation includes such matters as the personal background of the criminal, the reason for the crime, and the conduct of the convicted person after the crime.[102] In the case of Nazi defendants convicted for crimes of violence, it soon became apparent that most of the sentences were unusually mild, at the lower end of prescribed minimum penalties, and often inconsistent. Judges made great efforts to interpret the law in ways that benefited defendants, an attitude that reflected the mood of the German people in whose name they spoke. Holding Nazi defendants responsible for obeying an authority all had supported would have compelled poswar German society to scrutinize its own profound complicity with these crimes.[103]

One of the most frequently allowed mitigating facts has been the argument that defendants had grown up and lived in a society permeated with National Socialist ideas. It is no doubt true that crimes committed in a quasi-totalitarian system cannot be treated in the same way as offenses in a state committed to the rule of law, a *Rechtsstaat*.[104] At the same time, this difference much of the time has been given undue importance. In the trial of members of an Einsatzgruppe, the court noted that the accused had been "children of their time." They had violated the law "of a state that defied justice while at the same time it claimed to be a *Rechtsstaat*. It was in this kind of setting that they had become criminals, and this required that they be granted mitigating circumstances."[105]

In 1966, Alfred Karl Heinrich was accused of being an accessory to murder in several hundred cases. Even as a student he had been drawn to National Socialist ideas, and in 1923 he had joined the *Jungsturm*, which later became the Hitler Youth. He enlisted in the Nazi party in 1931 and became a member of the SD two years later. At that time, Heinrich took the oath of the SD: "I pledge allegiance to my Führer Adolf Hitler, to the SS, and all my superiors." In 1942, Heinrich was sent to Belarus, where he served as head of several SD offices and participated in the killing of Jews until the spring of 1944. The court considered itself unable to disprove Heinrich's claim that he had considered the operations against the Jews as "*unschön*" (not pretty) and that he had carried them out "grudgingly." The judges considered it a mitigating fact that Heinrich had been "caught up more and more in the maelstrom of the national socialist reign of force and had become influenced by its propaganda." He had become a loyal supporter of the Nazi regime and had unfailingly upheld his oath of loyalty. It appears, the court declared, that "he had carried out the criminal orders primarily because he had been a convinced supporter of the Third Reich" and therefore had considered it necessary to obey his Führer. Rewarded for having been a good Nazi, Heinrich was given a prison term of just five years.[106]

In a few cases, courts rejected the idea that indoctrination in Nazi ideology could be a mitigating factor. A court in Darmstadt declared that a defendant's commitment to National Socialist ideas could not lead to a reduction in sentence. Everyone who claims to be a decent person "must be expected to have enough knowledge of right and wrong to recognize injustice even if it is commanded by a reckless leader."[107] A Bochum court ruled that the accused had been a convinced Nazi who had identified himself with the Final Solution. Hence the fact that he had participated as a declared enemy of the Jewish people in the shooting of Jews had to be considered an aggravating fact.[108]

The Bundesgericht appeared to resolve this disagreement in a decision rendered in 1978. Wilhelm Eickhoff had been convicted by a Hamburg court of the murder of at least fifty Jews. He had chosen his victims and had participated in the shooting. For these crimes, he was sentenced to twelve years' imprisonment. The High Court ruled that the Hamburg judges should have punished Eickhoff with life imprisonment. That the defendant had become "entangled in a system of injustice" was not a valid reason for not imposing the penalty required by the law. "Members belonging to other groups that glorify and exercise violence could also make the claim that deeds of violence are approved in their circles." In the absence of valid mitigating factors, murder had to be punished with imprisonment for life.[109]

This decision of the Bundesgericht made an important legal point. Just as a young man growing up in a Mafia environment cannot excuse a subsequent murder on the grounds that he had been inculcated with a disregard for human life, Nazi criminals should not be allowed to plead indoctrination with Nazi ideology as an excuse for their criminal deeds. Presumably, adult individuals are not pawns or tools of their elders or superiors but individuals who are responsible for their actions. However, this potentially significant decision had no practical consequences. The irrelevance of entanglement in an unjust system was considered by other courts a mere obiter dictum (an inessential argument not establishing a precedent). The crucial point had been the High Court's determination that conviction for the crime of murder required the penalty of life imprisonment. Hence in subsequent years judges continued to hand down conflicting decisions on the question of whether being a committed Nazi, and thus lacking mens rea (a guilty state of mind), should be considered a mitigating fact. Article 17 of the penal code provided that a defendant who did not recognize that he was doing wrong was innocent if he could not avoid this error, and that he was to receive a lower sentence if he could have avoided the mistake.

Even in cases where the criminal nature of the deed should have been manifest, as in the killing of children, some judges granted defendants the excuse that they had lacked mens rea. The SD official Walter Thormeyer had ordered the shooting of Jews and usually had conducted himself in an especially brutal manner. In one instance, he had given the order to throw a sick victim into the pit since "a bullet would have been wasted." Nevertheless, Thormeyer was convicted as a mere accomplice and given a prison sentence of twelve years. His brutality had not been an indication that he was an excess perpetrator. He had not know-ingly done wrong but had "shared the attitude of the men then in power who considered Jews as inferior."[110] Instead of considering this posture an indication of base motives, it was seen as a sign of reduced responsibility.

Many judges went out of their way to justify a reduced sentence. The Cologne Gestapo official Franz Sprinz was held responsible for the deportation of more than 8,500 Jews to Auschwitz and other extermination camps. But after 1945, he had led an orderly life, and this was considered a factor reducing his guilt. It seemed to show that without entanglement in the Nazi system, he would not have become a criminal. Also mitigating was the "long psychological burden" he had suffered hiding for years in his apartment because he was "afraid that he would suffer unjust punishment if extradited to a foreign country."[111] Would a murderer or thief in German postwar society have received a lighter sentence because, until caught, he had successfully hidden from the authorities?

In another case tried in 1966, it was shown that a member of a police post involved in a large number of executions had a particularly high number of vic-tims. Reliable testimony established that the defendant had been known as a particularly "good shooter" and that many of those to be executed had asked to be shot by the accused "because they thus would be spared additional suffering." The court considered these facts mitigating.[112] Other factors seen as reducing guilt in such proceedings have been the facts that a defendant had been a pris-oner of war, had been interned, had been wounded in the war, had been expelled from Eastern Europe, or had lost family members and property.[113] Many courts also concluded that the need for retribution had lessened with the passage of time and for this reason imposed a lower sentence.[114]

Some judges ruled in ways that created win-win situations for defendants. Thus the youth of a Nazi criminal at the time the offense had been committed could be a mitigating factor, but so could advanced age at a postwar trial—a prolonged prison term would unduly impinge on a relatively short remaining life span. Defendants who had not had much education and therefore had more eas-ily succumbed to Nazi hate propaganda, a court ruled in 1966, deserved "human sympathy."[115] On the other hand, for accused civil servants and professional offi-cers, it was a relieving fact that they had "shown eagerness to fulfill their duty as part of their professional standing."[116] Neither the mildness nor the incon-sistency of sentences can be appealed. Unless a sentence involves a legal error, judges have wide discretion in deciding appropriate punishment.

The mild and often-inconsistent sentences handed down by the courts in Nazi crimes of violence have drawn criticism from various quarters. The Coordinating Council of the Societies for Christian-Jewish Cooperation addressed a letter to all German professors of law on March 12, 1963, in which it drew attention to the light sentences given to defendants convicted of the mass murder of Jews. The letter described twelve such cases and noted that the sentences averaged out to ten minutes of jail time for each person killed.[117] The Governing Council of the Evangelical Church of Germany issued a statement on March 13, 1963, in which the churchmen expressed their concern about the disparity between sentences handed down for ordinary crimes of violence and those for Nazi killings. It was imperative to restore justice that had been violated so egregiously by the Nazi rulers.[118] A bill introduced by all four parties represented in the state parliament of Württemberg on July 11, 1963, urged the state government, together with the governments of other Länder, to obtain a better juridical disposition of Nazi crimes. Public prosecutors were urged to work for punishments commensurate with the gravity of the offenses and to appeal sentences that violated decisions of the Bundesgerichtshof. The bill was approved unanimously.[119] Likewise, the *Deutsche Juristentag* of 1966 drew attention to the fact that the sentences handed down in the punishment of Nazi murders were usually at the lower end of the recommended range. This was inappropriate, especially where the perpetrators had held positions of responsibility or where the number of killed was very large.[120]

On the basis of 141 trial records, the Auschwitz survivor Hermann Langbein has noted numerous "ill-considered verdicts."[121] Other critics have used harsher language. Fritz Bauer called many of sentences a "mockery of the victims."[122] The way in which many of the judges have justified their mild sentences has been called a "trivialization of NS-crimes."[123] Another writer has argued that many of the mild penalties represent "mere symbolic punishment."[124]

Before 1933, German jurists, especially those serving in the universities, had shared in the development of National Socialist legal theory.[125] Following the Nazi seizure of power, a large number of judges joined the Nazi party and its affiliated formations. Many of the judges were conservatives who harbored antidemocratic and authoritarian sentiments, and this outlook predisposed them to accept Nazi ideology. If we add the widespread respect for authority and the lack of civil courage prevailing in Germany, it becomes evident why the German judiciary quickly and willingly carried out the repressive laws of the new regime.

After the victory over the Nazi regime in the spring of 1945, the Allies suspended all German courts, but by the end of that same year, local, district, and state courts were again functioning. The intention had been to allow only politically reliable judges and court personnel to serve, but that proved impossible. In Bremen, for example, only two judges with an untainted record could be found. By 1946, about 80 percent of Nazi-era judges again held office.[126] A report issued in 1949 by the American commissioner for Bavaria, entitled "Some Aspects of Re-Nazification in Bavaria," revealed that 752 of 924 judges and prosecutors (that is, 81 percent) were former Nazis. Similar conditions existed in the other Western zones of occupation.[127]

The reintegration of former members of the Nazi party into German society continued after the German Federal Republic came into being on May 23,

1949. There was much talk of the need to utilize the knowledge and experience of all Germans. On May 11, 1951, the Bundestag adopted a statute, colloquially known as "the 131 Law." Article 131 of the Basic Law had authorized the parliament to regulate the status of all civil servants who had not been given back their old positions. The law now accorded all public servants, with the exception of members of the Gestapo and other "major offenders," a legal claim to reemployment. The result was that fewer than 1,000 out of 345,000 Nazi-era civil servants failed to reclaim their former positions.[128]

In the state of North-Rhine Westphalia, twenty of thirty-three leading positions in the criminal police were held by former SS officers.[129] Even high officials of the Nazi state soon again occupied positions of seniority. Hans Globke, the man who had co-authored the Nuremberg race laws, headed Konrad Adenauer's chancellery office. In some *Länder*, 100 percent of Nazi judges were able to return to their former posts. Twenty-seven out of forty judges making up the Bundesgerichtshof in 1950 had served in the Nazi judiciary.[130] As of that date, 68 percent of all German judges had been Nazi-era judges.[131]

The widespread mood to let bygones be bygones benefited some of the most tainted Nazi judges and prosecutors. It was one thing to forgive membership in the NSDAP, the Nazi party—many Germans had joined the party not out of ideological conviction but to further their careers. It was an entirely different matter to give a pass to men who had served on the special courts of the Nazi state and who were responsible for thousands of death sentences meted out for the slightest offenses. The Nuremberg trial of some of these judges referred to these men as "carrying the dagger of the murderer under the robe of the judge."[132] Thus Kurt Bellmann, who as head of the Sondergericht of Prague was linked to at least 110 death sentences, now was a judge at the Landgericht Hannover. Eduard Dreher had served as prosecutor at the Sondergericht of Innsbruck, where he had argued for the death penalty for such minor offenses as stealing a bicycle. After the war, Dreher became a high official in the German Ministry of Justice and took a leading role in the development of criminal law.[133] In the state of North-Rhine Westphalia, twenty-four former members of the notorious *Volksgerichtshof* (people's court), the highest special court responsible for 5,243 death sentences, served as judges or prosecutors. Close behind were Baden-Württemberg with nineteen and Bavaria with fifteen former Volksgerichtshof officials.[134] Not one of the 106 judges and 179 prosecutors who served on the Volksgerichtshof was convicted by a German court for their regime of judicial terror, and the same holds true for the judges of the special courts.[135] Of the twenty-two prosecutors and judges who had served at the Sondergericht Kiel, by 1951 no fewer than twenty-one (95 percent) were back in various positions of the judiciary of Schleswig-Holstein, some of them at high ranks.[136]

Extensive and highly damaging publicity about these men eventually led to a half-hearted redress. In 1950, the Bundestag adopted as Article 116 of a new law about the judiciary a provision that judges and prosecutors who had served between September 1, 1939, and May 9, 1945, could apply for their retirement within nine months. The committee proposing this bill expressed "the expectation that judges and prosecutors who on account of a past role in death sentences could expect justified complaints, would be aware of their duty and retire."[137] Yet the great majority of affected judges either did not think that the law applied to them or regarded early retirement as a confession of guilt. At the end of the grace period, on June 30, 1962, only 149 judges had applied for early retirement.[138] The problem solved itself eventually because with the passage of time additional judges reached mandatory retirement age.

The tainted postwar judiciary has been held responsible for the many shortcomings in the prosecution of Nazi criminals. For example, on April 8, 1945, the Nazi judge Otto Thorbeck had condemned to death six members of the German resistance, including Wilhelm Canaris and Dietrich Bonhoeffer. But on June 19, 1956, the Bundesgerichtshof acquitted Thorbeck of the charge of having been an accomplice to murder on the grounds that, according to then-prevailing law, the resisters had committed treason.[139] The fact that four of the five members of the BGH handing down this judgment had been judges or prosecutors of the Nazi regime was surely not an irrelevant factor in this miscarriage of justice. In later years, the German courts recognized that resistance against the Nazi *Unrechtsstaat* was not only not a crime but a duty.[140]

The mildness of many verdicts has been attributed to the fact that many postwar judges had been active in the Nazi judiciary.[141] A historian who studied 142 verdicts in such proceedings has concluded that "the high ratio of former NS jurists is a principal reason for the retribution that failed to occur."[142] Another student of the subject has argued similarly that an important factor in the classification of so many Nazi criminals as mere accomplices was the attitude of the judges. Many of these judges had a personal stake in regarding Nazi offenders as "accomplices without a will of their own" and as victims of criminal leadership.[143]

Even the Bundesgerichtshof has finally rebuked the flawed record of earlier years. In 1995, the High Court upheld the conviction of a former East German judge for bending the law and imposing politically motivated death sentences. The court ruled that ideological blindness was no excuse for conduct that violated basic moral values, and it criticized the decisions of the BGH in the 1960s for not recognizing the necessity of applying this principle to Nazi judges. The Nazi regime had perverted the legal order with the result that one is justified to speak of *Blutjustiz* (blood justice). Yet, said the court, none of the judges responsible for these crimes had been convicted.[144] (This finding is not fully correct, but it is true that only a handful of Nazi judges were ever convicted for their terror sentences, and these cases involved summary trials during the final days of the war.[145])

The former Article 336 of the Penal Code (now Article 339) made it a criminal offense, punishable by a prison term of one to five years, for judges to engage in

Rechtsbeugung (perversion of justice, literally "bending of the law") to the detriment or favor of a party. In a decision handed down by the Bundesgericht in 1993, the High Court explained that such judicial misconduct would occur if, for example, there existed an "unacceptable discrepancy between the gravity of the crime and the penalty imposed."[146] Applying this yardstick and the reasoning of the BGH in its 1995 decision, a very large number of Nazi-era judges were guilty of a perversion of justice and should have been charged with violating article 336 of the Penal Code. Given the fact that many such tainted judges served at the highest level of the German judiciary, it is no surprise that such redress never took place. These judges acted in line with the well-known principle that "one crow does not peck out another's eyes."

The Ludwigsburg official Adalbert Rückerl has warned against blanket judgments. Not every judge or prosecutor who served during the Nazi era is on that account unfit to fill these posts in the democratic Germany of today.[147] It is also important to recognize that the attitude of the judges in the first four decades after the end of the war accurately mirrored the mood of the society of which they were a part. Yet whatever the many causes for this result, the fact remains that much of what transpired under the name of retribution for Nazi crimes in postwar Germany amounts to what the Holocaust survivor Ralph Giordano has called a farce and a second guilt. Herta Däubler-Gmelin, who served as German Minister of Justice between 1998 and 2002, viewed it as significant that not a single judge of the dreaded *Volksgerichtshof* has stood trial. The judiciary was successful in arranging for its own amnesty. According to appropriate standards of justice, Däubler-Gmelin concluded, the prosecution of Nazi crimes "has not been a success story."[148] In 1995 the BGH spoke of a basic "failure to condemn the NS-system of justice,"[149] and this assessment too would seem to be appropriate.

Explaining the Holocaust

There have been many attempts to explain why so many seemingly ordinary Germans became willing participants in the murder of the Jews. One scholar has tallied forty-one different theories.[1] These explanations include the potential for evil in human nature and the psychological characteristics of the perpetrators, as well as such situational factors as group pressure and the desire for conformity. Nearly all historical accounts also invoke the role of anti-Semitism in German society, ranging from mild prejudice to a strong hatred of Jews. Yet none of these alleged causal factors holds up under critical analysis. Many of these competing explanations are partly right, but none alone is sufficient to account for the phenomenon at issue.

The explanation of the Holocaust that posits individual pathology is probably the oldest, yet it is also one of the weakest. As evolutionary psychology shows us, in order to serve survival and reproduction, natural selection endowed human beings with certain patterns of behavior, and these include the potential for aggressive violence and evil. The capacity for extraordinary evil of the kind that manifested itself during the Holocaust, one psychologist writes, is "within us all. We have a hereditary dark side that is universal across humankind."[2] However, the universal capacity for evil does not explain why only some of us perpetrate extraordinary evil and why the great majority never do. There is no gene for genocide, and indeed we have an innate resistance to killing our own species. Moreover, human nature contains a mixture of good and evil. In addition to the proclivity for violence, we are able to learn to appreciate love and friendship, loyalty and cooperation, fairness, and even the capacity for self-sacrifice. Steven Pinker uses the phrase "the better angels of our nature" that subdue the demons of violence with which we are wired.[3] Finally, and most importantly, our behavior is not determined by our genetic programs. Our genetic makeup is not a straightjacket that triggers inevitable conduct. Genes do not cause behavior. Rather, they influence the way we live. As a result of the interworking of nature and nurture, we are able to, and do indeed, adopt a great variety of potential behaviors.[4]

The historical evidence confirms this insight. The perpetrators of the Final Solution were not mentally ill in any clinical sense, nor did they represent one psychological type. There was no unique murderous Nazi personality. The killers came from various backgrounds, had different psychological attributes, and acted out of a variety of motives. Some indeed killed eagerly, enjoyed being masters of life and death, and developed a capacity for brutality. Others killed to advance their careers or followed orders to kill because it was the easy way out. Still others refused to murder, and a few paid dearly for this act of conscience. Individual cases show a gulf between the situation that offered an opportunity and the deed itself. A small unpredictable factor remains, defying explanation: the freedom to act with violence or to refrain from it.[5]

Attempts to locate the reasons for the widespread participation in the Holocaust in certain specifically German characteristics fare no better. It is no doubt correct, as psychologists such as Alexander Mitscherlich have stressed, that German education, family life, and schooling encouraged an attitude of discipline and obedience to authority.[6] German history, it can be argued, followed a path that was different from much of Western Europe by stressing the moral superiority of the state and a preference for strong authority. The majority of Germans followed an almost linear autocratic tradition that resulted in a relatively weak and dependent conscience in public affairs.[7] This tradition does not necessarily suggest a causal link between Martin Luther and Adolf Hitler, nor does it mean that Hitler's ascent was inevitable. However, cultural belief systems certainly contribute to the shaping of individual behavior. Nazi ideology capitalized on this specifically German posture by cultivating the duty of absolute obedience to the commands of the Führer, and many Germans were predisposed to embrace this outlook.

Yet this theory too raises the question why only some Germans became the perpetrators of the Final Solution. As one scholar has put it, "Toilet training is not the key to genocide."[8] The same Germans who at best were silent bystanders to the persecution of the Jews expressed their anger at the euthanasia program, the killing of the physically handicapped and mentally ill. Their socialization in a culture of obedience did not prevent many of them from occasionally protesting a measure that they found morally unacceptable. While the majority culture supported authoritarian attitudes, the process of socialization did not automatically lead to genocide. A person could be an anti-Semite but decide not to participate in the murder of the Jews. The actions of individuals are not dictated by their history or culture.[9]

Daniel Goldhagen's 1996 book, *Hitler's Willing Executioners*, did well with the German public, in part because the young American praised the German people for the exemplary manner in which they had come to terms with their Nazi past. However, scholars of the Holocaust both in Germany and the United States have harshly criticized the work. According to Goldhagen, the Germans under Hitler were possessed of a special "racial eliminationist anti-Semitism," and this belief system, he maintained, constitutes a sufficient explanation of why individual

Germans willingly killed Jews.[10] Goldhagen's argument is contradicted by the fact that Lithuanians, Croats, Romanians, and other ethnic groups in Himmler's killing squads murdered Jews as efficiently as, and often with more brutality than, the Germans. Ukrainians, for example, were often enlisted when Germans were unwilling to take part in the killing of children.

Goldhagen's thesis also falsely assumes that a general eliminationist anti-Semitism prevailed in Germany. Even when the Nazi regime removed restraints on violent action against Jews, there were no spontaneous anti-Jewish eruptions. As the diary of the Holocaust survivor Victor Klemperer demonstrates, an uneven attitude toward the vilified Jews continued even during the war years, when the Jews had become complete outcasts. Goldhagen's argument also is unable to account for the differences in conduct that characterized the actions of the Germans in the East, and it revives the discredited notion of Germany's collective guilt. It leaves out the many different situational factors without which the conduct of ordinary Germans loses its context. "By eschewing subtlety and nuance," writes a historian, "Goldhagen is actually appealing to a public that wants to hear what it already believes. By doing so, he obscures the fact that the Holocaust was too murky and too horrible to be reduced to simplistic interpretations that rob it of its pertinence in our time."[11] The genocides of Cambodia and Rwanda are a reminder that mass killing is not the sole prerogative of Germans.[12]

Theodor Adorno and several other former members of the Frankfurt Institute for Social Research undertook to locate a predisposition to anti-Semitic conduct in certain character traits. In their study *The Authoritarian Personality*, the émigré German researchers argued that individuals high on the so-called "F-scale" had an affinity for the fascist ideology. Such persons had a character often called the "bicycle type": they buckled under those above them and trampled upon those below them. They also transferred their unconscious hate of dictatorial family members to hostility to Jews and other minorities.[13] Critics have pointed out that authoritarian attitudes are not limited to the political right, and that at the left there is an authoritarianism impressively like the authoritarianism of the right.[14] More importantly, we know that the authoritarian character type has no predictive value. A study of the SS security personnel examined the sociocultural environment from which these men had come. This included deprivation considered conducive to the development of an authoritarian personality, such as a low level of education, rural background, dogmatic religion, authoritarian family background, and more. The author of this study concluded that there was no single sociocultural environment that characterized the majority of the security service, and that no particular personality, authoritarian or otherwise, was typical for what the author called "Hitler's Enforcers." The causes of their behavior could not be found in defective personalities but rather in a situation that legitimized participation in mass murder.[15] The conduct of the perpetrators shows the great significance of the belief that the Holocaust represented state policy, allegedly ordered by Hitler himself, though this conviction does not provide either moral or legal exculpation.

The importance of the context in which the mass killings took place is thus another reason why mere dispositional explanations that invoke specific psychological characteristics fail to account for the murders. Collective crimes under totalitarian rule cannot be explained by the usual reasons that account for the offenses committed by people in ordinary society. Individual acts of murder or mass shootings in Paris or Orlando inspired by radical Islamist ideas take place in violation of legal and societal norms, whereas the massacres of the Holocaust were organized, directed, and legitimated by the state. Ignoring this important fact leads to overdrawn conclusions from psychological experiments such as the Milgram study on obedience.

The social psychologist Stanley Milgram asked a group of volunteers to administer what appeared to be increasingly more powerful electric shocks to a man tied to a chair. Even though no actual shocks were involved, the pretended victim cried and pleaded for relief. Yet the volunteers obeyed the instructor's command to ignore these pleas and continued applying shocks, even as the instrument indicated possible lethal consequences. Milgram concluded from this experiment that when an individual views himself as carrying out the wishes of a person in authority, he regards himself as no longer responsible for the action. Ordinary people can thus become agents of terrible destruction.[16] The Milgram experiment was repeated in many other countries, characterized by quite different histories, including Italy, South Africa, Australia, Spain, Germany, Jordan, and the Netherlands, and these replications appeared to confirm Milgram's conclusions.[17]

Milgram's study seemed to prove that any person at any time can be transformed into a mass murderer and become a perpetrator of genocide. Milgram himself affirmed this conclusion. When he appeared on the television program *60 Minutes* in 1979, he was asked whether the Holocaust could happen in the United States. Milgram replied that one could find enough personnel for a death camp in any medium-sized American town.[18] Others have similarly maintained that the vice of blind obedience can make us all into criminals. In a book entitled *Are We All Nazis?*, the author Hans Askenasy argued that *we* would almost certainly have done the same things Milgram's subjects did. Potentially we are all Nazis.[19] And yet this conclusion is not warranted by the Milgram study or any other psychological experiment.

There are several important differences between the Holocaust and the circumstances of the Milgram study, and the evidence confirms the crucial importance of these discrepancies. First, Milgram's subjects were assured by the authority figure conducting the experiment that no permanent physical damage would result from their actions. The perpetrators of genocide had no such assurance and knew that they were destroying human life. Second, many of the perpetrators of the Holocaust did not kill simply as a result of obedience but acted with anti-Jewish fervor. Milgram's subjects not only had no hostile feelings toward their victims but probably were strongly opposed to harming them. Finally, Milgram's subjects exhibited anguish and conflict while administering dangerous electric shocks. Many of the killers of the Holocaust, by contrast, acted with conviction, cruelty, and sadism.[20]

In all, then, both the laboratory setting and the historical facts of the Holocaust raise serious doubts about the relevance of the Milgram experiment. It fails to explain the many hate-driven cruelties that characterized the mass murder of the Jews.[21] There is no reason to believe that any participants in the Milgram study would have stood at an execution pit in the East and shot naked men, women, and children or dropped pellets of poison into the gas chambers. Milgram draws our attention to the social and situational pressures that can lead ordinary people to commit extraordinary evil.[22] However, most individuals are not potential genocidal perpetrators, and the worst that *can* occur fortunately does not happen very often. The horrors of the Holocaust took place not because of the psychological dispositions of those who engaged in it, but because the Nazi state put at the disposal of its followers means of violence beyond the reach of other people, ordinary or not.[23]

Other psychological experiments fail similarly to prove man's inevitable predilection for evil. The social psychologist Philip Zimbardo divided a group of volunteers into "guards" and "prisoners" and put them into a mocked-up prison wing. The guards were instructed to serve meals and ensure an orderly routine, but otherwise were free to act as they chose. As it turned out, many soon began to tyrannize the prisoners. Some of their victims, too, changed their behavior and abandoned all solidarity with each other. The experiment, planned for two weeks, had to be halted after only seven days because of the sadistic conduct of some of the guards and the occurrence of depression and other disturbances among the prisoners. Zimbardo noted how easy it was for normal people to behave sadistically when put into an appropriate environment,[24] and the experiment certainly demonstrates how being in a certain situation influences persons to adjust their conduct. People indeed often do evil because of where they are, and not who they are.[25] Yet the circumstances of the study could not explain why not all of the subjects behaved in unexpected ways. As with the Milgram study, the artificial conditions of the Zimbardo experiment pose another problem. The subjects of the experiment knew that they were participating in a game, and that things would not be allowed to get out of hand. The many different elements that made up the complex events of the Holocaust cannot be replicated in an experiment. The gap between the laboratory and real life is just too large to bridge.[26]

Bearing in mind the inherent limits of experimental studies, social psychology can nevertheless contribute to our understanding of the dynamics of participation in the Holocaust. A large body of evidence, based on observation and controlled studies, shows that situational elements exert a powerful influence on human behavior. For example, the experiments conducted by Solomon Asch at Swarthmore College in the 1950s demonstrated the powerful human tendency to conform. Some of these factors, as Christopher Browning has shown, were at work in Reserve Police Battalion 101. Members of the battalion who had doubts about killing defenseless human beings took solace in the fact that others seemed to have no problem in carrying out these murders. At least initially, almost all of the men were horrified and disgusted by what they were doing, but for the great majority, to break ranks and adopt overtly nonconformist behavior was simply unimaginable. It was easier for them to shoot.[27] To refuse participation amounted to leaving the unpleasant assignment of murder to one's comrades, and that meant being seen as abandoning the solidarity and equal acceptance of burdens expected of all members of the unit.[28]

Moreover, being in a group diffuses responsibility. Groups suppress dissent and provide a dominant moral authority that shields the individual. Comradeship in the East operated as a lubricant for the machinery of destruction and as relief from the burden of guilt. It meant joining in whatever the group deemed to be right and appropriate.[29] Group members, it has been pointed out, may become capable of conduct of which they are incapable individually.[30]

Identification with a group also increases a judgmental attitude toward outsiders, which in extreme cases can lead to dehumanizing the "other." For many men of Police Battalion 101, Browning writes, the Jews stood outside their circle of human obligation and responsibility. They were the enemy, and the commander of the battalion appealed to this notion of the dangerous Jew when he explained to his men why it was necessary to kill women and children.[31] Nazi propaganda regularly denounced Jews as parasites, vermin, and a plague, and this dehumanization made it easier for their killers. The dehumanized victim is deprived of his human status and is no longer perceived as a feeling or suffering person. Dehumanization creates psychological distance between the perpetrator and the evildoing. The victim becomes expendable. Dehumanization also implies that the victims deserve such extreme measures as death. When they are depicted as demons or other threatening types, whatever is done to them is justified. Seen against an imagined deadly menace, deportation and mass murder could become pre-emptive self-defense.[32] The best way of protecting us from the effect of witnessing the pain and suffering of others is to convince ourselves that the victims must have done something to bring it on themselves.[33]

Still another psychological mechanism that influenced the conduct of the men of Police Battalion 101 was the fact that they acted on the orders of their superiors. Following orders strengthened the tendency to conform to the behavior of one's comrades.[34] When commanded to perform a certain act, the individual does not see himself as personally responsible.[35] The existence of superior orders becomes one of many possible rationalizations that help a perpetrator to reconcile killing with his other values.[36] And then there was the effect of cumulative killing. The violent milieu in which these men lived could not but have a brutalizing effect. "As in combat," observes Browning, "the horrors of the initial encounter eventually become routine, and the killing becomes progressively easier." Habituation played its part. "Like much else, killing was something one could get used to."[37] Actions that are routine no longer invite moral deliberation. Killing is seen as part of one's normal job, "all in a day's work." Normal inhibitions against violence weaken, helped along by euphemisms like *Sonderbehandlung* (special treatment) that hide the true meaning of murder.[38]

As helpful as these psychological insights are, it must be remembered that situational factors no more than genes dictate or determine behavior. Different individuals react differently in identical circumstances. People sometimes do evil in the absence of specific external influences, and they sometimes refrain from doing evil when such influences are present.[39] As we have seen, even in the horrible circumstances of the killing units and death factories, there were those who refused to take life. The social context in which people live leaves them with a margin of discretion within which perpetrators could exercise freedom of choice. These margins are expanded in the case of people who have a high degree of moral and social intelligence.[40] All this reminds us that the explanation of why some men succumb to outside pressures and others resist them successfully is highly complex. It should make us suspicious of monocausal constructs that simplify the human condition. The answer we seek can be found only in the interaction of many different factors.

From early on, anti-Semitism was a major component of Nazi ideology. For tactical reasons, Hitler at times would change the severity of his anti-Jewish measures, but the strength of his hatred of Jews was never in doubt. When Hitler took power on January 30, 1933, a "Germany without Jews" became state policy. Those anti-Semites who during the days of the Weimar Republic may have hesitated to vent their hostile feelings toward the Jews publicly now felt free to do so. At that point in time, nobody yet envisioned mobile killing units or gas chambers. Yet from the moment that a world without Jews was contemplated as a reality, a decisive break with the most basic values of Western civilization had taken place.[41]

Prior to 1933, the Germans arguably were among the least anti-Semitic people in Europe, though hostility to the Jews had existed for centuries. Christian anti-Judaism, it is generally recognized, provided a reservoir of loathing and contempt that facilitated the emergence of racial anti-Semitism during the nineteenth century. The demonological view of the Jews inherited from Christian theology easily merged with the new secular anti-Jewish sentiments. The New Testament mixed, however grotesquely, with Aryan myths and a Darwinian view of history, in which the strongest were destined to win by eliminating the inferior and impure. During the Weimar Republic, many Germans resented the Jews as economic rivals, be they doctors, lawyers, shopkeepers, or tradesmen. The Nazis knew how to tap into and encourage this animosity.[42] What had long been latent was now allowed to emerge into the open. "The appeal from above," writes the German Holocaust survivor Ralph Giordano, "met its counterpart from below."[43]

The first anti-Jewish measures taken by the new government—Jewish civil servants and university professors lost their jobs and Jewish businesses were boycotted—appeared to be not very drastic and dangerous, but along with these official actions there began a steady drumbeat of hatred calling for the elimination of the Jews from German society. Anyone who heard Nazi stormtroopers chanting in the streets "*Juda verrecke!*" (Jewry perish!) and "*Wenn das Judenblut vom Messer spritzt, dann geht's noch mal so gut*" (When Jewish blood spurts from the knife, then all goes doubly well) should have realized that worse was to come. The Nazi hate-rag *Der Stürmer* had at its height a circulation of 1.5 million readers, and it was posted in public places all over Germany. When this odious publication pronounced with every issue "*Die Juden sind unser Unglück*" (The Jews are our misfortune), it should have been clear that the Nazis saw no place for Jews in German society. The *Entjudung* (de-Jewification) of Germany was seen as the precondition and basis of a racially homogeneous *Volksgemeinschaft* (people's community), limited to the Aryans. The Nazis had created a culture that made it possible to imagine a Germany without Jews and Judaism. And from here it was but a short step to the determination that the Jews had no place among human beings altogether and must be physically destroyed.[44]

When specific anti-Jewish policies such as boycott, deprivation of citizenship, aryanization, and emigration failed to solve the "Jewish problem," more extreme measures came to be adopted.[45] This onslaught on the Jews took place in full public view, but no social group in German society openly opposed it. The view that the Jews exerted undue influence on German society appears to have been widespread. For most Germans, anti-Semitism may have gone no further than the belief that German Jews were not really German and that a reduction of the Jewish influence was desirable. But even such muted prejudice was enough to let Germans react with indifference as their Jewish neighbors were persecuted in the 1930s and deported and murdered in the 1940s.[46] Neither the Nuremberg Laws of 1935, which in effect reduced the Jews to pariah status, nor the forced aryanization of Jewish businesses in late 1938 caused much of a reaction among the German public.[47] Not a few Germans privately found fault with the burning of the synagogues and the plundering of Jewish businesses during Kristallnacht of November 9, 1938. And yet, on that day, writes historian Alon Confino, "one could imagine a German world in which Jews and Judaism were terminated by fire and violence."[48] Nearly one hundred Jews were murdered during the violence of the Night of Glass, but the police did not interfere with these killings. The highest party court ruled subsequently that the men who, acting without or against orders, had killed Jews had believed that they were serving the Führer and therefore were not to be expelled from the Nazi party.[49] In his speech on January 30, 1939, Hitler told the German people that in the event that world Jewry were to succeed once again in plunging the world into war, the result would be not the victory of the Jews but their "annihilation." Even though neither Hitler nor any of his entourage at this point had a specific plan for the achievement of "annihilation," the Holocaust had become imaginable.

When war broke out in 1939, a majority of Germans had come to accept the belief that the Jews constituted a problem that awaited a solution, and that the best solution would be the disappearance of the Jews from Germany. The barrage of Jew-baiting had left its imprint on popular attitudes. A careful study of German public opinion concludes that by this time a majority of Germans had become hostile to the Jews. "The Nazi policy succeeded because it was anchored in deeply rooted anti-Jewish sentiments which permeated all classes." Because most Germans did not reject the persecution of the Jews on grounds of principle, their potential resistance to the genocidal means that were being prepared was low.[50] In some places, German onlookers applauded the deportation of the Jews; in others they voiced disquiet. But the most prevalent attitude was unconcern. Evidence from Jewish eyewitness accounts and recollections as well as the reports of the Security Service about popular attitudes show that the most widespread posture among the German population was apathy and indifference regarding the treatment and fate of the Jews. The Jews were out of sight and out of mind. But as Hitler's biographer Ian Kershaw has pointed out, "This was not a neutral stance. It was a deliberate turning away from any personal responsibility."[51] It left the Jews at the mercy of a state that had no mercy.

The German people embraced an anti-Jewish posture without being terrorized or brainwashed. The very idea of brainwashing a nation of sixty million people is of course entirely implausible. The notion probably gained acceptance because it helped coping with the full enormity of the fact that so many atrocities had been committed by, and with the support of, so many Germans.[52]

Hitler always asserted that in fighting the Jews he was doing the work of God, and many Germans indeed came to see in Hitler a messianic figure.[53] He was regarded as the God-appointed savior who, by fighting a cosmic struggle against Jewish evil, would redeem Germany. Ian Kershaw has called the bond between Hitler and the German people an example of charismatic authority. Hitler was endowed with heroic qualities. His leadership offered the prospect of national salvation and redemption.[54] Faith in the Führer created a situation in which the state could mobilize the consciences of a broad cross-section of citizens in the service of a moral catastrophe. Hitler's role as the sole source of law and political legitimacy dissolved moral norms as well as any doubt about the rightness of the orders for the murder of the Jews.[55] The German soldiers who invaded Soviet territory in June of 1941 were primed to kill unarmed Jewish men, women, and children. They had been prepared to embrace racial murder by a six-year campaign of relentless vilification that had depicted the Jews as Germany's misfortune and as a dangerous bacillus that threatened mankind.

The readiness of the Germans to expel Jews from their universe of moral obligation evolved as a result of knowledge disseminated by institutions they respected—churches, schools, universities, and the scientific establishment.[56] Eminent theologians such as Ethelbert Stauffer and Gerhard Kittel argued that every good Christian had the duty to support the National Socialist anti-Jewish policies. After the violent events of Kristallnacht in 1938, the Protestant bishop Martin Sasse distributed a collection of Luther's anti-Semitic passages with the triumphant announcement, "On November 10, the birthday of Luther, German synagogues are burning."[57] In a book published in 1937, *The Jew as a Criminal*, two criminologists argued that just "like the spirochete bacteria that carries syphilis, so the Jews are the carriers of criminality in its political and apolitical form." The Jew, they wrote, "is the embodiment of evil that rises against God and nature."[58] A few years later in the Bergen-Belsen concentration camp, the SS doctor Fritz Klein took this argument to its logical conclusion: "Out of respect for human life, I would remove a purulent appendix from a deceased human body." For the same reason, the Jews, a "purulent appendix in the body of Europe," had to be eradicated from the body of the continent.[59]

German participants in the Final Solution could do their dirty work without being fanatic anti-Semitic ideologues, though many were certainly that and worse. Ideological commitment varied, but the great majority of Germans had arrived at the conviction that the Jews were a menace that had to be countered. This view was part of a frame of reference that steered their perceptions and through which they interpreted the events they witnessed. This frame of reference at times made them criticize the way mass murder was taking place but not the fact that it was happening.[60] Years of anti-Semitic agitation had lowered the barriers to murder.[61] Most of the men serving in the East had internalized the Nazi morality that allowed the killing of racially inferior and subhuman individuals. They did not perceive the killing operations as atrocities but as necessary brutal tactics against people who had been officially designated as Germany's dangerous enemy.[62] The starved Jews they encountered fit the image of Nazi propaganda. Equating Jews with Bolsheviks and partisans further facilitated their readiness to kill. A former member of a police battalion recalled in 1961 that at the time he fully believed the propaganda that declared the Jews to be criminal and subhuman: "The thought that one should oppose or evade the order to take part in the extermination of Jews never entered my head."[63]

Anti-Semitism can lead to pogroms, but in order to carry out mass murder on the gigantic scale of the Final Solution, the directing hand of the state was necessary. The Nazi regime provided this organization with deadly efficiency. The Nazis hunted down their victims over an entire continent with a persistence and fanaticism that has few parallels. During the 1980s, conservative German historians such as Andreas Hillgruber proposed that the Holocaust be treated not like a "singular event" but as "normal history."[64] The debate about this issue became known as the *Historikerstreit* (the historians' dispute), and those who shared Hillgruber's position talked of the need to "historicize" the Holocaust. But while the attempted destruction of the Jewish people was carried out by generally normal individuals, it was anything but "normal history." The Holocaust was unprecedented because never before had a state undertaken to kill all members of a group—man, woman, and child—and hunt them down over an entire continent. In contrast to mass killings in earlier centuries, Nazi genocide was genocide with an ideological purpose; it served no pragmatic interests. The Holocaust evolved as part of the Nazis' vision of building a racially pure Aryan world in which the Jew had no place.[65] Members of the SS, at all levels of this organization, were deeply involved in carrying out what the regime called the Final Solution of the Jewish Question. The way in which these men rationalized the program of mass murder, their moral compass, was shared by other perpetrators of the Holocaust.

Membership in the SS involved a way of life. The SS had its own worldview and system of values, a mixture of nationalism, racism, and a cult of youth and manliness. Considered an elite force, service in the SS afforded prestige. Himmler called the SS a "knighthood," a "new nobility."[66] "We were the best and the toughest," Johannes Hassebrock, one of the commandants of the concentration camp Gross Rosen, declared after the war, still very proud.[67] Others have called the SS "the model citizens of a murderous regime,"[68] with unconditional obedience being one of the most important virtues.[69] The oath of the SS declared, "I pledge to you, Adolf Hitler, Führer and Chancellor of the Reich, my loyalty and bravery. I will obey you and those whom you have designated as my superiors until the death, so help me God."[70] A handbook of conduct expected from the SS man put it as follows: "Obedience is based on the conviction that the national socialist ideology will rule supreme."[71]

The Nazi regime organized ideological indoctrination at all levels of society and especially for those serving in the security services and the armed forces. A publication issued for the SS in 1943 entitled *Der Untermensch* (The Subhuman) characterized the Soviet people, and the Jews among them, as "being on a level below animals." Pictures, allegedly taken in the occupied eastern territories, showed monstrous-looking persons clad in rags and contrasted these to beautiful Aryan types.[72] It is difficult to know how effective this propaganda was; it may simply have strengthened already existing prejudice. Whatever the answer, it is clear that this indoctrination confirmed the hostility toward Jews and thus contributed to the readiness to murder them. It expanded the boundaries of acceptable and desirable behavior, and it weakened traditional views of right and wrong.[73] Not surprisingly, Himmler repeatedly called for a strengthening of ideological instruction.[74] The Jewish question was at the center of this schooling, and as the Final Solution unfolded, the destructive aim of this undertaking was acknowledged more and more openly. A police publication for ideological instruction issued in December 1941 stated, "What even two years ago appeared to be impossible, is now being realized step by step: at the end of the war, Europe will be free of Jews."[75]

Increasingly, Nazi rhetoric at the highest levels included references to the destruction of the Jews that was underway and praised it as an all-important historic deed, a cleansing operation against evil. In a message read at a ceremony marking the anniversary of the founding of the Nazi party on February 24, 1942, Hitler declared, "My prophecy will be fulfilled that in this war it is not the Aryans who will be exterminated but the Jew who will be eradicated. Whatever the battle will bring or however long it may last, this will be the ultimate legacy of this war. And then finally, after the elimination of these parasites, a long suffering world will experience a long period of brotherhood among nations and true peace."[76] And in an editorial for the Nazi weekly *Der Angriff,* published on February 23, 1943, Robert Ley, the head of the Nazi labor organization, wrote, "Finally the Jew has been selected to be exterminated for his scandalous misdeeds and crimes. We Germans have been assigned by destiny to carry out this verdict of providence."[77]

Himmler expressed a similar sentiment in a speech to a group of SS officers in Poznan (occupied Poland) on October 4, 1943: "In our history, this [the extermination of the Jews] is an unwritten and never-to-be-written page of glory."[78] And yet the fact that Himmler referred to the murder of the Jews as an "unwritten and never-to-be-written" series of events indicated that the organizer of the Final Solution was unwilling to allow the massacres to be openly acknowledged. While Hitler too repeatedly spoke abstractly of "extermination," the fate of the Jews was not an acceptable topic of conversation in his headquarters.[79] Their reluctance to confront the reality of the mass murders, Confino suggests, would seem to indicate that Hitler and Himmler had "a sense of transgression." Both avoided describing what really happened not only to others but also to themselves because they sensed that they were breaking a taboo.[80] In his diary entry for March 27, 1942, Goebbels speaks of the extermination of the Jews as "a barbaric undertaking that need not be described more fully."[81] At the onset of Operation Reinhard in 1942, Himmler reportedly invoked the need for "superhuman acts of inhumanity."[82] As one SS officer is said to have stated, "While on duty I am a swine, and I am almost always on duty."[83] As much as the Nazi regime sought to achieve a total transformation of values, it never succeeded in fully achieving this goal. Even Hitler and the members of his immediate entourage probably knew deep down that they were doing wrong.[84]

The moral unease experienced by these leaders is reflected in the euphemisms they employed in describing the horrors of the mass murders. It began with terms like *Sonderbehandlung* (special treatment), *Endlösung* (final solution), and *Umsiedlung* (resettlement), but even this terminology came to be considered too concrete. For a statistical report about the Final Solution composed on April 4, 1943, Himmler gave orders that the destruction of the Jews was nowhere to be described as "*Sonderbehandlung der Juden.*" Instead, the annihilation was to be referred to as "transportation of Jews in the Eastern provinces to the Russian East" and as "guiding through." The concern with regulating language is further evidence of the survival of old standards of morality that made it unacceptable to call things by their real names.[85]

Himmler's repeated insistence that the extermination of the Jews be carried out in an orderly fashion and that the executioners stay "decent" is another indication that the leader of the SS never fully abandoned the values of his upbringing. We find it impossible to link decency and wholesale murder, but the very fact that Himmler used a word like decency, a term belonging to the moral language of his past, is what is significant here. In an order issued on December 12, 1941, Himmler imposed upon his subordinates the "sacred duty personally to make sure that none of our men who have to carry out this difficult duty [to kill the Jews] is brutalized or suffers damage to his spirit or character."[86] A guide for the ideological education of the SS and police, designed to delineate the moral code of that black-clothed elite, invoked values such as "cleanliness" and "chivalry."[87]

At the same time, the context of these exhortations made it clear that members of foreign races were excluded from this moral universe and the reach of human solidarity. There was no need to treat the Jews as human, and indeed it would be outright wrong. The killing of the Jews was not seen as murder. In the light of the new morality, it was a moral duty. The importance of this conceptual link is crucial. Without such a moral underpinning, the mass murder would have been impossible.[88] The strong hold that hatred of the Jews had on the mentality of the SS is shown by the fact that even after Himmler in 1945 had ordered an end to the killing of Jews, it continued during the death marches to which the inmates of the camps were subjected in the spring of 1945.

In several semi-public speeches, Himmler acknowledged that the killing his men had to carry out was indeed terrible, but that it needed to be done without personal enrichment. On February 29, 1940, Himmler spoke to *Gauleiters* (the leaders of Nazi party districts) and other party functionaries and defended the killing of the Polish intelligentsia. The executions, he declared, were terrible. "It is an awful and hideous experience for a German to have to be present at this horror. This is so, and if it were otherwise we would no longer be German or Germanic."[89] On October 4, 1943, at Poznan, Himmler again addressed high-ranking SS officers on the subject of the massacres. The evacuation and extermination of the Jewish people is a "difficult subject," Himmler declared, about which we do not speak in public. "Most of you will know what it means when 100 bodies lie together, when 500 are there, or when there are 1,000. To have seen this through and, with the exception of human weakness, to have remained decent, has made us hard." We have taken the riches of the Jews, Himmler continued, and have delivered it to the state treasury. However, "[W]e have taken nothing from them for ourselves. A few, who have offended against this, will be judged in according with an order that I gave at the beginning: He who takes one Mark of this is a dead man. . . . We have the moral right, we have the duty to do it, to kill this people who would kill us. We however do not have the right to enrich ourselves with even one fur, with one Mark, with one cigarette, with one watch, with anything. . . . We have carried out this most difficult task for the love of our people. And we have suffered no defect within ourselves, or in our character."[90]

Himmler's notion that it was possible to engage in wholesale murder and remain decent was of course a fiction. Everything we know about the implementation of the Final Solution makes it clear that the Holocaust included barbaric orgies of violence and gratuitous cruelty aplenty. Wanton anti-Jewish brutality was an inevitable accompaniment of the campaign of murder against the Jews. The Nazi leadership motivated the killers by branding the Jews as subhuman parasites and threats to the very survival of the German people. Whatever Himmler's personal preference may have been, given this virulent campaign of hate, it was impossible to execute the Final Solution in an orderly fashion. In an organization set up for mass murder, there was no chance to prevent arbitrary murder. According to Himmler, one could murder thousands of Jews and yet remain a decent German. At the same time, neither Himmler nor his followers fully believed in this maxim, and they engaged in various verbal subterfuges to quiet a conscience that they were never able to silence completely.

The Jews in the East were fair game. Yet killers of Jews could run into trouble if their debauched actions became too public. The *public exposure* of the murder of Jews, not the act itself, led to a prison term for Max Taubner, the commander of a technical supply unit with the First SS Infantry Brigade in Ukraine. Täubner had joined the SS in January 1933 and volunteered for the Waffen-SS a few days before the invasion of the Soviet Union in June 1941. A German court in 1973 characterized him as a "fanatic enemy of Jews."[91] After the start of the war in the East, Täubner let it be known that he would "finish off" twenty thousand Jews if at all possible, but much to his disappointment, the auxiliary unit he headed had hardly any contact with Jews. Täubner thereupon developed his own game plan for murdering the hated opponent.

When Täubner's unit reached the town of Zwiahel (Novograd Volynsky) west of Kiev, most of the Jewish inhabitants had already been murdered by EG C on September 12, 1941, or during subsequent "cleansing operations." However, some 300 had been incarcerated by a local Ukrainian militia and were being kept in an improvised prison close to town. Täubner marched his men to the prison and had the 319 Jewish inmates shot at an execution pit. Täubner's unit arrived in Scholochowo on October 17, where they shot 191 Jews of all ages. On Täubner's orders, one of the SS men took pictures of the shooting. Later that month, because of heavy rainfall, Täubner's unit was stuck in the small town of Alexandria, northeast of Kirowograd, for a few weeks. To pass the time, Täubner's unit shot all the Jews they could find—a total of 459.

Täubner and some of his men also brutalized their victims before killing them. The SS court that eventually tried Täubner described these deeds: "Jews, who had been ordered to saw wood in the yard of the quarters, were beaten on the pretext that they did not work in an orderly manner. On this occasion they were also hit with spades." One of the SS men "induced the Jews to beat each other to death by promising that the survivor would not be shot. The Jews did in fact knock each other down, even though they did not kill each other." Täubner joined in the beatings "and also hit Jewish women with a whip. . . . On one occasion, a couple of Jews were ordered to tear down a wooden shed. It was arranged so that the shed collapsed on top of them, burying them under the debris." One night, when Täubner's men had been feasting, he invited them to go with him to the basement where some twenty Jewish prisoners, including women and elderly men, were being held. Täubner beat the terrified prisoners with a wooden club until two of the victims were dead; several others were left wounded. A few days later, he had a group of ten to fifteen orphaned children executed together with the elderly nurse caring for them. An SS man grabbed the children by the hair, lifted them up one by one, shot them through the back of the head, and then tossed them into the grave. All of the killings were photographed and duly noted in the unit's logbook.[92]

It was the documentation of his actions that led to Täubner's downfall. After his unit had been recalled from Ukraine and reassigned to East Prussia, the enthusiastic Jew hater began to boast of his deeds and show off the pictures he had ordered to be taken. Prevailing regulations prohibited such photography, and he and four of his men were arrested. Since October 17, 1939, members of the SS and police had been subject to special courts, with Himmler the chief legal authority.[93] On Himmler's orders, the proceedings against Täubner's accomplices were dropped in late 1942, and Täubner's own case was referred to the Supreme SS Court (*Hauptamt SS-Gericht*) in Munich. Here he faced charges not for murder but only for "breach of troop discipline." The verdict of the SS court of May 24, 1943 noted:

> The defendant should not be punished for the actions against the Jews as such. The Jews must be exterminated; there is no loss in any of the killed Jews. Even though the defendant should have recognized that the extermination of the Jews is the task of Kommandos especially set

up for this purpose, it should be assumed in his favor that he may have considered himself authorized to participate in the extermination of the Jews himself. The driving motivation of the defendant has been genuine hatred of Jews.[94]

The court indicated that Täubner had to be punished not for the killings themselves but for the manner in which the executions had been carried out. "The conduct of the defendant," the Munich SS court declared, "is in the highest degree unworthy of an honor-loving and decent German man." The court explained:

> It is not the German way to apply Bolshevist methods during the necessary extermination of the worst enemy of our people. The action of the defendant borders on such methods.
>
> The defendant allowed the men under his command to become brutalized so that they conducted themselves like a savage horde. The defendant has endangered the discipline among his men in the worst imaginable way. Even though the defendant has taken care of his men in every other way, by this conduct he has grossly failed his supervisory duties, among which, according to SS guidelines, is not to let his men degenerate morally.[95]

In the eyes of his judges, Täubner suffered from "severe character defects." He had ordered pictures be taken of "images conveying the most evil excesses," and he had shown these pictures to his wife and acquaintances. Illustrative of his degeneracy was the fact "that the defendant showed himself particularly pleased with a picture that showed a Jewish woman largely naked." All this also represented a serious breach of security. "How easy it would it have been [for these pictures] to pass from Southern Germany through Switzerland into the hands of enemy propaganda." For the various offenses he had committed, Täubner was sentenced to ten years' imprisonment, expelled from the SS, and declared unfit for military duty. The disgraced SS man served only a little more than a year in the penitentiary before he was pardoned by Himmler in January 1945.[96] But when prosecutors in the early 1970s sought to try Täubner for the numerous murders he had committed, a district court rebuffed them on the grounds that such a prosecution would constitute double jeopardy.[97]

The verdict of the SS court was based on a legal principle Himmler had established in a similar case on October 26, 1942, to wit, in instances of unauthorized shootings of Jews, the decisive question was the motive. No punishment was to be imposed for "politically motivated" killings unless the maintenance of military discipline was at stake or it was a case of "selfish or sadistic or sexual motives."[98] A person involved in such crimes, as the SS judge Konrad Morgen put it, "manifests by his act severe character flaws that make him intolerable to the German *Volksgemeinschaft* [people's community]."[99]

And yet what Täubner and his men had done was not all that unusual. We know that the treatment of Jews before they were shot was nearly always incredibly brutal and cruel. With alcohol flowing freely, troop discipline, too, was usually extremely loose. It would appear that Täubner had had the bad luck of being caught for taking pictures and showing these pictures to a large number of individuals. He had caused a scandal, and that was his real offense. Neither Himmler nor any of his underlings cared one whit about the killing of the Jews, no matter how dreadful the circumstances. Neither were they excessively concerned about military discipline as long as the business of murdering the Jews was attended to more or less efficiently. What was unacceptable was to have these proceedings documented in photographs and circulated freely. We know that many other soldiers violated the prohibition of taking pictures of executions. The Red Army found thousands of images of such killings in the pockets of German prisoners.[100] However, these photos for the most part stayed in the families. Moreover, they generally did not portray brutal excesses of the kind committed by Täubner.

During the course of the war, SS and police courts several times tried and convicted members of the SS who had killed Jews without orders. In the fall of 1944, Maximilian Grabner, the head of the Gestapo in Auschwitz, was charged with arbitrarily killing prisoners, but his trial was adjourned and never resumed.[101] It would seem that Himmler did not really care about the brutalities that almost always accompanied the killing of Jews as long as these atrocities did not endanger the orderly progress of the Final Solution and did not lead to unwelcome publicity. Even in these cases, Himmler usually pardoned the offenders, for he was willing to accept that they had acted in the right spirit.[102] Täubner, for example, who had been sentenced to ten years' imprisonment, served little more than one year of his sentence. In other words, and not surprisingly, the jurisprudence of the SS served not the protection of innocent human life and the punishment of those who violated this elementary human value, but rather the maintenance of order and discipline in an organization of murderers.

Despite Himmler's warning of the severe punishment awaiting those who stole Jewish property and valuables, thievery was rampant. It included the simple grunt who grabbed the fur-lined boots of a Jewish victim as well as SS officers who shipped home entire suitcases of stolen Jewish jewelry and gold. Eighty percent of all cases tried and 25 percent of all convictions handed down by SS courts in 1943 involved property delicts. The seriousness with which the leadership of the SS regarded violations of the norms of this elite formation is shown by the fact that between 1939 and 1944, there were 1,001 implemented death sentences.[103] Among those executed for property crimes was Karl Otto Koch, the commandant of Buchenwald, where an extensive system of graft had been in operation.[104] The former Buchenwald inmate Eugen Kogon speaks of "an abscess on the rotten body" that finally burst open.[105] After Oswald Pohl had become head of the new Economic and Administrative Main Office of the SS in February 1942, he removed one-third of the concentration camp commandants for corruption.[106]

In the fall of 1944, the post office discovered an overweight package containing dental gold from Auschwitz, and Himmler ordered a special commission to investigate the practices of the SS guards at Auschwitz. The commission was headed by the SS judge Konrad Morgen, who had been dealing with corruption in the ranks of the SS since early 1942. Morgen searched the rooms and lockers of the rank-and-file guards and found heaps of stolen gold and jewelry. More than twenty SS men were turned over to the SS courts. He was not allowed to search the dwellings of the higher officers.[107] Moreover, when Morgen began to look into the source of the pilfered gold and into allegations of excessive brutality, his investigation was blocked. From the very beginning, Heydrich and Himmler had reserved for themselves control over the proceedings of the SS and police courts. They could remove "unsuitable" judges, reduce sentences, and stop investigations altogether. This is what happened here. As Morgen testified at the postwar Auschwitz trial, "It was not possible for me to press charges against people who had carried out the orders of my superiors, for example the executions that had been ordered by Reichsführer Himmler."[108] Another member of the special Auschwitz commission, the SS judge Gerhard Wiebeck, told the Auschwitz court that "the investigation of general killing was not authorized. I heard that the extermination of the Jews had been verbally ordered by Hitler."[109]

Himmler wanted his elite to remain decent. The fact that there existed a huge gap between the Reichsführer's expectations and the actual conduct of his men—whether in regard to the gratuitous brutalities of the mass killings or the greedy pilfering of Jewish property—is another reason why the conduct of the perpetrators cannot be explained solely on the basis of ideological elements, including anti-Semitism. The desire for personal enrichment and the satisfaction of violent cravings were omnipresent elements of the Holocaust. At the same time, anti-Semitism, the result of years of propaganda and indoctrination, served as the underlying belief system of the Final Solution and as a convenient rationalization. In the eyes of most perpetrators, helping solve the Jewish problem justified whatever they were doing and provided a general absolution.[110]

"However one may wish to draw the line of active participation," wrote Raul Hilberg, the dean of Holocaust research, "the machinery of destruction was a remarkable cross-section of the German population. Every profession, every skill, and every social status was represented in it."[111] The actual perpetrators acted out of a variety of motives. Some were convinced haters of Jews, while others killed out of a sense of duty, to advance their career, because they followed orders, or because they wanted to conform to the group. There was no uniform

Nazi perpetrator type. The majority of the killers were not sadists, though some types of individuals probably were more readily recruited into the routine of murder. Leadership was an important factor: units led by particularly brutal men became particularly brutal.[112] Time and again, the scope and speed of the mass killing, and thus the fate of tens of thousands of human beings, depended on the energy with which leading, and even subordinate, commanders pursued the murder of the Jews.[113] Finally, in addition to dispositional elements, we must reckon with situational factors. The Holocaust took place as part of a war of extermination in the East, for which Hitler had suspended the conventions of humanitarian law. At least two million Russian prisoners of war were left to die of starvation in a conflict that lowered the value of human life generally.

None of these factors creates causality or dictates a person's behavior. They tell us how we are likely to act, not the way we must act, or, as the language of science puts it, the prediction is probabilistic rather than deterministic. Human beings are not Pavlovian dogs who react with conditional reflexes to stimuli. They are not captives of either psychic forces or outside circumstances. Even in collective crimes like the Holocaust, there exists an individual dimension that will determine the degree of entanglement in evil. Whatever human beings do, they can always act differently. Even if people's perceptions and actions are affected by social, cultural, and biological circumstances, human beings at all times enjoy freedom of action.[114] Depending on their particular personalities, humans react differently to diverse external pressures. They are influenced but not coerced by them.[115] There remains an element of personal agency.

What we have learned of the biographical background of the perpetrators and their subsequent conduct confirms that at several different stages in their life, they had to decide on a course of action. At the time, they may not have been aware that they had a moral decision to make, but whether they knew it or not, they did make a choice. Most of them became executioners, and that is the truth with which they had to live for the rest of their lives.[116] After the war had ended, the ordinary Germans who had committed these deeds returned to their families and resumed their normal lives. Whether they were tried and punished for their crimes or, as happened more frequently, they escaped unscathed, it is clear that wholesale murder necessarily left the killers with a serious taint on their character. We do not expect the average person to commit suicide in order to maintain his personal integrity. But even in the worst corners of the Nazi system, there existed the possibility of avoiding the extraordinary evil ordered from above. The fact that so few availed themselves of this possibility remains an ineradicable blot on an entire German generation and a cross that their descendants continue to bear.

ABBREVIATIONS AND GLOSSARY

Alter Kämpfer	longtime member of the Nazi party (lit., "old fighter")
BA	*Bundesarchiv* (Federal Archive)
BDC	Berlin Document Center
Befehlsnotstand	defense of superior orders
Beihilfe zum Mord	aiding and abetting murder
BGH	*Bundesgerichtshof* (Germany's highest court)
Bunker	concentration camp jail
DAF	*Deutsche Arbeitsfront* (German Labor Front)
EG	*Einsatzgruppe* (special task force playing a key role in the murder of the Jews)
EK	*Einsatzkommando* (subunit of *Einsatzgruppe*)
Fr.	frame
FRG	Federal Republic of Germany
Führerbefehl	order of the Führer
Gauleiter	leader of an NSDAP *Gau* (party district)
Gehilfe	accomplice
Generalgouvernement	general government (administrative unit of German-occupied Poland)
Gestapa	*Geheimes Staatspolizeiamt* ([head] office of the Gestapo)
Gestapo	*Geheime Staatspolizei* (secret state police)
Gleichschaltung	compulsory reorganization to bring institutions or organizations under Nazi control
Heer	German army
Hiwis	*Hilfswillige* (auxiliaries recruited from Soviet prisoners of war and other volunteers)
HJ	*Hitler Jugend* (Hitler Youth)
Judenfrei	free of Jews
JUNSV	*Justiz und NS-Verbrechen* (Justice and National Socialist Crimes, title of collection of German court cases published by University of Amsterdam Press)
Kapo	concentration camp inmate acting as part of the camp staff
Kommando	squad
KZ	*Konzentrationslager* (concentration camp)
Land	German state
Landgericht	German court at the state level
MStGB	*Militärstrafgesetzbuch* (military penal code)
NA	National Archives, College Park, MD
NJW	*Neue Juristische Wochenschrift*

n.p.	no pagination
NSDAP	*Nationalsozialistische Deutsche Arbeiterpartei* (National Socialist German Workers Party)
NSFO	*Nationalsozialistischer Führungsoffizier* (National Socialist Ideological Guidance Officer)
OKH	*Oberkommando des Heeres* (High Command of the Army)
OKW	*Oberkommando der Wehrmacht* (High Command of the Armed Forces)
par.	paragraph
Pg.	*Parteigenosse* (party comrade)
Rechtsbeugung	perversion of justice
Rechtsstaat	state based on the rule of law
Reichsführer SS und Chef der deutschen Polizei	title of Himmler as head of the SS and police
Revier	concentration camp hospital
RGBl	*Reichsgesetzblatt* (German law gazette)
Rollkommando	mobile unit
RSHA	*Reichssicherheitshauptamt* (German Main Security Office)
SA	*Sturmabteilung* (lit. "storm detachment," the paramilitary) organization of the Nazi party)
SD	*Sicherheitsdienst* (lit. "security service," the intelligence service of the SS)
SK	*Sonderkommando* (special detachment, subunit of Einsatzgruppe)
Sonderbehandlung	special treatment (Nazi euphamism for the killing of the Jews)
Sondergericht	special court
SPD	*Sozialdemokratische Partei Deutschlands* (German Social Democratic Party)
Sport	sport, punishment drill in the concentration camps
SS	*Schutzstaffel* (lit., "shield squadron," the Nazi party's elite force commanded by Himmler)
StGB	*Strafgesetzbuch* (German penal code)
Täter	perpetrator
Trawniki	German auxiliary force recruited from Soviet prisoner of war
Unrechtsstaat	state based on systematic injustice and lacking legitimacy
Untermensch	subhuman creature
USHMM	United States Holocaust Memorial Museum
Vergangenheitsbewältigung	coming to terms with the past
Völkische	militant nationalists
Volksdeutsche	ethnic Germans from Eastern Europe
Volksgemeinschaft	people's community
Volksgerichtshof	Nazi special court dealing with security crimes
Wehrmacht	German Armed Forces
Zentrale Stelle der Landesjustizverwaltungen zur Aufklärung nationalsozialistischer Verbrechen	Central Office of the State Administrations of Justice for the Investigation of National Socialist Crimes

NOTES

Introduction

1. Cited by Confino, *A World without Jews*, p. 205.
2. Cited by Laqueur, *The Terrible Secret*, p. 2.
3. Allen, *The Business of Genocide*, p. 275. Allen himself does not share this view.
4. Arendt, *The Origins of Totalitarianism*, p. 416.
5. De Mildt, *In the Name of the People*, p. 15.
6. Brunner, "'Oh Those Crazy Cards Again,'" pp. 342–344.
7. Gilbert, *Nuremberg Diary*, p. 11.
8. Dicks, *Licensed Mass Murder*, p. 17.
9. Wittmann, *Beyond Justice*, p. 32.
10. Rupnow, "Das unsichtbare Verbrechen," p. 91.
11. Frei, *Vergangenheitspolitik*, p. 77. In fairness to men like Adenauer, one should note that even Eisenhower shared the view of the honorable German soldier. See Large, "Reckoning without the Past," p. 111.
12. Stargardt, *The German War*, p. 559.
13. Walter von Molo to Thomas Mann, August 4, 1945, quoted in Bermann-Fischer, *Bedroht-bewahrt*, p. 547.
14. Quoted in Stern, *The Whitewashing of the Yellow Badge*, p. 367.
15. Quoted in Besier, *Neither Good nor Bad*, p. 37.
16. Kershaw, *Hitler, the Germans, and the Final Solution*, p. 140.
17. Volker Ullrich, "'Wir haben nichts gewusst,'" p. 44.
18. Giordano, *Die zweite Schuld*, p. 33.
19. Rückerl, *NS-Verbrechen vor Gericht*, p. 324.
20. University of Amsterdam, *Justiz und NS-Verbrechen: Sammlung deutscher Strafurteile wegen nationalsozialistischer Tötungsverbrechen, 1945–2012*, hereafter JUNSV, vol. 15, case 465a.
21. JUNSV, vol. 21, case 595.
22. See especially Broszat, "Nationalsozialistische Konzentrationslager 1933–1945," pp. 11–133.
23. "'Holocaust': Die Vergangenheit kommt zurück," *Spiegel*, January 29, 1979.
24. Celan, *The Poems of Paul Celan*, pp. 60–62.
25. Buruma, *The Wages of Guilt*, pp. 88–91.
26. See Szejnmann, "Perpetrators of the Holocaust," pp. 25–54.
27. Orth, "The Concentration Camp Personnel," p. 46.
28. Lasik, "Historical-Sociological Profile of the Auschwitz SS," p. 274.
29. Mann, *The Dark Side of Democracy*, p. 263. See also Westermann, *Hitler's Police Battalions*.
30. See, for example, Heer and Naumann, eds., *Vernichtungskrieg*.
31. Bartov, *Germany's War and the Holocaust*, p. 158.

Chapter 1

1. Wünschmann, *Before Auschwitz*.
2. Morsch and Ohm, eds., *Terror in der Provinz Brandenburg*, p. 70.
3. Orth, *Die Konzentrationslager-SS*, p. 99.
4. Broszat, "Nationalsozialistische Konzentrationslager 1933–1945," p. 39.
5. Richardi, *Schule der Gewalt*.
6. Dillon, *Dachau and the SS*, p. 1.
7. Quoted in a German court verdict of May 28, 1965, JUNSV, vol. 21, case 591, p. 123.
8. Kaienburg, "KZ-Terror und Kriegsgewalt," pp. 38–39, 46.
9. Smelser and Syring, eds., *Die SS Elite unter dem Totenkopf*, p. 18.
10. Allen, *The Business of Genocide*, p. 39.
11. Broszat, "Nationalsozialistische Konzentrationslager 1933–1945," p. 65.
12. Ibid., p. 131.
13. Krakowski, "The Satellite Camps," p. 50.
14. Phillips, ed., *The Trial of Joseph Kramer and Forty-Four Others*, pp. 47, 123.
15. Kogon, *The Theory and Practice of Hell*, p. 80.
16. Sofsky, *The Order of Terror*, p. 113.
17. One of the many camp inmates who has ably described the regime of terror is Kogon, *The Theory and Practice of Hell*, chap. 9.
18. Quoted in the verdict of the Auschwitz trial, August 20, 1965, JUNSV, vol. 21, case 595, p. 406.
19. Buchheim et al., *Anatomie des SS-Staates*, vol. 1, p. 320.
20. Wachsmann, *KL*, p. 107.
21. BA, NS added 7/1020, n.p.
22. Wachsmann, *KL*, pp. 108, 727.
23. Hugo was convicted of murder and sentenced to life imprisonment by a German court in 1967. See JUNSV, vol. 26, case 650.
24. For accounts by survivors, see Kautsky, *Teufel und Verdammte*; Neurath, *Die Gesellschaft des Terrors*; Kielar, *Anus Mundi*; Wiesel, *Night*.
25. Sofsky, *The Order of Terror*, p. 247.
26. Weiss, *Journey through Hell*, quoted in Schoenberner, ed., *Wir haben es gesehen*, p. 258.
27. Kogon, *The Theory and Practice of Hell*, chap. 14.
28. Helm, *If This Is a Woman*, pp. 227–228.
29. BA, NS 7/355, p. 2.
30. BA, NS 7/355, pp. 6–14.
31. Levi, *Survival in Auschwitz*, p. 89.
32. Herbert, "Arbeit und Vernichtung," p. 228.
33. Ulrich Fritz, "Wachmannschaften im Konzentrationslager Flossenbürg," p. 38. See also Erpel, *Zwischen Vernichtung und Befreiung*, chap. 4.
34. Stargardt, *The German War*, p. 299.
35. Wünschmann, *Before Auschwitz*, p. 155
36. Kogon, *The Theory and Practice of Hell*, p. 29.
37. Riedel, *Ordnungshüter und Massenmörder im Dienst der "Volksgemeinschaft,"* p. 186.
38. Matthäus et al., *Ausbildungsziel Judenmord*, p. 50. Matthäus notes that this disregard of Himmler's orders throws an interesting light on the claim of Nazi defendants after the war that they had functioned under a regime of "absolute obedience" that had forced them into violence against Jews.
39. Orth, "The Concentration Camps," p. 51.
40. Wünschmann, *Before Auschwitz*, p. 161.
41. Dieter Pohl, "The Holocaust and the Concentration Camps," pp. 160–161; Garbe, "Absonderung, Strafkommandos und spezifischer Terror," pp. 176–177; Pingel, *Häftlinge unter SS-Herrschaft*, pp. 92–93.
42. Wünschmann, *Before Auschwitz*, p. 203.
43. Dillon, *Dachau and the SS*, p. 177.

44. Matthäus et al., *Ausbildungsziel Judenmord*, pp. 56–57.
45. Wünschmann, *Before Auschwitz*, p. 227.
46. Horwitz, *In the Shadow of Death*, pp. 14–16, 20–21.
47. Garbe, "Absonderung, Strafkommandos und spezifischer Terror," p. 190.
48. Dieter Pohl, "The Holocaust and the Concentration Camps," p. 151.
49. Orth, "Die Kommandanten der nationalsozialistischen Konzentrationslager," p. 769.
50. Ibid., p. 159.
51. Schwarberg, *The Murders at Bullenhuser Damm*, p. 119.
52. Ibid., pp. 40–46. See also Alexandre, *Der Judenmord*, p. 124.
53. Orth, "The Concentration Camp Personnel," pp. 47–48.
54. Buchheim, *Anatomie des SS-Staates*, vol. 1, pp. 376–379.
55. Riedel, *Ordnungshüter und Massenmörder im Dienst der "Volksgemeinschaft,"* p. 9.
56. Langbein, *Im Namen des deutschen Volkes*, p. 93.
57. Baron-Cohen, *The Science of Evil*, p. 20.
58. Besier, *Neither Good nor Bad*, p. 270.
59. Welzer, *Täter*, p. 11.
60. Verdict of Landgericht Stuttgart, May 18, 1992, in JUNSV, vol. 48, case 911.
61. Kogon, *The Theory and Practice of Hell*, pp. 232–235.
62. Hackett, ed., *The Buchenwald Report*, p. 154.
63. BA, NS 7/1020, n.p.
64. Verdict of Landgericht Bayreuth, July 3, 1958, JUNSV, vol. 14, case 484a.
65. Verdict of Landgericht Ansbach, April 11, 1961, JUNSV, vol. 17, case 505.
66. Verdict of Landgericht Saarbrücken, July 10, 1978, JUNSV, vol. 42, case 849a.
67. Verdict of Landgericht Frankfurt/M, August 19–20, 1965, JUNSV, vol. 21, case 595.
68. Wittmann, *Beyond Justice*, p. 140.
69. Demant, *Auschwitz*, p. 8.
70. Werle and Wandres, *Auschwitz vor Gericht*, pp. 152–153.
71. Wittmann, *Beyond Justice*, p. 285.
72. German privacy law required that his name be given in abbreviated form.
73. Verdict of Landgericht Frankfurt/M, February 27, 1981, JUNSV, vol. 44, case 866.
74. Crowe, *Oskar Schindler*, p. 74.
75. Sofsky, *The Order of Terror*, p. 115.
76. Kautsky, *Teufel und Verdammte*, p. 83.
77. Anna Pawelczynska, quoted in Todorov, *Facing the Extreme*, p. 181.
78. Verdict of Landgericht Bonn, February 6, 1959, JUNSV, vol. 15, case 473, p. 655. See also Riedle, *Die Angehörigen des Kommandostabs im KZ Sachsenhausen*, pp. 204–219.
79. Verdict of Landgericht Cologne, May 28, 1965, JUNSV, vol. 21, case 591.
80. Distel, "Frauen in nationalsozialistischen Konzentrationslagern," p. 204.
81. Buber-Neumann, *Als Gefangene bei Stalin und Hitler*, p. 314.
82. Tillion, *Frauenkonzentrationslager Ravensbrück*, p. 154.
83. Mailänder, *Female SS Guards and Workaday Violence*, p. 280.
84. Langbein, *People in Auschwitz*, p. 396.
85. Müller, "Die Oberaufseherin Maria Mandl," pp. 52–54.
86. Dublon-Knebel, "'Erinnern kann ich mich nur an eine Frau Danz,'" p. 308.
87. Phillips, ed., *The Trial of Joseph Kramer and Forty-Four Others*, p. xli.
88. Wenck, "Verbrechen as 'Pflichterfüllung'?," p. 38.
89. Verdict of Landgericht Berlin, September 5, 1957, JUNSV, vol. 14, case 450.
90. Verdict of Landgericht Heidelberg, December 16, 1949, JUNSV, vol. 5, case 188.
91. Verdict of Landgericht Cologne, May 28, 1965, JUNSV, vol. 21, case 591. See also Riedle, *Die Angehörigen des Kommandostabs im KZ Sachsenhausen*, pp. 237–241, 257.
92. Venezia, *Inside the Gas Chambers*, pp. 74–75.
93. Dillon, *Dachau and the SS*, pp. 133–134.
94. Lingens, *Prisoner of Fear*, p. 139. On the Babitz camp, see also Zieba, "'Wirtschaftshof' Babitz," pp. 73–87.

95. See, e.g., the case of SS-Unterscharführer Palmier, who was transferred out of Sachsenhausen, in the Verdict of Landgericht Düsseldorf, October 15, 1960, JUNSV, vol. 16, case 497, p. 713.

96. Langbein, *People in Auschwitz*, pp. 287, 419, 422–426, 429.

97. Ibid., pp. 437–38.

98. Naumann, *Auschwitz*, p. 93.

Chapter 2

1. Mallmann, "Die Türöffner der 'Endlösung,'" p. 438.

2. Kershaw, *Hitler, the Germans, and the Final Solution*, p. 270.

3. Hilberg, *Perpetrators, Victims, Bystanders*, p. 16.

4. Schleunes, *The Twisted Road to Auschwitz*, p. 257.

5. Cited in Kershaw, *Hitler, the Germans, and the Final Solution*, p. 104.

6. Kershaw, *Hitler 1889–1936: Hubris*, p. 527.

7. Browning, ed., *The Origins of the Final Solution*, p. 425.

8. Quoted in Krausnick, "Hitler und die Morde in Polen," p. 205.

9. Ibid., p. 206.

10. Heiber, ed., *Reichsführer!*, p. 167.

11. Browning, *Collected Memories*, p. 23.

12. Kershaw, *Hitler, the Germans, and the Final Solution*, pp. 108–109.

13. Schramm, ed, *Kriegstagebuch des Oberkommandos der Wehrmacht*, vol. 1, p. 341.

14. See the affidavit of Walter Blume in the *Einsatzgruppen Case* in *Trials of War Criminals before the Nuernberg Military Tribunals*, vol. 4, p. 140, and the affidavit of Wilhelm Förster, Nuremberg document NO-5520, NA Washington, RG 238, box 95.

15. The letter is reprinted in Klein, ed., *Die Einsatzgruppen in der besetzten Sovietunion 1941–42*, pp. 324–327.

16. Kwiet, "From the Diary of a Killing Unit," p. 81.

17. Matthäus et al., eds., *War, Pacification and Mass Murder 1939*, p. 3.

18. BA, NS 2, p. 123.

19. MacLean, *The Field Men*, p. 132.

20. Christian Ingrao, *Believe and Destroy*, p. vii.

21. Sydnor Jr., *Soldiers of Destruction*, p. 346.

22. Hilberg, *The Destruction of the European Jews*, p. 189; Krausnick and Wilhelm, *Die Truppe des Weltanschauungskrieges*, p. 281; Earl, *The Nuremberg SS-Einsatzgruppen Trials 1945–58*, pp. 4–5. See also Longerich, *Der ungeschriebene Befehl*, p. 97.

23. Quoted in Angrick, *Dokumente der Einsatzgruppen in der Sowjetunion*, vol. 2, p. 266.

24. Mallmann et al., eds., *Die 'Ereignismeldungen UdSSR' 1941*, vol. 1, p. 8, gives the estimate of 535,000.

25. Fritsche, "Holocaust and the Knowledge of Murder," p. 600.

26. Dieter Pohl, *Verfolgung und Massenmord in der NS-Zeit 1933–1945*, p. 83.

27. Langerbein, *Hitler's Death Squads*, pp. 15–16.

28. Ingrao, *Believe and Destroy*, p. 293.

29. Mallmann, "Der qualitative Sprung im Vernichtungsprozess," p. 254.

30. Westermann, *Hitler's Police Battalions*, p. 165.

31. Birn, *Die Höheren SS- und Polizeiführer*, pp. 392–393.

32. Longerich, *Der ungeschriebene Befehl*, p. 109.

33. Himmler's words—we cannot afford "to let the chidren grow up, who then will kill our children and grandchildren"—are quoted in Welzer, *Täter*, p. 173.

34. Angrick et al., eds., *Dokumente der Einsatzgruppen in der Sowjetunion*, vol. 1, pp. 243–244.

35. This figure comes from a lengthy document, known as the "Stahlecker-Bericht," which was also used at the Nuremberg trial. It can be found in International Military Tribunal, *Trial of the Major War Criminals*, vol. 37, document 180-L. It is cited here by Jäger, *Verbrechen unter totalitärer Herrschaft*, p. 336.

36. Quoted in Langbein, *Im Namen des deutschen Volkes*, p. 128.

37. Arad, *The Holocaust in the Soviet Union*, p. 131.

38. "Stahlecker-Bericht," cited by Angrick et al., eds., *Dokumente der Einsatzgruppen in der Sowjetunion*, vol. 1, p. 172.
39. Herbert, *"Vernichtungspolitik,"* pp. 49–50.
40. Ibid., p. 115.
41. Verdict of Landgericht Munich I, July 21, 1961, JUNSV, vol. 17, case 519, pp. 669–670.
42. Earl, *The Nuremberg SS-Einsatzgruppen Trials 1945–58*, p. 6.
43. Ingrao, *Believe and Destroy*, p. 196.
44. Matthäus, "What about the 'Ordinary Men'?," p. 139.
45. Verdict of Landgericht Aurich, May 29, 1961, JUNSV, vol. 17, case 511a, p. 446.
46. Verdict of Landgericht Tübingen, May 10, 1961, JUNSV, vol. 17, case 509, p. 345.
47. Nuremberg document PS-2992, quoted in www.HolocaustResearchProject.org. This document, with a few changes to the official translation, is also reproduced in Reitlinger, *The SS*, pp. 184–185. The translation includes some grammatical mistakes.
48. Höfer's statement, August 27, 1959, Bundesarchiv Ludwigsburg, 2 AR-Z 21/58, vol. vi, p. 4035ff., quoted in Klee et al., eds., *"The Good Old Days,"* pp. 63–66.
49. Quoted in Earl, *The Nuremberg SS-Einsatzgruppen Trials 1945–58*, p. 164.
50. Verdict of Landgericht Darmstadt, November 29, 1968, JUNSV, vol. 31, case 694a, p. 183.
51. Westermann, "Stone-Cold Killers or Drunk with Murder?," p. 10.
52. Verdict of Landgericht Darmstadt, November 29, 1968, JUNSV, vol. 31, case 694a, p. 160.
53. Ingrao, *Believe and Destroy*, p. 200.
54. Burds, *Holocaust in Rovno*, p. 13.
55. Pohl, "Ukrainische Hilfskräfte beim Mord an den Juden," p. 219; Heer, *Vom Verschwinden der Täter*, p. 119.
56. Heer, "Extreme Normalität," p. 732.
57. Verdict of Landgericht Hamburg, December 21, 1979, JUNSV, vol. 43, case 856.
58. MacQueen, "The Context of Mass Destruction," p. 27.
59. Angrick et al., eds., *Dokumente der Einsatzgruppen in der Sowjetunion*, vol. 1, p. 259.
60. Ibid.
61. Todorov, *Facing the Extreme*, p. 160.
62. Stang, *Kollaboration und Massenmord*, p. 167.
63. Weiss-Wendt, *Murder without Hatred*.
64. Browning, *Nazi Policy, Jewish Workers, German Killers*, p. 150.
65. Verdict of Landgericht Stuttgart, July 15, 1966, JUNSV, vol. 24, case 634a, p. 16.
66. Westermann, *Hitler's Police Battalions*, pp. 15–16; Matthäus, "Die Beteiligung der Ordnungspolizei am Holocaust," p. 176.
67. Klemp, *Nicht ermittelt*, p. 71.
68. Westermann, "'Ordinary Men' or 'Ideological Soldiers'?," pp. 45–50; Curilla, *Der Judenmord in Polen und die deutsche Ordnungspolizei 1939–1945*, pp. 916–919.
69. Matthäus, "Die 'Judenfrage' als Schulungsthema von SS and Polizei," p. 49.
70. Angrick, "'Da hätte man schon ein Tagebuch führen müssen,'" p. 325.
71. Browning, *Ordinary Men*, p. 73.
72. Mallmann et al., eds., *Deutscher Osten 1939–1945*, p. 70.
73. Verdict of Landgericht Wuppertal, May 24, 1973, JUNSV, vol. 38, case 792, p. 790.
74. Ibid., pp. 798–802.
75. Mallmann et al., eds., *Deutscher Osten 1939–1945*, p. 71.
76. Schäfer, *"Jedenfalls habe ich auch mitgeschossen,"* p. 531.
77. Verdict of Landgericht Frankfurt/M, February 6, 1973, JUNSV, vol. 38, case 787, p. 319.
78. Verdict of Landgericht Münster, May 6, 1968, JUNSV, vol. 28, case 675a, p. 276.
79. Freundlich, *Die Ermordung einer Stadt namens Stanislau*, p. 158.
80. Browning, ed., *The Origins of the Final Solution*, p. 349.
81. Wolfgang Benz et al., eds., *Einsatz im 'Reichskommissariat Ostland,'* p. 76.
82. Schneider, *"Auswärts eingesetzt,"* p. 471.
83. Angrick and Prehn, *Besatzungspolitik und Massenmord*, pp. 348–349.
84. Mallmann et al., eds. *Deutscher Osten*, pp. 46–47.

85. Grabowski, *Hunt for the Jews*, p. 3.
86. Matthäus, "What about the 'Ordinary Men'?," p. 139.
87. Dieter Pohl, *Verfolgung und Massenmord in der NS-Zeit*, p. 74.
88. Hürter, *Hitlers Heerführer*, p. 531. The same conclusion is reached by Stephen G. Fritz, *Ostkrieg*, p. 104.
89. The leaflets were composed by the Psychological Laboratory of the Ministry of War. The quotations used above are in Krausnick, "Kommissarbefehl und 'Gerichtsbarkeitserlass Barbarossa' in neuer Sicht," pp. 721–722.
90. Quoted in Messerschmidt, *Militarismus, Vernichtungskrieg, Geschichtspolitik*, p. 229.
91. Manoschek, "'Wo der Partisan ist, ist der Jude,'" p. 178.
92. Bartov, *Germany's War and the Holocaust*, p. 26.
93. Besson, "Zur Geschichte des nationalsozialistischen Führungsoffiziers."
94. Messerschmidt, *Die Wehrmachtjustiz 1933–1945*, pp. 33–38.
95. Quoted in Messerschmidt, "Wehrmacht und Nationalsozialismus," p. 21.
96. Quoted in Messerschmidt, *Die Wehrmacht im NS-Staat*, pp. 327 and 355.
97. Dieter Pohl, "Die Wehrmacht und der Mord an den Juden in den besetzten sowjetischen Gebieten," p. 50.
98. Longerich, *Der ungeschriebene Befehl*, p. 94.
99. Jacobsen, "Kommissarbefehl und Massenexekutionen sowjetischer Kriegsgefangener," p. 187.
100. Full text in Jacobsen, "Kommissarbefehl und Massenexekutionen," pp. 181–184.
101. Full text in Jacobsen, "Kommissarbefehl und Massenexekutionen," pp. 188–191.
102. Messerschmidt, *Die Wehrmacht im NS-Staat*, p. 400.
103. Beorn, *Marching into Darkness*, pp. 52–53.
104. Bartov, *Hitler's Army*, p. 131.
105. Quoted in von Lingen, "Partisanenkrieg und Wehrmachtjustiz am Beispiel Italien 1943–1945," p. 16.
106. Longerich, *Heinrich Himmler*, p. 543.
107. Quoted in Kay, *The Making of an SS Killer*, p. 69
108. Quoted in Messerschmidt, *Militarismus, Vernichtungskrieg, Geschichtspolitik*, p. 232.
109. Manoschek, "'Wo der Partisan ist, ist der Jude,'" pp. 176–177.
110. Töpperwien, *"Erschiessen will ich nicht!,"* p. 247.
111. "Verhalten der Truppe im Ostraum," reprinted in Klee and Dressen, eds., *"Gott mit uns,"* p. 39.
112. Ibid., pp. 41–42. See also Stephen G. Fritz, *Frontsoldaten*, p. 199.
113. Quoted by Gerlach, *Kalkulierte Morde*, p. 619.
114. Quoted in Richter, "Die Wehrmacht und der Partisanenkrieg in den besetzten Gebieten der Sowjetunion," p. 847.
115. Klein, "Die Erlaubnis zum grenzenlosen Massenmord," p. 929.
116. Hürter, *Hitlers Heerführer*, p. 532.
117. Mallman et al., eds., *Die 'Ereignismeldungen UdSSR' 1941*, p. 171.
118. Ereignismeldung 28, July 20, 1941, ibid., p. 151.
119. Ereignismeldung 58, August 20, 1941, ibid., p. 321.
120. Ingrao, *Hitler's Elite*, p. 271.
121. Longerich, *Heinrich Himmler*, pp. 535–536.
122. Quoted in Berkhoff, "The Mass Murder of Soviet Prisoners of War and the Holocaust," p. 795.
123. Staff, ed., *Justiz im Dritten Reich*, p. 251. The entire verdict is reproduced on pp. 249–252.
124. Messerschmidt, *Wehrmachtjustiz 1933–1945*, p. 292.
125. Manoschek, "'Wo der Partisan ist, ist der Jude,'" p. 173.
126. Friedrich, *Das Gesetz des Krieges*, p. 795.
127. Ibid., p. 172.
128. Quoted in Engert, ed., *Soldaten für Hitler*, p. 142.
129. Mallmann, "Die Türöffner der 'Endlösung,'" p. 447.
130. Dieter Pohl, "Die Wehrmacht und der Mord an den Juden," pp. 44–45.

131. Richter, "Die Wehrmacht und der Partisanenkrieg in den besetzten Gebieten der Sowjetunion," p. 848.

132. Quoted in Heer, *Vom Verschwinden der Täter*, p. 130.

133. Beorn, *Marching into Darkness*, p. 240.

134. Fuchs, *Your Loyal and Loving Son*, pp. 118–22.

135. Römer, "Truppenführer als Täter," pp. 70–71, 78.

136. See, for example, Hürter, *Ein deutscher General an der Ostfront*.

137. Quoted in Krausnick, "Kommissarbefehl und 'Gerichtsbarkeitserlass Barbarossa,'" p. 737.

138. Angrick, *Dokumente der Einsatzgruppen in der Sowjetunion*, vol. 2, p. 263. See also Krannhals, "Die Judenvernichtung in Polen und die Wehrmacht," p. 575.

139. Messerschmidt, *Wehrmachtjustiz 1933–1945*, p. 316.

140. Quoted in Stargardt, *The German War*, p. 196.

141. Mallman et al., eds., *Die 'Ereignismeldungen UdSSR' 1941*, p. 745.

142. Quoted in Manoschek, "'Wo der Partisan ist, ist der Jude,'" pp. 182–183.

143. Osterloh, "'Hier handelt es sich um die Vernichtung einer Weltanschauung,'" p. 794.

144. Polian, "First Victims of the Holocaust," p. 771.

145. See, for example, the order of the commanding general for the army rear area south of September 1, 1941, quoted in Krausnick, "Kommissarbefehl und 'Gerichtsbarkeitserlass Barbarossa,'" p. 709.

146. Wüllner, *Die NS-Militärjustiz*, pp. 380–382.

147. This case too is described in Wüllner, *Die NS-Militärjustiz*, pp. 423–430.

148. Keilig, *Das deutsche Heer, 1939–1945*, sect. 141, p. 1.

149. Cüppers, *Wegbereiter der Shoah*, pp. 85, 98–99.

150. Rohrkamp, "*Weltanschaulich gefestigte Kämpfer*," p. 69.

151. Messerschmidt, *Die Wehrmachtjustiz*, p. 168.

152. Stein, *The Waffen-SS*, p. 286.

153. Absolon, *Wehrgesetz und Wehrdienst 1935–1945*, p. 96.

154. Cüppers, "Auf den Weg in den Holocaust," pp. 290–291.

155. Browning, *The Origins of the Final Solution*, p. 310.

156. Weinberg, *Crossing the Line in Nazi Genocide*, p. 6.

Chapter 3

1. A similar typology is developed by Paul, "Von Psychopathen, Technokraten des Terrors und 'ganz gewöhnlichen' Deutschen," pp. 61–62, and Mann, "Were the Perpetrators of Genocide 'Ordinary Men' or 'Real Nazis'?," pp. 332–333.

2. Perels and Pohl, *NS-Täter in der deutschen Gesellschaft*, p. 10.

3. Jäger, *Verbrechen unter totalitärer Herrschaft*, p. 77.

4. Browning, "Ideology, Culture, Situation, and Dispositions," p. 74.

5. Goldhagen, *Hitler's Willing Executioners*, p. 23.

6. Kershaw, *Hitler, the Germans, and the Final Solution*, p. 73.

7. Verdict of Landgericht Hildesheim, May 3, 1968, JUNSV, vol. 28, case 674a.

8. Stang, "Dr. Oskar Dirlewanger," pp. 66–75.

9. Tec, *In the Lion's Den*, p. 103.

10. Paul and Mallmann, "Sozialisation, Milieu und Gewalt," p. 12; Neitzel and Walzer, *Soldaten*, p. 52.

11. Vest, *Genozid durch organisatorische Machtapparate*, p. 141.

12. Earl, *Nuremberg SS-Einsatzgruppen Trials 1945–58*, p. 68.

13. Weber, "Normalität und Massenmord," pp. 49–50.

14. *Goldensohn, The Nuremberg Interviews*, pp. 390–391.

15. *Trials of War Criminals before the Nuernberg Military Tribunals*, vol. 4, p. 542.

16. Linck, "Ernst Szymanowski alias Biberstein," p. 226.

17. Heer, "Extreme Normalität," pp. 750–751, 753.

18. Bartov, *Hitler's Army*, p. 152.

19. Latzel, "Wehrmachtsoldaten zwischen 'Normalität' und NS-Ideologie," p. 577.

20. Stephen G. Fritz, *Frontsoldaten*, pp. 198, 195.
21. Buchbender and Sterz, eds., *Das andere Gesicht des Krieges*, p. 171.
22. Linck, "Ordnung und Sauberkeit," p. 43.
23. Manoschek, ed., *"Es gibt nur eines für das Judentum—Vernichtung,"* p. 18.
24. Quoted in Raim, *Justiz zwischen Diktatur und Demokratie*, p. 1138.
25. Quoted in Gerlach, ed., *Durchschnittstäter*, pp. 588–589.
26. Jäger, *Verbrechen unter totalitärer Herrschaft*, p. 44.
27. Angrick, "'Da hätte man schon ein Tagebuch führen müssen,'" p. 360.
28. Neitzel and Walzer, *Soldaten*, pp. 149–151.
29. Ullrich, "'Wir haben nichts gewusst,'" p. 21.
30. Browning, *Ordinary Men*, p. 201.
31. Quoted in Angrick, "'Da hätte man schon ein Tagebuch führen müssen,'" p. 354.
32. Quoted in Angrick, "'Da hätte man schon ein Tagebuch führen müssen,'" p. 341.
33. Golovchansky et al., eds. *"Ich will raus aus diesem Wahnsinn,"* p. 314.
34. Welzer, *Täter*, pp. 218–219; Browning, *Origins of the Final Solution*, p. 429.
35. Verdict of Landgericht Freiburg, July 12, 1963, JUNSV, vol. 19, case 555a, p. 455.
36. Verdict of Landgericht Munich I, February 26, 1970, JUNSV, vol. 33, case 724a, p. 458.
37. Verdict of Landgericht Essen, March 29, 1965, JUNSV, vol. 20, 588a, p. 805.
38. Verdict of Landgericht Hamburg, April 24, 1972, JUNSV, vol. 37, case 772, p. 193.
39. Longerich, *"Davon haben wir nichts gewusst!,"* p. 240.
40. Order of December 12, 1941, quoted in Kwiet, "Erziehung zum Mord," p. 449.

Chapter 4

1. Hilberg, *The Destruction of the European Jews*, pp. 218–219.
2. Sofsky, *Order of Terror*, p. 43.
3. For a vivid description of one such gassing, see Verdict of Landgericht Karlsruhe, December 20, 1961, JUNSV, vol. 18, case 826a, p. 100.
4. Quoted in Earl, *The Nuremberg SS-Einsatzgruppen Trials 1945–58*, p. 165.
5. Quoted in Ingrao, *Believe and Destroy*, p. 194.
6. Arad, *Belzec, Sobibor, Treblinka*, p. 377.
7. Friedrich, *Die kalte Amnestie*, p. 355. See also Landgericht Düsseldorf, September 3, 1965, JUNSV, vol. 22, case 596a.
8. Verdict of Landgericht Düsseldorf, September 3, 1965, JUNSV, vol. 22, case 596a, pp. 108–113.
9. Frank diary, September 9, 1941, quoted in Poliakov and Wulf, eds., *Das Dritte Reich und die Juden*, pp. 181–182.
10. Quoted in Arad, *Belzec, Sobibor, Treblinka*, p. 68.
11. Ibid., pp. 69–71, 175.
12. Dieter Pohl, "Die Trawniki-Männer im Vernichtungslager Belzec 1941–43," p. 285.
13. Friedländer, *Kurt Gerstein*, pp. 109–110.
14. Tregenza, "Belzec," p. 242.
15. Sofsky, *Order of Terror*, p. 43.
16. Schwan and Heindrichs, eds., *Der SS-Mann*, p. 95.
17. Glazar, *Trap with a Green Fence*, p. 11.
18. Rajchman, *The Last Jew of Treblinka*, p. 67.
19. Orth, "Experten des Terrors," p. 103.
20. Diner, "Negative Symbiosis," p. 252.
21. Gutman and Berenbaum, eds., *Anatomy of the Auschwitz Death Camp*, p. 30.
22. Piper, "The Number of Victims," p. 71.
23. Peri Broad in Bezwinska, ed., *KL Auschwitz Seen by the SS*, p. 179.
24. Smale, "Judging the Guilt of a Man Who Admits Complicity at Auschwitz."
25. Broad in Bezwinska, ed., *KL Auschwitz Seen by the SS*, p. 179.
26. Sofsky, *Order of Terror*, p. 252.
27. Gross and Renz, eds., *Der Frankfurter Auschwitz-Prozess (1963–1965)*, vol. 1, p. 39.

28. Greif, *We Wept without Tears*, pp. 194–195, 298; Venezia, *Inside the Gas Chambers*, pp. 66–67; Broad in Bezwinska, ed., *KL Auschwitz Seen by the SS*, pp. 175–176.

29. Lifton, *The Nazi Doctors*, p. 162.

30. Hoess, *Commandant of Auschwitz*, p. 198.

31. Greif, *We Wept without Tears*, p. 112.

32. Venezia, *Inside the Gas Chambers*, p. 64.

33. Nyiszli, *Auschwitz*, p. 52.

34. Ibid., pp. 54–55. Piper, "Gas Chambers and Crematoria," pp. 170–171.

35. Verdict of Landgericht Frankfurt/M, February 26, 1976, JUSNSV, vol. 40, case 829, p. 800.

36. Gross and Renz, eds., *Der Frankfurter Auschwitz-Prozess (1963–1965)*, vol. 1, p. 262.

37. Alexandre, *Der Judenmord*, pp. 117–118, 122.

38. Hördler, *Ordnung und Inferno*, pp. 304–305.

39. For additional details on the fate of the Gypsies in Auschwitz, see Lewy, *The Nazi Persecution of the Gypsies*, ch. 10.

40. Ibid., p. 160.

41. Ibid., pp. 161–162.

42. Todorov, *Facing the Extreme*, p. 141.

43. Hoess, *Commandant of Auschwitz*, pp. 31–32, 42, 44–45, 65.

44. Fest, *Face of the Third Reich*, pp. 278–279.

45. Lifton, *The Nazi Doctors*, p. 419.

46. Ibid., p. 284.

47. Goldensohn, *The Nuremberg Interviews*, p. 315.

48. Hoess, *Commandant of Auschwitz*, pp. 144–145.

49. Fest, *Face of the Third Reich*, p. 285.

50. Hoess, *Commandant of Auschwitz*, pp. 130–132.

51. Fest, *Face of the Third Reich*, p. 285.

52. Koop, *Rudolf Höss*, p. 282.

53. Verdict of Landgericht Frankfurt/M, August 20, 1965, JUNSV, vol. 21, case 595, p. 430.

54. Sereny, *Into the Darkness*, p. 229.

55. Verdict of Landgericht Düsseldorf, December 22, 1970, JUNSV, vol. 3, case 746, p. 776.

56. Webb and Chocholaty, *The Treblinka Death Camp: History, Biographies, Remembrance*, p. 19.

57. Verdict of Landgericht Düsseldorf, September 3, 1945, JUNSV, vol. 22, case 596a, pp. 41, 50, 60, 177.

58. Müller, *Eyewitness Auschwitz*, p. 125.

59. Greif, *We Wept without Tears*, p. 203.

60. Schmid, "Otto Moll," p. 138.

61. Verdict of Landgericht Düsseldorf, September 3, 1945, JUNSV, vol. 22, case 596a.

62. Ibid., p. 188.

63. Verdict of Landgericht Frankfurt/M, September 16, 1966, JUNSV, vol. 24, case 637a, pp. 627–628.

64. Demant, *Auschwitz*, pp. 40, 45.

65. Fahlbusch, "Im Zentrum des Massenmordes," pp. 63, 69, 71.

66. Müller, *Eyewitness Auschwitz*, p. 93.

67. Lingens, *Prisoner of Fear*, p. 133.

68. Rückerl quoted in De Mildt, *In the Name of the People*, p. 311.

69. Arad, *Belzec, Sobibor, Treblinka*, p. 198.

70. Ibid., p. 312.

71. Hilberg, *Perpetrators, Victims, Bystanders*, p. 54.

72. Naumann, *Auschwitz*, pp. 95–96.

73. Arad, *Belzec, Sobibor, Treblinka*, p. 196.

74. Rückerl, *Nationalsozialistische Vernichtungslager im Spiegel deutscher Strafprozesse*, pp. 72–73.

75. Wachsmann, *KL*, p. 371.

76. De Mildt, *In the Name of the People*, p. 310.

77. Lüdtke, "Der Bann der Wörter," p. 11.

78. Stargardt, *The German War*, pp. 241–242.

79. Strzelecki, "The Plunder of the Victims and Their Corpses," p. 248.
80. Friedländer, *The Years of Extermination*, p. 498.
81. De Mildt, *In the Name of the People*, p. 245.
82. Strzelecki, "The Plunder of the Victims and Their Corpses," pp. 251–254, 260–261.
83. Goldensohn, *The Nuremberg Interviews*, p. 403.

Chapter 5

1. Kwiet, "Erziehung zum Mord," p. 451.
2. Buchheim, "Befehl und Gehorsam," pp. 257–380.
3. Jäger, *Verbrechen unter totalitärer Herrschaft*, part 2. See also the list of such cases in Verdict of Landgericht Darmstadt, July 28, 1967, JUNSV, vol. 26, case 657a, p. 450.
4. Jäger, *Verbrechen unter totalitärer Herrschaft*, pp. 141, 149–151.
5. Quoted in Buchheim, "Befehl und Gehorsam," p. 273.
6. Grossman, *On Killing*. See also the discussion of Waller, *Becoming Evil*, p. 236.
7. Milgram, *Obedience to Authority*.
8. MacNair, "Psychological Reverberations for the Killers," p. 276.
9. Lifton, *Nazi Doctors*, p. 15.
10. Ronald Smelser and Syring, eds., *Die SS-Elite unter dem Totenkopf*, p. 39.
11. Angrick, "Erich von dem Bach-Zelewski," pp. 31, 42.
12. Heiber, ed., *Reichsführer!*, p. 131.
13. Quoted in Birn, *Die Höheren SS- und Polizeiführer*, p. 387.
14. Verdict of Landgericht Berlin, June 22, 1962, JUNSV, col. 18, case 540a, p. 627.
15. Cf. Schwan, *Politics and Guilt*, pp. 58–63.
16. Oleschinski, "Ein Augenzeuge des Judenmord desertiert," p. 54.
17. Quoted in Klee et al., eds., *"The Good Old Days,"* p. 62.
18. Verdict of Landgericht Tübingen, May 10, 1981, JUNSV, vol. 17, case 509, p. 353.
19. Quoted in Ingrao, *Believe and Destroy*, p. 194.
20. Ibid., p. 192.
21. Quoted in Angrick, "'Da hätte man schon ein Tagebuch führen müssen,'" p. 350.
22. See, e.g., Curilla, *Die deutsche Ordnungspolizei und der Holocaust*, pp. 931–933.
23. Browning, *Reserve Police Battalion 101*, pp. 57, 113.
24. Mallman et al., eds., *Deutscher Osten*, p. 86.
25. Angrick and Prehn, *Besatzungspolitik und Massenmord*, pp. 432–433.
26. Browning, *Nazi Policy, Jewish Workers, German Killers*, p. 175.
27. Cüppers, *Wegbereiter der Shoah*, p. 210.
28. Quoted in Höhne, *The Order of the Death's Head*, p. 364.
29. Quoted in Rümer, *Kameraden*, p. 457.
30. Ziemann, "Fluchten aus dem Konzens zum Durchhalten," p. 607.
31. Klee et al., eds., *"The Good Old Days,"* p. 204.
32. Quoted in Browning, *Nazi Policy, Jewish Workers, German Killers*, p. 159.
33. Streim, "Zum Beispiel," p. 99.
34. Angrick, "'Da hätte man schon ein Tagebuch führen müssen,'" p. 361.
35. Verdict of Landgericht Munich I, February 26, 1970, JUNSV, vol. 33, case 724a, p. 443.
36. Alexandre, *Judenmord*, pp. 67, 72.
37. Ibid., pp. 62–66. For further details, see Ueberschär, "Der Polizeioffizier Klaus Hornig," pp. 77–93.
38. Lasik, "Historical-Sociological Profile of the Auschwitz SS," p. 288.
39. Gross and Renz, eds., *Der Frankfurter Auschwitz-Prozess (1963–1965)*, vol. 2, p. 912.
40. Naumann, *Auschwitz*, pp. 95–96.
41. Beorn, *Marching into Darkness*, pp. 174–175.
42. Haase, "Oberleutnant Dr. Albert Battell und Major Max Liedtke," p. 200. See also Verdict of Landgericht Hamburg, January 14, 1969, JUNSV, vol. 31, case 699, p. 559.
43. Goshen, "Albert Battels Widerstand gegen die Judenvernichtung in Przemysl," p. 488.
44. Wette, *Feldwebel Anton Schmid*, passim.

45. Hosenfeld, *"Ich versuche jeden zu retten,"* pp. 627–628.
46. Heinrichs, "Hauptmann d. R. Wilm Hosenfeld," p. 76.
47. www.yadvashem.org/yv/righteous/stories/hosenfeld.asp.
48. Wette, ed., *Retter in Uniform*, pp. 16–17.
49. Wette and Vogel, eds., *Das letzte Tabu*, pp. 101–102, 241.
50. Haase, "Wehrmachtsangehörige vor dem Kriegsgericht," p. 479.
51. Wette, ed., *Retter in Uniform*, pp. 20, 25.
52. Hilberg, *The Destruction of the European Jews*, p. 253.
53. *Westfälische Landeszeitung*, May 19, 1945, quoted in Heiber, "Dokumentation," p. 68, n. 3.
54. Quoted in Browning, *Ordinary Men*, pp. 21–23.
55. This letter is reproduced in Verdict of Landgericht Kassel, January 9, 1963, JUNSV, vol. 18, case 546a, p. 808.
56. Heiber, "Dokumentation," p. 79.
57. Curilla, *Die deutsche Ordnungspolizei und der Holocaust*, p. 939.
58. Steinbach, *Ein Volk, ein Reich, ein Glaube?*, p. 221.
59. Tec, *In the Lion's Den*, pp. 74, 102.
60. Bankier, *The Germans and the Final Solution*, p. 135.
61. Friedländer, *Years of Extermination*, pp. 215–218. Reichenau's statement is on p. 216.
62. Verdict of Landgericht Darmstadt, November 29, 1968, JUNSV, vol. 31, case 694a, p. 160.
63. Gorscurth, *Tagebücher eines Abwehroffiziers*, p. 51.
64. Quoted in Friedländer, *The Years of Extermination*, p. 218.
65. Stargardt, *The German War*, p. 174.
66. Jäger, *Verbrechen unter totalitärer Herrschaft*, pp. 203–204.
67. Klee et al., eds., *"The Good Old Days,"* p. 5.
68. Quoted in Stahl, "Generaloberst Johannes Blaskowitz," p. 23.
69. Matthäus et al., eds., *War, Pacification and Mass Murder 1939*, p. 29.
70. Wetter and Vogel, eds., *Das letzte Tabu*, p. 32.
71. Jäger, *Verbrechen unter totalitärer Herrschaft*, pp. 205–220.
72. Kitterman, "Those Who Said 'No!,'" 248.
73. Rossi, *Wehrmacht Priests*, p. 246.
74. Bergen, "Between God and Hitler," pp. 123–38.
75. Blass, "Psychological Perspectives on the Perpetrators of the Holocaust," p. 40.
76. Quoted in Kempner, *SS im Kreuzverhör*, p. 281.

Chapter 6

1. Sandkühler, "Die Täter des Holocaust," p. 41.
2. Giordano, *Die zweite Schuld*.
3. Görtemaker and Safferling, eds., *Die Rosenburg*.
4. Giordano, *Der perfekte Mord*, p. 21.
5. Eichmüller, "Die Strafverfolgung von NS-Verbrechen durch westdeutsche Justizbehörden seit 1945," pp. 630–632.
6. Ibid., p. 636.
7. Nehmer, "Täter als Gehilfen?," pp. 644–645.
8. Ibid., p. 636.
9. Wette, "Das Bild der Wehrmacht-Elite nach 1945," p. 301.
10. Hoffmann, *Stunden Null?*, p. 15.
11. Schneider, *"Auswärts eingesetzt,"* p. 563.
12. Müller, *Hitler's Justice*, pp. 259–260.
13. See the introductory remarks to the East German section of JUNSV.
14. Lichtenstein, "NS-Prozesse," p. 166.
15. Phillips, ed., *Trial of Joseph Kramer and Forty-Four Others*, p. 13.
16. Sigel, *Im Interesse der Grechtigkeit*, p. 55; Lessing, *Der erste Dachauer Prozess (1945/46)*, p. 141.

17. Lessing, *Der erste Dachauer Prozess (1945/46)*, pp. 106, 208–209, 267; Sigel, *Im Interesse der Gerechtigkeit*, p. 44.
18. Sigel, *Im Interesse der Gerechtigkeit*, pp. 105–107.
19. Ibid., p. 77.
20. Earl, *The Nuremberg SS-Einsatzgruppen Trials 1945–58*, p. 259.
21. *Trials of War Criminals before the Nuernberg Military Tribunals*, vol. 4, pp. 373–377.
22. Earl, *The Nuremberg SS-Einsatzgruppen Trials 1945–58*, p. 249.
23. Mallmann et al., eds., *Die 'Ereignismeldungen UdSSR' 1941*, p. 16.
24. Ibach, *Kemna Wuppertaler Konzentrationslager 1933–1934*, p. 126.
25. Kruse, "NS-Prozesse und Restauration," p. 132.
26. Verdict of Landgericht Frankfurt/M, March 3, 1951, JUNSV, vol. 8, case 270a, pp. 269–270.
27. Verdict of BGH, November 25, 1964, 2 StR 71/64, par. 42c.
28. Verdict of Landgericht Hagen, December 20, 1966, JUNSV, vol. 25, case 642a, p. 217.
29. Verdict of BGH, 4 StR 47/69, March 25, 1971, par. 102.
30. Müller-Hohagen, *Verleugnet, verdrängt, verschwiegen*, p. 85.
31. Perels, "Die Aushöhlung des Rechtsstaates durch die Umwandlung von NS-Tätern in Gehilfen," p. 204.
32. Memo of Cardinal Frings of August 2, 1945, quoted in Görtemaker and Safferling, eds., *Die Rosenburg*, pp. 45–46.
33. Verdict of Landgericht Bremen, November 27, 1953, JUNSV, vol. 11, case 379, p. 567.
34. Longerich, *"Davon haben wir nichts gewusst!,"* p. 240. See also Johnson, *Nazi Terror*.
35. Frei, ed., *Karrieren im Zwielicht*, p. 310.
36. De Mildt, *In the Name of the People*, p. 23.
37. Quoted in Buruma, *The Wages of Guilt*, p. 13.
38. Sigel, *Im Interesse der Gerechtigkeit*, pp. 112–113; Earl, *The Nuremberg SS-Einsatzgruppen Trial 1945–58*, p. 266.
39. Friedlander, "The Judiciary and Nazi Crimes in Postwar Germany," p. 4.
40. Ratz et al., eds., *Die Justiz und die Nazis*, p. 78.
41. Quoted in Anne Sa'adah, *Germany's Second Chance*, p. 170.
42. Werle, "Der Holocaust als Gegenstand der bundesdeutschen Strafjustiz," p. 2531.
43. Pendras, *The Frankfurt Auschwitz Trial, 1963–65*, pp. 54–55.
44. *Strafgesetzbuch* (StGB), Articles 25–27. See also Verdict of Oberlandesgericht Frankfurt/M, April 16, 1948, JUNSV, vol. 1, case 14b, pp. 268–269.
45. Absolon, *Das Wehrmachtstrafrecht im 2*, Articles 47.
46. Greve, "Täter oder Gehilfen?," p. 206.
47. Entscheidungen des Reichsgerichts in Strafsachen 74, 84. See the discussion in Nehmer, "Täter als Gehilfen?," p. 638.
48. BGH, 5 StR 529/55.
49. BGH 9 StE 4/62, in *Neue Juristische Wochenschrift* 8 (1963), p. 358. A rather poor translation of this decision can be found in Dubber and Hörnle, *Criminal Law: A Comparative Approach*, pp. 312–315.
50. Bryant, *Eyewitnesses to Genocide*, p. 214.
51. Quoted in Wittke, "Teilexkulpation von NS-Tätern?," p. 587.
52. Friedrich, *Die kalte Amnestie*, p. 365.
53. Greve, *Der justitielle und rechtspolitische Umgang mit den NS-Gewaltverbrechen in den sechziger Jahren*, p. 193.
54. Wittke, "Teilexkulpation von NS-Tätern?," p. 580.
55. Baumann, "Beihilfe bei eigenhändiger voller Tatbestandserfüllung," p. 561.
56. Friedlander, "Nazi Crimes and the German Law," p. 32.
57. Wittman, *Beyond Justice*, pp. 220–221. See also Dencker, "Täterschaft und Beihilfe bei NS-Gewaltverbrechen," p. 55.
58. Fritz Bauer, "Ideal-oder Realkonkurrenz bei nationalsozialistischen Verbrechen?," p. 628.
59. Renz, *Fritz Bauer und das Versagen der Justiz*, p. 34.
60. Fritz Bauer, "Im Namen des Volkes," p. 307.

61. Verdict of BGH, February 20, 1969, in JUNSV, vol. 21, case 595b, p. 125.
62. Kurz, "Paradigmenwechsel bei der Strafverfolgung des Personals in den deutschen Vernichtungslagern?," p. 124.
63. Verdict of Landgericht Münster, May 6, 1968, JUNSV, vol. 28, cse 675a, p. 647.
64. Perels, *Entsorgung der NS-Herrschaft?*, pp. 20–21.
65. Noll, "Die NS-Verbrecherprozesse strafrechtsdogmatisch und gesetzgebungspolitisch betrachtet," pp. 46–47.
66. Gross and Renz, eds., *Der Frankfurter Auschwitz-Prozess*, pp. 939, 951, 960–961, 1366. See also Friedrich, *Die kalte Amnestie*, p. 359.
67. Gross and Renz, eds., *Der Frankfurter Auschwitz-Prozess*, pp. 918–919, 1367. See also Friedrich, *Die kalte Amnestie*, p. 358.
68. Verdict of Landgericht Munich I, July 21, 1961, JUNSV, vol. 17, case 519, p. 693.
69. Quoted in Mallmann et al., eds., *Deutscher Osten 1939–1945*, p. 131.
70. Verdict of Landgericht Munich I, July 21, 1961, JUNSV, vol. 17, case 519, p. 705.
71. Greve, "Täter oder Gehilfen?," p. 209.
72. Verdict of Landgericht Kiel, April 8, 1964, JUNSV, vol. 19, case 567a, pp. 802–805. See also Greve, "Täter oder Gehilfen?," pp. 202–207.
73. Verdict of Landgericht Wuppertal, May 24, 1973, JUNSV, vol. 38, case 792, pp. 316–317.
74. Verdict of Landgericht Düsseldorf, September 3, 1965, JUNSV, vol. 22, case 596a. See also Perels, "Die Aushöhlung des Rechtsstaates durch die Umwandlung von NS-Tätern in Gehilfen," p. 217. Friedrich, *Die kalte Amnestie*, p. 355.
75. BGH 5 StR 114/65, August 25, 1965, JUNSV, vol. 20, case 579b.
76. Perels, "Die Aushöhlung des Rechtsstaates durch die Umwandlung von NS-Tätern in Gehilfen," p. 205.
77. See United States Holocaust Memorial Museum, "John Demjanjuk: Prosecution of a Nazi Collaborator," http://www.ushmm.org/wlc/en/article.php?ModuleId=10007956.
78. Verdict of Landgericht Munich II, December 5, 2011, JUNSV, vol. 49, case 924, pp. 229, 247, 355, 378. See also Wefing, *Der Fall Demjanjuk*.
79. For a detailed account of the Demjanjuk trial, see Douglas, *The Right Wrong Man*.
80. Kurz, "Paradigmenwechsel bei der Strafverfolgung des Personals in den deutschen Vernichtungslagern," pp. 128–129.
81. Crossland, "Late Push on War Crimes."
82. Eddy, "Chasing Death Camp Guards in Germany with New Tools for Prosecutors."
83. Smale, "Judging the Guilt of a Man Who Admits Complicity at Auschwitz."
84. "'Bookkeeper of Auschwitz' Found Guilty by German Court," *Reuters World News online*.
85. "Woman, 91, Charged over Auschwitz Role," *Wall Street Journal*; Smale, "Survivors of Auschwitz Seek Action in Nazi Case."
86. Eddy, "'Sincerely Sorry,' Ex-Auschwitz Guard Says at Trial."
87. Absolon, ed., *Das Wehrmachtstrafrecht im 2. Weltkrieg*, p. 14.
88. Rittau, *Militärstrafgesetzbuch*, p. 108.
89. Grau, *Wehrstrafrecht und allgemeines Strafrecht*, p. 39.
90. BGH, March 29, 1963, 4 StR 500/62.
91. Verdict of Landgericht Essen, February 10, 1966, JUNSV, vol. 23, case 620, p. 182.
92. Radbruch, "Statutory Lawlessness and Supra-Statutory Law," p. 231.
93. Verdict of Landgericht Wuppertal, April 30, 1970, JUNSV, vol. 33, case 730, p. 755.
94. Quoted in Naumann, *Auschwitz*, p. xxiv.
95. Rückerl, *The Investigation of Nazi Crimes 1945–1978*, pp. 82–83.
96. Verdict of Landgericht Bochum, June 6, 1968, JUNSV, vol. 29, case 678.
97. Verdict of Landgericht Frankfurt/M, August 20, 1965, in Gross and Renz, eds. *Der Frankfurter Auschwitz-Prozess*, pp. 896–898.
98. BGH, February 20, 1969, 2 StR 280/67, in Gross and Renz, eds. *Der Frankfurter Auschwitz-Prozess*, p. 1242.
99. Verdict of Landgericht Frankfurt/M, October 8, 1970, in Gross and Renz, eds. *Der Frankfurter Auschwitz-Prozess*, pp. 1331, 1350.

100. Jäger, *Verbrechen unter totalitärer Herrschaft*, p. 154.
101. Deutscher Juristentag, *Probleme der Verfolgung und Ahndung von nationalsozialistischen Gewaltverbrechen*, p. 9.
102. StGB, Articles 46–49.
103. Mildt, *In the Name of the People*, p. 325.
104. This point has been stressed by Ernst-Walter Hanack. See, e.g., Horstmann and Litzinger, *An den Grenzen des Rechts*, p. 69.
105. Verdict of Landgericht Hannover, October 14, 1971, JUNSV, vol. 36, case 760a, p. 275.
106. Verdict of Landgericht Munich I, January 21, 1966, JUNSV, vol. 23, case 617, pp. 5–6, 37, 40.
107. Verdict of Landgericht Darmstadt, July, 16, 1948, quoted in Hirsch, *Die Strafzumessung bei nationalsozialistischen Gewalt- und Kriegsverbrechen*, p. 155.
108. Verdict of Landgericht Bochum, July 22, 1966, quoted in Hirsch, *Die Strafzumessung bei nationalsozialistischen Gewalt- und Kriegsverbrechen*, p. 214.
109. Verdict of BGH, February 23, 1978, JUNSV, vol. 40, case 830b, p. 867.
110. Verdict of Landgericht Freiburg/Br, May 18, 1967, quoted in Greve, *Täter oder Gehilfen?*, p. 220.
111. Verdict of Landgericht Cologne, July 9, 1954, JUNSV, vol. 12, case 403a, p. 599.
112. Verdict of Landgericht Bochum, July 22, 1966, JUNSV, vol. 24, case 635, p. 476.
113. Greve, *Täter oder Gehilfen?*, p. 217.
114. See, for example, Verdict of Landgericht Verden, June 6, 1962, JUNSV, vol. 18, case 537.
115. Verdict of Landgericht Stuttgart, July 15, 1966, JUNSV, vol. 24, case 634, p. 257.
116. Greve, *Der justitielle und rechtspolitische Umgang mit den NS-Gewaltverbrechen*, p. 164.
117. Henkys, *Die nationalsozialistischen Gewaltverbrechen*, pp. 346–349.
118. Ibid., pp. 339–342.
119. Just-Dahlmann and Just, *Die Gehilfen*, p.124.
120. Deutscher Juristentag, *Probleme der Verfolgung und Ahndung von nationalsozialistischen Gewaltverbrechen*, p. 9. See also Just-Dahlmann and Just, *Die Gehilfen*, pp. 248–249.
121. Langbein, *Im Namen des deutschen Volkes*, p. 119. The same term is used by Hey, "Die NS-Prozesse," p. 352.
122. Bauer, *Die Humanität der Rechtsordnung*, p. 84.
123. Wolfrum, "Täterbilder," p. 134.
124. Henkys, *Die nationalsozialistischen Gewaltverbrechen*, p. 234.
125. Messerschmidt, *Militarismus, Vernichtungskrieg, Geschichtspolitik*, p. 117.
126. Von Miquel, "Juristen," p. 188.
127. Müller, *Hitler's Justice*, pp. 202–203. See also Diestelkamp, "Die Justiz nach 1945 und ihr Umgang mit der eigenen Vergangenheit," p. 145.
128. Müller, *Hitler's Justice*, p. 205.
129. Okroy, "'. . . kann nicht bezeifelt werden,'" p. 108.
130. Rüthers, "Die Gesetzgebung," p. 138.
131. Von der Ohe, "Der Bundesgerichtshof und die NS-Justizverbrechen," p. 314.
132. *The United States vs. Josef Alstötter et al.*, cited by Hankel, "Die NS-Militärjustiz in den Nürnberger Urteilen," p. 47.
133. Helmut Kramer, "Entlastung als System," pp. 109, 117.
134. Rottleuthner, *Karrieren und Kontinuitäten deutscher Justizjuristen vor und nach 1945*, p. 124.
135. Lamprecht, "Lesarten für Rechtsbeugung," p. 562. See also Friedrich, *Freispruch für die Nazi-Justiz*.
136. Godau-Schüttke, *"Ich habe nur dem Recht gedient,"* p. 130.
137. Quoted in Ratz, *Die Justiz und die Nazis*, p. 66.
138. Von Miquel, "'Wir müssen mit den Mördern zusammenleben!,'" p. 217.
139. BGH 1 StR 50/56, June 19, 1956.
140. Fröhlich, "Freispruch für Bonhoeffers Richter," pp. 241–242.
141. Rottleuthner, *Karrieren und Kontinuitäten deutscher Justizjuristen vor und nach 1945*, p. 100.
142. Freudiger, "Die blockierte Aufarbeitung von NS-Verbrechen in der Bundesrepublik," p. 130.
143. Greve, "Täter oder Gehilfen?," p. 221.

144. BGH, StR 747/94, November 16, 1995, par. 75–76.
145. Spendel, *Rechtsbeugung durch Rechtsprechung*, pp. 17–18.
146. BGH decision of December 13, 1993, quoted in Lamprecht, "Lesarten für Rechtsbeugung," p. 562.
147. Rückerl, *NS-Verbrechen vor Gericht*, pp. 310–311.
148. Introduction to Perels, *Das juristische Erbe des "Dritten Reiches,"* p. 10.
149. *Neue Juristische Wochenschrift* 49 (1996), p. 863.

Chapter 7

1. Heinsohn, *Warum Auschwitz?*, chap. 3.
2. Waller, *Becoming Evil*, pp. 152, 166–167. See also Kekes, *Facing Evil*.
3. Pinker, *The Better Angels of Our Nature*, p. 569.
4. Waller, *Becoming Evil*, p. 152.
5. Sofsky, *Violence*, pp. 20–21. See also Newman and Erber, *Understanding Genocide*, pp. 326, 340.
6. Mitscherlich and Mitscherlich, *The Inability to Mourn*.
7. Elias, *The Germans*, p. 401.
8. Zukier, "The 'Mindless Years'?," pp. 207–208.
9. Jones, *Moral Responsibility in the Holocaust*, p. 111; Zukier, "The 'Mindless Years'?," p. 204.
10. Goldhagen, *Hitler's Willing Executioners*, pp. 416–417.
11. Bartov, *Germany's War and the Holocaust*, p. 136.
12. We have several collections dealing with the Goldhagen thesis: Schoeps, ed., *Ein Volk von Mördern?*; Heil and Erb, eds., *Geschichtswissenschaft und Öffentlichkeit*; Finkelstein and Birn, eds., *A Nation on Trial*.
13. Adorno et al., *The Authoritarian Personality*.
14. Shils, "Authoritarianism, 'Right' and 'Left,'" p. 38.
15. Browder, *Hitler's Enforcers*, p. 168. See also Rippl, ed., *Autoritarismus*, and the discussion by Waller, *Becoming Evil*, pp. 76–86.
16. Milgram, *Obedience to Authority*.
17. Neubacher, "Verbrechen aus Gehorsam," pp. 54–55.
18. Blass, ed., *Obedience to Authority*, p. 36.
19. Askenasy, *Are We All Nazis?*, p. 83.
20. Waller, *Becoming Evil*, pp. 107–108.
21. Blass, "Psychological Perspectives on the Perpetrators of the Holocaust," pp. 37.
22. Waller, *Becoming Evil*, p. 108.
23. Wolfe, *Political Evil*, p. 75. See also de Swaan, *The Killing Compartments*.
24. Zimbardo, "Pathology of Imprisonment," pp. 4, 6, 8.
25. Waller, *Becoming Evil*, p. 227.
26. Wolfe, *Political Evil*, p. 71. See also Fenigstein, "Were Obedience Pressures a Factor in the Holocaust?"
27. Browning, *Ordinary Men*, p. 184.
28. Kühne, *Kameradschaft*, p. 187.
29. Kühne, "Male Bonding and Shame Culture," p. 74.
30. Waller, *Becoming Evil*, pp. 34–35.
31. Browning, *Ordinary Men*, p. 73.
32. Koonz, *The Nazi Conscience*, p. 259.
33. Waller, *Becoming Evil*, pp. 248–249, 255; Kelman, "Violence without Moral Restraint," pp. 49–50. See also Kelman and Hamilton, *Crimes of Obedience*.
34. Browning, *Ordinary Men*, p. 87.
35. Kelman, "Violence without Moral Restraint," p. 39.
36. Basic and Welzer, "Die Bereitschaft zum Töten," p. 88.
37. Browning, *Ordinary Men*, pp. 161, 85.
38. Kelman, "Violence without Moral Restraint," pp. 46–48.
39. Kekes, *Facing Evil*, p. 128.

40. Waller, *Becoming Evil*, p. 229.

41. Confino, *A World without Jews*, pp. 8–9.

42. Kater, "Everyday Anti-Semitism in Prewar Nazi Germany," p. 136.

43. Giordano, *Erinnerungen eines Davongekommenen*, p. 119.

44. Confino, *A World without Jews*, pp. 154–155.

45. Schleunes, *Twisted Road to Auschwitz*, p. 260.

46. McMillan, *How Could This Happen?*, p. 152.

47. Burrin, *Warum die Deutschen?*, pp. 88–89.

48. Confino, *A World without Jews*, p. 10.

49. Quoted in Sellert and Rüping, *Studien- und Quellenbuch zur Geschichte der deutschen Strafrechtspflege*, vol. 2, p. 277.

50. Bankier, *The Germans and the Final Solution*, pp. 121, 156.

51. Kershaw, *Hitler, the Germans, and the Final Solution*, p. 229.

52. Gelately, *Backing Hitler: Consent and Coercion in Nazi Germany*, p. 259.

53. Schoeps, *Das Gewaltsyndrom*, p. 87.

54. Kershaw, *Hitler, the Germans, and the Final Solution*, pp. 348–349.

55. McMillan, *How Could This Happen?*, p. 135.

56. Koonz, *The Nazi Conscience*, pp. 272–273.

57. Sasse, ed., *Martin Luther über die Juden*, p. 2, cited by Schoeps, *Das Gewaltsyndrom*, p. 89.

58. Quoted in Confino, *A World without Jews*, p. 7.

59. Lingens, *Prisoner of Fear*, pp. 1–2.

60. Neitzel and Walzer, *Soldaten*, p. 120.

61. Kochinka and Straub, "'Dämonologie' oder psychologisches Denken," pp. 104–106.

62. Jones, *Moral Responsibility in the Holocaust*, p. 163.

63. Quoted in Westermann, *Hitler's Police Battalions*, p. 12.

64. Hillgruber, "Jürgen Habermas, Karl-Heinz Janssen, and the Enlightenment in the Year 1986," p. 233.

65. Cf. Bauman, *Modernity and the Holocaust*, pp. 91–92.

66. Wegner, "Anmerkungen zur Geschichte der Waffen-SS aus organisatorischer- und funktionsgeschichtlicher Sicht," p. 410.

67. Segev, *Soldiers of Evil*, pp. 62–63.

68. Allen, *The Business of Genocide*, p. 5.

69. Reichsorganisationsleiter der NSDAP, *Organisationsbuch der NSDAP*, p. 418.

70. Quoted in Simmel, "Wir haben nur unsere Pflicht getan," p. 17.

71. Quoted in Langerbein, *Hitler's Death Squads*, p. 20.

72. Reichsführer SS und Chef der Deutschen Polizei, SS Hauptamt, *Der Untermensch*, p. 16.

73. Bauman, *Modernity and the Holocaust*, p. 7.

74. See his memo to Theodor Eicke on April 30, 1942, in Heiber, ed., *Reichsführer!*, p. 145.

75. *Mitteilungsblatt für weltanschauliche Schulung*, 27 (December 1, 1941), quoted in Matthäus, "'Warum wird über das Judentum geschult?,'" p. 122. See also Banach, *Heydrichs Elite*.

76. Quoted in Browning, *The Origins of the Final Solution*, p. 547, n. 2.

77. Quoted in Longerich, *"Davon haben wir nichts gewusst!,"* p. 263.

78. Quoted in Confino, *A World without Jews*, p. 196.

79. Longerich, *Der ungeschriebene Befehl*, pp. 24–25.

80. Confino, *A World without Jews*, p. 197.

81. Quoted in Longerich, *Der ungeschriebene Befehl*, p. 154.

82. Friedländer, "From Anti-Semitism to Extermination," p. 44.

83. Rückerl, *NS-Verbrechen vor Gericht*, p. 279.

84. Jäger, *Verbrechen unter totalitärer Herrschaft*, pp. 201–202.

85. Ibid., pp. 238–239.

86. Quoted in Kwiet, "Erziehung zum Mord," p. 449.

87. SS-Hauptamt, *Lehrplan für die weltanschauliche Erziehung in der SS und Polizei*.

88. Welzer, *Täter*, p. 40.

89. Himmler, *Geheimreden 1933 bis 1945 und andere Ansprachen*, p. 128.

90. There exists a written as well as a recorded version of this speech, which was introduced at the Nuremberg trial as document PS-1919. The above English translation was made by four persons of Project Nizkor and can be found at www.jewishvirtuallibrary.org.

91. JUNSV, Landgericht Heilbronn, May 24, 1973, vol. 38, case 793, p. 835.

92. Quoted in de Mildt, "Getting Away with Murder," pp. 102–104 (translation modified). See also ernst Klee et al., eds., *The Good Old Days,*" p. 197.

93. For a summary discussion, see Buchheim et al., *Anatomie des SS-Staates*, vol. 1, pp. 181–190.

94. De Mildt, "Getting Away with Murder," p. 104.

95. Ibid., p. 105.

96. Ibid.

97. Ibid., p. 110.

98. Quoted in Vieregge, *Die Gerichtsbarkeit einer "Elite,"* p. 263.

99. Quoted in Pauer-Studer and Velleman, *Konrad Morgen*, p. 31.

100. Stargardt, *The German War*, p. 233.

101. Wachsmann, *KL*, pp. 388–389.

102. Wachsmann, *KL*, p. 389.

103. Wegner, "Die Sondergerichtsbarkeit von SS und Polizei," p. 256; Scheffler, "Zur Praxis der SS- und Polizeigerichtsbarkeit im Dritten Reich," p. 232.

104. Weingartner, "Law and Justice in the Nazi SS," pp. 290–291.

105. Kogon, *The Theory and Practice of Hell*, pp. 297–298.

106. Orth, "Die Kommandanten der nationalsozialistischen Konzentrationslager," pp. 758–759.

107. Langbein, *People in Auschwitz*, pp. 300–301.

108. Quoted by Wittmann, *Beyond Justice*, p. 162.

109. Ibid., p. 173.

110. Mallmann, "'Mensch, ich feiere heute den tausendsten Genickschuss,'" p. 124.

111. Hilberg, *The Destruction of the European Jews*, p. 649.

112. Beorn, *Marching into Darkness*, p. 7.

113. Jäger, *Verbrechen unter totalitärer Herrschaft*, p. 54.

114. Neitzel and Walzer, *Soldaten*, p. 8.

115. Waller, *Becoming Evil*, p. 16.

116. De Swaan, *The Killing Compartments*, pp. 39–40.

BIBLIOGRAPHY

Absolon, Rudolf. *Das Wehrmachtstrafrecht im 2. Weltkrieg: Sammlung der grundlegenden Gesetze*. Kornelimünster: Bundesarchiv, 1958.

———, ed. *Wehrgesetz und Wehrdienst 1935–1945: Das Personalwesen in der Wehrmacht*. Boppart am Rhein: Harald Boldt, 1960.

Adorno, Theodor W. *The Authoritarian Personality*. New York: Norton, 1950.

Alexander, Leo. "War Crimes and Their Motivation: The Socio-Psychological Structure of the SS and the Criminalization of a Society." *Journal of Criminal Law and Criminology* 39 (1948): 298–326.

Alexandre, Michel. *Der Judenmord: Deutsche und Österreicher berichten*. Cologne: VGS, 1998.

Alford, C. Fred. "'Hitler's Willing Executioners': What Does 'Willing' Mean?" *Theory and Society* 26 (1997): 719–738.

Allen, Michael Thad. *The Business of Genocide: The SS, Slave Labor and the Concentration Camps*. Chapel Hill: University of North Carolina Press, 2002.

Altemeyer, Robert Anthony. *The Authoritarian Specter*. Cambridge, MA: Harvard University Press, 1996.

Alvarez, Alex. *Governments, Citizens, and Genocide: A Comparative and Interdisciplinary Approach*. Bloomington: Indiana University Press, 2001.

Aly, Götz. *Biedermann und Schreibtischtäter: Materialien zur deutschen Täter-Biographie*. Berlin: Rotbuch, 1989.

———. *Hitler's Beneficiaries: Plunder, Racial War, and the Nazi Welfare State*. Translated by Jefferson Chase. New York: Henry Holt, 2007.

———. "Theodor Schieder, Werner Conze oder die Vorstufen der physischen Vernichtung." In *Deutsche Historiker im Nationalsozialismus*, edited by Winfried Schulze and Otto Gerhard Oexle, pp. 163–182. Frankfurt/M: Fischer, 1999.

———. *Why the Germans? Why the Jews? Envy, Race Hatred, and the Prehistory of the Holocaust*. Translated by Jefferson Chase. New York: Metropolitan Books, 2014.

Améry, Jean. *At the Mind's Limits: Contemplations by a Survivor on Auschwitz and Its Realities*. Translated by Sidney and Stella P. Rosenfeld. Bloomington: Indiana University Press, 1980.

Angrick, Andrej. "'Da hätte man schon ein Tagebuch führen müssen': Das Polizeibataillon 322 und die Judenmorde im Bereich der Heeresgruppe Mitte während des Sommers und Herbstes 1941." In *Die Normalität des Verbrechens: Festschrift für Wolfgang Scheffler zum 65. Geburtstag*, edited by Helga Grabitz, Klaus Bästlein, and Johannes Tuchel, pp. 325–385. Berlin: Edition Hentrich, 1994.

———. *Dokumente der Einsatzgruppen in der Sowjetunion*. 2 vols. Darmstadt: Wissenschaftliche Buchgesellschaft, 2011.

———. "Erich von dem Bach-Zelewski: Himmlers Mann für alle Fälle." In *Die SS Elite unter dem Totenkopf*, edited by Ronald M. Smelser and Enrico Syring, pp. 28–44. Paderborn: Ferdinand Schöningh, 2000.

Angrick, Andrej, and Ulrich Prehn. *Besatzungspolitik und Massenmord: Die Einsatzgruppe D in der südlichen Sowjetunion 1941–1943.* Hamburg: Hamburger Edition, 2003.

Arad, Yitzhak. *Belzec, Sobibor, Treblinka: The Operation Reinhard Death Camps.* Bloomington: University of Indiana Press, 1987.

———. *The Holocaust in the Soviet Union.* Lincoln: University of Nebraska Press, 2009.

Arendes, Cord. *Zwischen Justiz und Tagespresse: "Durchschnittstäter" in regionalen NS-Verfahren.* Paderborn: Ferdinand Schöningh, 2012.

Arendt, Hannah. "Organisierte Schuld." *Die Wandlung* 4 (1945/46): 333–344.

———. *The Origins of Totalitarianism.* New York: Harcourt Brace, 1951.

Arndt, Ivo, and Wolfgang Scheffler. "Organisierter Massenmord an Juden in nationalsozialistischen Vernichtungslagern: Ein Beitrag zur Richtigstellung apologetischer Literatur." *Vierteljahrshefte für Zeitgeschichte* 24 (1976): 105–135.

Asher, Harvey, Kimberley Robert, and Corey Hudson. "Ganz normale Täter: Variablen sozialpsychologischer Analysen." *Zeitschrift für Genozidforschung* 3 (2001): 81–115.

Askenasy, Hans. *Are We All Nazis?* Secaucus, NJ: Lyle Stuart, 1978.

Bald, Detlef, and Wolfram Wette. *Zivilcourage: Helfer und Retter aus Wehrmacht, Polizei und SS.* Frankfurt/M: Fischer, 2004.

Banach, Jens. *Heydrichs Elite: Das Führerkorps der Sicherheitspolizei und der SD 1936–1945.* Paderborn: Ferdinand Schöningh, 1998.

Bandura, Albert. "Mechanisms of Moral Disengagement." In *Origins of Terrorism*, edited by Walter Reich, pp. 161–191. New York: Cambridge University Press, 1990.

Bankier, David. *The Germans and the Final Solution: Public Opinion under Nazism.* Oxford: Blackwell, 1992.

———. *Holocaust and Justice: Representation and Historiography of the Holocaust in Post-War Trials.* Jerusalem: Yad Vashem, 2010.

———, ed. *Probing the Depth of German Antisemitism: German Society and the Persecution of the Jews.* New York: Berghahn Books, 2000.

Bar-On, Daniel. "The Bystander in Relation to the Victim and the Perpetrator: Today and During the Holocaust." *Social Justice Research* 14 (2001): 125–148.

———. "Holocaust Perpetrators and Their Children: A Paradoxical Mentality." In *The Collective Silence*, edited by Barbara Heimannsberg and Christian J. Schmidt, pp. 195–208. San Francisco, CA: Jossey-Bass, 1993.

Baron-Cohen, Simon. *The Science of Evil: On Empathy and the Origins of Cruelty.* New York: Basic Books, 2011.

Bartov, Omer. "Forum Essay." *American Historical Review* 103 (1998): 1191–1194.

———. *Germany's War and the Holocaust: Disputed Histories.* Ithaca, NY: Cornell University Press, 2003.

———. *Hitler's Army: Soldiers, Nazis, and War in the Third Reich.* New York: Oxford University Press, 1991.

Barzun, Jacques. *Clio and the Doctors: Psycho-History, Quanto-History, and History.* Chicago: University of Chicago Press, 1974.

Basic, Natalija, and Harald Welzer. "Die Bereitschaft zum Töten: Überlegungen zum Zusammenspiel von Sinn, Mord und Moral." *Zeitschrift für Genozidforschung* 1 (2000): 78–100.

Bauer, Fritz. *Die Humanität der Rechtsordnung: Ausgewählte Schriften.* Edited by Joachim Perel and Irmtrud Wojak. Frankfurt/M: Campus, 1998.

———. "Ideal- oder Realkonkurrenz bei nationalsozialistischen Verbrechen?" *Juristen Zeitung* 22 (1967): 625–628.

———. "Im Namen des Volkes: Die strafrechtliche Bewältigung der Vergangenheit." In *Zwanzig Jahre danach*, edited by Helmut Hammerschmidt, pp. 301–314. Munich: Kurt Desch, 1965.

Bauer, Fritz, Peter Schneider, and Hermann J. Meyer. *Rechtliche und politische Aspekte der NS-Verbrecherprozesse.* Mainz: Johannes-Gutenberg-Universität, 1968.

Bauer, Yehuda. "Einige Überlegungen zur Shoah." *Zeitschrift für Geschichtswissenschaft* 54 (2006): 542–549.

———. "Is the Holocaust Explicable?" *Holocaust and Genocide Studies* 5 (1990): 145–155.

———. *Rethinking the Holocaust.* New Haven, CT: Yale University Press, 2001.

Baum, Steven K. *The Psychology of Genocide: Perpetrators, Bystanders and Rescuers.* Cambridge: Cambridge University Press, 2008.

Bauman, Zygmunt. *Modernity and the Holocaust.* Ithaca, NY: Cornell University Press, 1989.

Baumann, Jürgen. "Beihilfe bei eigenhändiger voller Tatbestandserfüllung." *Neue Juristische Wochenschrift* 16 (1963): 561–565.

———. "Die strafrechtliche Problematik der nationalsozialistischen Gewaltverbrechen." In *Die nationalsozialistischen Gewaltverbrechen*, edited by Reinhard Henkys, pp. 267–321. Stuttgart: Kreuz, 1965.

Baumeister, Roy F. *Evil: Inside Human Violence and Cruelty.* New York: W. H. Freeman, 1997.

———. "The Holocaust and the Four Roots of Evil." In *Understanding Genocide*, edited by Leonard S. Newman and Ralph Erber, pp. 241–258. New York: Oxford University Press, 2002.

Bazyler, Michael, and Frank Tuerkheimer. *Forgotten Trials of the Holocaust.* New York: New York University Press, 2014.

Bennhold, Martin, ed. *Spuren des Unrechts: Recht und Nationalsozialismus. Beiträge zur historischen Kontinuität.* Cologne: Pahl-Rugenstein, 1989.

Benz, Angelika. *Der Henkersknecht: Der Prozess gegen John Iwan Demjanjuk in München.* Berlin: Metropol, 2011.

———. "Exzesstäter, Schreibtischtäter oder Durchschnittsbürger? Täterbilder in Forschung und Öffentlichkeit." *Informationen* 35 (2010): 3–6.

Benz, Angelika, and Marija Vulesika, eds. *Bewachung und Ausführung: Alltag der Täter in national-sozialistischen Lagern.* Berlin: Metropol, 2011.

Benz, Wolfgang, and Barbara Distel, eds. *Der Ort des Terrors: Geschichte der nationalsozialistischen Konzentrationslager.* Vol. 5. Munich: C. H. Beck, 2005.

Benz, Wolfgang, Bernhard Diestelkamp, and Michael Stolleis, eds. *Justizalltag im Dritten Reich.* Frankfurt/M: Fischer, 1968.

Benz, Wolfgang, ed. *Legenden, Lügen, Vorurteile: Ein Lexikon zur Zeitgeschichte.* Munich: Moos und Partner, 1990.

Benz, Wolfgang, Hans Buchheim, and Hans Mommsen, eds. *Der Nationalsozialismus: Studien zur Ideologie und Herrschaft.* Frankfurt/M: Fischer, 1993.

Benz, Wolfgang, Konrad Kwiet, and Jürgen Matthäus. *Einsatz im "Reichskommissariat Ostland": Dokumente zum Völkermord im Baltikum und in Weissrussland 1941–1944.* Berlin: Metropol, 1998.

Beorn, Waitman Wade. *Marching into Darkness: The Wehrmacht and the Holocaust in Belarus.* Cambridge, MA: Harvard University Press, 2014.

Bergen, Doris. "Between God and Hitler: Military Chaplains and the Crimes of the Third Reich." In *In God's Name: Genocide and Religion in the Twentieth Century*, edited by Omer Bartov and Phyllis Mack, pp.123–138. New York: Berghahn, 2001.

Bergen, Peter. "Why the Terrorists Commit Terrorism?" *New York Times*, June 15, 2016.

Berger, Leslie. "A Psychological Perspective on the Holocaust: Is Mass Murder Part of Human Behavior?" In *Perspectives on the Holocaust*, edited by Randolph L. Braham, pp. 19–32. Boston: Kluwer-Nijhoff, 1983.

Bergmann, Werner, and Rainer Erb. *Anti-Semitism in Germany: The Post-Nazi Epoch since 1945.* Translated by Belinda Cooper and Allison Broun. New Brunswick, NJ: Transaction, 1997.

Berkhoff, Karel C. "The Mass Murder of Soviet Prisoners of War and the Holocaust: How Were They Related?" *Kritika: Explorations in Russian and Eurasian History* 6 (2005): 789–796.

Bermann-Fischer, Gottfried. *Bedroht—bewahrt: Der Weg eines Verlegers.* Frankfurt/M: Fischer, 1967.

Bernstein, Michael André. *Foregone Conclusions: Against Apocalyptic History.* Berkeley, CA: University of California Press, 1994.

Besier, Gerhard. *Neither Good nor Bad: Why Humans Behave How They Do.* Newcastle upon Tyne: Cambridge Scholars Publishing, 2014.

Besson, Waldemar. "Zur Geschichte des nationalsozialistischen Führungs-Offiziers." *Vierteljahr-shefte für Zeitgeschichte* 9 (1961): 76–116.

Best, Werner. "Die Geheime Staatspolizei." *Deutsches Recht* 6 (1936): 125–128.

Bezwinska, Jadwiga, ed. *KL Auschwitz Seen by the SS: Höss, Broad, Kramer.* New York: Howard Fertig, 1984.

Birn, Ruth Bettina. *Die Höheren SS- und Polizeiführer: Himmlers Vertreter im Reich und in den besetzten Gebieten.* Düsseldorf: Droste, 1986.

Birn, Ruth Bettina, and Volker Riess. "Nachgelesen: Goldhagen und seine Quellen." In *Geschichtswissenschaft und Öffentlichkeit,* edited by Johannes Heil and Rainer Erb, pp. 38–62. Frankfurt/M: Fischer, 1998.

Blass, Thomas. "Perpetrator Behavior as Destructive Obedience: An Evaluation of Stanley Milgram's Perspective, the Most Influential Psychological Approach to the Holocaust." In *Understanding Genocide,* edited by Leonard S. Newman and Ralph Erber, pp. 91–109. New York: Oxford University Press, 2002.

———. "Psychological Perspectives on the Perpetrators of the Holocaust: The Role of Situational Pressures, Personal Dispositions and Their Interaction." *Holocaust and Genocide Studies* 7 (1993): 30–50.

———, ed. *Obedience to Authority: Current Perspectives on the Milgram Paradigm.* Mahwah, NJ: Lawrence Erlbaum, 2000.

Bloxham, Donald. "The Genocidal Past in Western Germany and the Experience of Occupation." *European History Quarterly* 34 (2004): 305–335.

———. "The Organisation of Genocide: Perpetration in Comparative Perspective." In *Ordinary People as Mass Murderers,* edited by Claus-Christian Jensen and W. Szejnmann, pp. 185–200. New York: Palgrave Macmillan, 2008.

———. "Organized Mass Murder: Structure, Participation, and Motivation in Comparative Perspective." *Holocaust and Genocide Studies* 22 (2008): 203–245.

Boehnert, Gunnar. "Rudolf Höss: Kommandant of Auschwitz." In *Die SS Elite unter dem Totenkopf,* edited by Ronald M. Smelser and Enrico Syring, pp. 254–266. Paderborn: Ferdinand Schönigh, 2000.

Braun, Hans, Uta Gerhardt, and Everhard Holtmann, eds. *Die lange Stunde Null: Gelenkter sozialer Wandel in Westdeutschland nach 1945.* Baden-Baden: Nomos, 2007.

Breitmann, Richard. *The Architect of Genocide: Himmler and the Final Solution.* New York: Alfred A. Knopf, 1991.

———. "'Gegen Nummer Eins': Antisemitische Indoktrination in Himmlers Weltanschauung." In *Ausbildungsziel Judenmord?,* edited by Jürgen Matthäus, Konrad Kwiet, Jürgen Förster, and Richard Breitman, pp. 21–34. Frankfurt/M: Fischer, 2003.

———. "Himmler and the 'Terrible Secret' among the Executioners." *Journal of Contemporary History* 26 (1991): 431–451.

Broszat, Martin. "Nationalsozialistische Konzentrationslager 1933–1945." In *Anatomie des SS Staates,* edited by Hans Buchheim, vol. 2, pp. 11–133. Freiburg: Walter, 1965.

———. "Siegerjustiz oder strafrechtliche 'Selbstreinigung': Aspekte der Vergangenheitsbewältigung der deutschen Justiz während der Besatzungszeit 1945–1949." *Vierteljahrshefte für Zeitgeschichte* 29 (1981): 477–544.

Browder, George C. *Hitler's Enforcers: The Gestapo and the SS Security Services in the Nazi Revolution.* New York: Oxford University Press, 1996.

———. "Perpetrator Character and Motivation: An Emerging Consensus." *Holocaust and Genocide Studies* 17 (2003): 480–497.

Brown, Daniel Patrick. *The Camp Women: The Female Auxiliaries Who Assisted the SS in Running the Nazi Concentration Camps.* Atglen, PA: Schiffer Military History, 2002.

Browning, Christopher R. *Collected Memories: Holocaust History and Postwar Testimony.* Madison: University of Wisconsin Press, 2003.

———. "Die Debatte über die Täter des Holocaust." In *Nationalsozialistische Vernichtungspolitik 1939–1945,* edited by Ulrich Herbert, pp. 148–169. Frankfurt/M: Fischer, 1998.

———. "Ideology, Culture, Situation, and Disposition: Holocaust Perpetrators and the Group Dynamics of Mass Killing." In *NS-Gewaltherrschaft,* edited by Alfred Bernd Gottwald, Norbert Kampe, and Peter Klein, pp. 66–76. Berlin: Edition Hentrich, 2005.

———. *Nazi Policy, Jewish Workers, German Killers.* Cambridge: Cambridge University Press, 2000.

————. *Ordinary Men: Reserve Police Battalion 101 and the Final Solution in Poland.* New York: Harper, 1992.

————. *Remembering Survival: Inside a Nazi Slave Labor Camp.* New York: W. W. Norton, 2010.

————. "Vernichtung und Arbeit: Zur Fraktionierung der planenden deutschen Intelligenz im besetzten Polen." In *"Vernichtungspolitik": Eine Debatte über den Zusammenhang von Sozialpolitik und Genozid im nationalsozialistischen Deutschland*, edited by Wolfgang Schneider, pp. 37–51. Hamburg: Junius, 1991.

————, ed. *The Origins of the Final Solution: The Evolution of Nazi Jewish Policy, September 1939–March 1942.* Lincoln: University of Nebraska Press, 2004.

Brunner, José. "'Oh Those Crazy Cards Again': A History of the Debate on the Nazi Rohrschachs, 1946–2001." *Political Psychology* 22 (2001): 233–261.

Brunner, Markus, Jan Lohl, Winter Sebstian, Rolf Pohl, Sascha Howin, Isabelle Hannemann, and Marc Schwietring, eds. *Volksgemeinschaft, Täterschaft und Nationalsozialismus: Beiträge zur psychoanalytischen Sozialpsychologie des Nationalsozialismus und seiner Nachwirkungen.* Giessen: Psychosozial Verlag, 2011.

Bryant, Michael S. *Eyewitnesses to Genocide: The Operation Reinhard Death Camp Trials 1955–1966.* Knoxville: University of Tennessee Press, 2014.

Buchbender, Ortwin, and Reinhold Sterz, eds. *Das andere Gesicht des Krieges: Deutsche Feldpostbriefe 1939–1945.* Munich: C. H. Beck, 1982.

Buchheim, Hans. "Befehl und Gehorsam." In *Anatomie des SS-Staates*, edited by Hans Buchheim, Martin Broszat, Hans-Adolf Jacobsen, and Helmut Krausnick, pp. 255–380. Vol. 1. Freiburg: Walter, 1965.

Buchheim, Hans, Martin Broszat, Hans-Adolf Jacobsen, and Helmut Krausnick, *Anatomie des SS-Staates.* 2 vols. Freiburg: Walter, 1965–1967.

Büchler, Yehoshua. "Kommandostab Reichsführer-SS: Himmler's Personal Murder Brigades in 1941." *Holocaust and Genocide Studies* 1 (1986): 11–25.

————. "'Unworthy Behavior': The Case of SS Officer Max Täubner." *Holocaust and Genocide Studies* 17 (2003): 409–429.

Bundesminister der Justiz. *Im Namen des deutschen Volkes: Justiz und Nationalsozialismus. Katalog zur Ausstellung des Bundesministers der Justiz.* Cologne: Wissenschaft und Politik, 1989.

Burds, Jeffrey. *Holocaust in Rovno: The Massacre at Sosenki Forest, November 1941.* New York: Palgrave Macmillan, 2013.

Burleigh, Michael. *Ethics and Extermination: Reflections on Nazi Genocide.* Cambridge. Cambridge University Press, 1997.

Burrin, Philippe. *Warum die Deutschen? Antisemitismus, Nationalsozialismus, Genocide.* Translated by Michael Bischoff. Berlin: Prophyläen, 2004.

Buruma, Ian. *The Wages of Guilt: Memories of War in Germany and Japan.* London: Orion House, 2002.

Caplan, Jane, and Nikolaus Wachsmann, eds. *Concentration Camps in Nazi Germany: The New Histories.* London: Routledge, 2010.

Carey, Sabine C., and Steven C. Poe, eds. *Understanding Human Rights Violations: New Systematic Studies.* Aldershot: Ashgate, 2004.

Celan, Paul. *The Poems of Paul Celan.* Translated by Michael Hamburger. New York: Perseus, 1972.

Cesarani, David. *Becoming Eichmann: Rethinking the Life, Crimes and Trial of a "Desk Murderer."* Cambridge, MA: Da Capo, 2007.

Charny, Israel W. *How Can We Commit the Unthinkable? Genocide: The Human Cancer.* Boulder, CO: Westview Press, 1982.

Chirot, Daniel, and Clark McCauley. *Why Not Kill Them All? The Logic and Prevention of Mass Political Murder.* Princeton, NJ: Princeton University Press, 2006.

Christie, Richard, and Marie Jahoda, eds. *Studies in the Scope and Method of "The Authoritarian Personality."* Glencoe, IL: Free Press, 1954.

Cohen, Elie A. *Human Behavior in the Concentration Camp.* Translated by M. H. Braaksma. Westport, CT: Greenwood Press, 1953.

Confino, Alon. *A World without Jews: The Nazi Imagination from Persecution to Genocide.* New Haven, CT: Yale University Press, 2014.

Conroy, John. *Unspeakable Acts, Ordinary People: The Dynamics of Torture.* New York: Alfred A. Knopf, 2000.

Coppi, Hans, and Kamil Majchrzak, eds. *Das Konzentrationslager und Zuchthaus Sonnenburg.* Berlin: Metropol, 2015.

Corino, Karl, ed. *Intellektuelle im Bann des Nationalsozialismus.* Hamburg: Hoffmann und Campe, 1980.

Crossland, David. "Late Push on War Crimes: Prosecutions to Probe SS Auschwitz Guards." *Spiegel Online,* April 8, 2013. www.spiegel.de.

Crowe, David M. *Oskar Schindler: The Untold Story of His Life, Wartime Activities, and the True Story behind the List.* Cambridge, MA: Westview Press, 2004.

Cüppers, Martin. "Auf dem Weg in den Holocaust: Die Brigaden des Kommandostabes Reichsführer-SS im Sommer 1941." In *Die Waffen-SS: Neue Forschungen,* edited by Jan Erik Schulte, Peter Lieb, and Bernd Wegner, pp. 286–301. Paderborn: Ferdinand Schöningh, 2014.

————. *Wegbereiter der Shoah: Die Waffen-SS, der Kommandostab Reichsführer-SS und die Judenvernichtung, 1939–1945.* Darmstadt: Wissenschaftliche Buchgesellschaft, 2005.

Curilla, Wolfgang. *Der Judenmord in Polen und die deutsche Ordnungspolizei 1939–1945.* Paderborn: Ferdinand Schöningh, 2011.

————. *Die deutsche Ordnungspolizei und der Holocaust im Baltikum und in Weissrussland 1941–1944.* Paderborn: Ferdinand Schöningh, 2006.

Dabag, Mihran, and Kristin Platt, eds. *Genozid und Moderne: Strukturen kollektiver Gewalt im 20. Jahrhundert.* Opladen: Leske and Budrick, 1998.

Dam, H. G. van, and Ralph Giordano, eds. *KZ-Verbrechen vor deutschen Gerichten: Dokumente aus den Prozessen gegen Sommer, Sorge, Schubert, Unkelbach.* Frankfurt/M: Europäische Verlagsanstalt, 1962.

Demant, Ebbo, ed. *Auschwitz—"Direkt von der Rampe weg . . ." Kaduk, Erber, Klehr: Drei Täter geben zu Protokoll.* Reinbek bei Hamburg: Rowohlt, 1979.

Dencker, Friedrich. "Täterschaft und Beihilfe bei NS-Gewaltverbrechen." *Zeitschrift für neuere Rechtsgeschichte* 27 (2005): 49–61.

————. "Vergangenheitsbewältigung durch Strafrecht: Lehren aus der Justizgeschichte der Bundesrepublik." *Kritische Vierteljahrsschrift für Gesetzgebung und Rechtswissenschaft* 73 (1990): 299–312.

Desbois, Patrick. *The Holocaust by Bullets: A Priest's Journey to Uncover the Truth behind the Murder of 1.5. Million Jews.* Translated by Catherine Spencer. New York: Palgrave Macmillan, 2008.

Deselaers, Manfred. *"Und Sie hatten nie Gewissensbisse?" Biografie von Rudolf Höss, Kommandant von Auschwitz, und die Frage nach seiner Verantwortung vor Gott und den Menschen.* 2nd rev. ed. Leipzig: St. Benno, 2001.

De Swaan, Abram. *The Killing Compartments.* New Haven, CT: Yale University Press, 2014.

Deutscher Juristentag. *Probleme der Verfolgung und Ahndung von nationalsozialistischen Gewaltverbrechen.* Munich: C. H. Beck, 1967.

Dicks, Henry Victor. *Licensed Mass Murder: A Social-Psychological Study of Some SS Killers.* New York: Basic Books, 1972.

Diercks, Herbert, and KZ-Gedenkstätte Neuengamme. *Entgrenzte Gewalt: Täterinnen und Täter im Nationalsozialismus.* Bremen: Temmen, 2002.

Diestelkamp, Bernhard. "Die Justiz nach 1945 und ihr Umgang mit der eigenen Vergangenheit." *Rechtshistorisches Journal* 5 (1986): 153–174.

Dillon, Christopher. *Dachau and the SS: A Schooling in Violence.* Oxford: Oxford University Press, 2015.

Dimsdale, Joel E., ed. *Survivors, Victims, and Perpetrators: Essays on the Nazi Holocaust.* Washington, DC: Hemisphere, 1980.

Diner, Dan. "Negative Symbiosis: Germans and Jews after Auschwitz." *Babylon* 1 (1986): 251–261

————, ed. *Ist der Nationalsozialismus Geschichte? Zu Historisierung und Historikerstreit.* Frankfurt/M: Fischer, 1987.

Dirks, Christian. *Die Verbrechen der anderen: Auschwitz und der Auschwitz-Prozess der DDR. Das Verfahren gegen den KZ-Arzt Dr. Horst Fischer.* Paderborn: Ferdinand Schöningh, 2006.

Distel, Barbara. "Frauen in nationalsozialistischen Konzentrationslagern: Opfer und Täterinnen." In *Der Ort des Terrors*, edited by Wolfgang Benz and Barbara Distel, pp. 195–209. Munich: C. H. Beck, 2005.

Douglas, Lawrence. *The Right Wrong Man: John Demjanjuk and the Last Great Nazi War Crimes Trial*. Princeton, NJ: Princeton University Press, 2016.

Dowe, Dieter, ed. *Die Deutschen, ein Volk von Tätern?* Bonn: Friedrich Ebert-Stiftung, 1996.

Drobisch, Klaus, and Günther Wieland. *System der NS-Konzentrationslager 1933–1939*. Berlin: Akademischer Verlag, 1993.

Dubber, Markus, and Tatjana Hörnle. *Criminal Law: A Comparative Approach*. Oxford: Oxford University Press, 2014.

Dublon-Knebel, Irith. "'Erinnern kann ich mich nur an eine Frau Danz . . .': Die Aufseherin Luise Danz in der Erinnerung ihrer Opfer." In *Im Gefolge der SS*, edited by Simone Erpel, pp. 299–315. Berlin: Metropol, 2007.

Du Perez, Petrus. *Genocide: The Psychology of Mass Murder*. London: Boyars/Bowerdean, 1994.

Dutton, Donald G. *The Psychology of Genocide: Massacres and Extreme Violence. Why 'Normal' People Come to Commit Atrocities*. Westport, CT: Praeger, 2007.

Earl, Hilary. *The Nuremberg SS-Einsatzgruppen Trials 1945–58: Atrocity, Law, and History*. Cambridge: Cambridge University Press, 2009.

Eddy, Melissa. "Chasing Death Camp Guard in Germany with New Tools for Prosecutors." *New York Times*, May 6, 2014.

———. "'Sincerely Sorry': Ex-Auschwitz Guard Says at Trial." *New York Times*, April 30, 2016.

Ehrenburg, Ilya, and Vasily Grossman. *The Complete Black Book of Russian Jewry*. Translated by David Patterson. New Brunswick, NJ: Transaction, 2002.

Eiber, Ludwig. "'. . . ein bisschen die Wahrheit': Briefe eines Bremer Kaufmanns von seinem Einsatz beim Polizei Reserve Bataillon 105 in der Sowjetunion 1941." *1999: Zeitschrift für Sozialgeschichte des 20. und 21. Jahrhunderts* 6 (1991): 58–83.

———. *Verfolgung—Ausbeutung—Vernichtung: Die Lebens- and Arbeitsbedingungen der Häftlinge in deutschen Konzentrationslagern 1933–1945*. Hannover: Fackelträger, 1985.

Eichmüller, Andreas. "Die Strafverfolgung von NS-Verbrechen durch westdeutsche Justizbehörden seit 1945: Eine Zahlenbilanz." *Vierteljahrshefte für Zeitgeschichte* 58 (2008): 621–640.

Elias, Norbert. *The Germans: Power Struggles and the Development of Habitus in the Nineteenth and Twentieth Centuries*. Translated by Eric Dunning and Stephen Mennell. New York: Columbia University Press, 1996.

Elster, Jon. *Die Akten schliessen: Recht und Gerechtigkeit nach dem Ende von Diktaturen*. Translated by Andreas Wirthensohn. Frankfurt/M: Campus, 2005.

Engert, Jürgen, ed. *Soldaten für Hitler*. Berlin: Rowohlt, 1998.

Erpel, Simone. *Im Gefolge der SS: Aufseherinnen des Frauen-KZ Ravensbrück*. Berlin: Metropol, 2007.

———. *Zwischen Vernichtung und Befreiung: Das Frauen-Konzentrationslager Ravensbrück in der letzten Kriegsphase*. Berlin: Metropol, 2005.

Ezergailis, Andrew. *The Holocaust in Latvia 1941–1944*. Riga: Historical Institute of Latvia, 1996.

Fahlbusch, Jan Henrik. "Im Zentrum des Massenmordes: Ernst Zierke im Vernichtungslager Belzec." In *KZ-Verbrechen*, edited by Wojciech Lenarczyk, pp. 53–72. Berlin: Metropol, 2007.

Feest, Johannes. "Die Bundesrichter: Herkunft, Karriere und Selektion der juristischen Elite." In *Beiträge zur Analyse des deutschen Oberschicht*, edited by Wolfgang Zapf, pp. 127–156. Tübingen: Soziologisches Seminar der Universität Tübingen, 1964.

Fenigstein, Allan. "Were Obedience Pressures a Factor in the Holocaust?" *Analyse und Kritik* 20 (1998): 54–73.

Fest, Joachim C. *The Face of the Third Reich: Portraits of the Nazi Leadership*. Translated by Michael Bullock. New York: Pantheon, 1970.

Finkelstein, Norman G., and Ruth Bettina Birn. *A Nation on Trial: The Goldhagen Thesis and Historical Truth*. New York: Henry Holt, 1998.

Forck, Bernhard Heinrich, ed. *. . . und folget ihrem Glauben nach: Gedenkbuch für die Blutzeugen der Bekennenden Kirche*. Stuttgart: Evangelisches Verlagswerk, 1949.

Frank, Hans. *Das Diensttagebuch des deutschen Generalgouverneurs in Polen 1939–1945*. Edited by Werner Präg and Wolfgang Jacobmeyer. Stuttgart: Deutsche Verlagsanstalt, 1975.

————. *Im Angesicht des Galgens: Deutung Hitlers und seiner Zeit auf Grund eigener Erlebnisse und Erkenntnisse*. Munich: Friedrich Alfred Bach, 1953.

Frank, Petra, and Stefan Hördler, eds. *Der Nationalsozialismus im Spiegel des öffentlichen Gedächtnisses: Formen der Aufarbeitung des Gedenkens*. Berlin: Metropol, 2005.

Frankl, Victor E. *Trotzdem Ja zum Leben sagen*. Vienna: Franz Deutiche, 1947.

Frei, Norbert, ed. *Geschichte vor Gericht: Historiker, Richter und die Suche nach Gerechtigkeit*. Munich: C. H. Beck, 2000.

————. *Karrieren im Zwielicht: Hitlers Eliten nach 1945*. Frankfurt/M: Campus, 2001.

————. *Vergangenheitspolitik: Die Anfänge der Bundesrepublik und die NS-Vergangenheit*. Munich: C. H. Beck, 2012.

Freudiger, Kerstin. "Die blockierte Aufarbeitung von NS-Verbrechen in der Bundesrepublik." In *NS-Täter in der deutschen Gesellschaft*, edited by Joachim Perels and Rolf Pohl, pp. 119–135. Hannover: Offizin, 2002.

————. *Die juristische Aufarbeitung von NS-Verbrechen*. Tübingen: J. C. B. Mohr, 2002.

Freundlich, Elisabeth. *Die Ermordung einer Stadt namens Stanislau: NS-Vernichtungspolitik in Polen*. Vienna: Österreichischer Bundesverlag, 1986.

Freyberger, Hellmuth, and Harald J. Freyberger. "Ganz normale Männer und ganz normale Familien? Ein Beitrag zur Nazitäter Psychologie unter Einfluss von zwei Buchrezensionen." *Psychosozial* 30 (2007): 85–99.

Friedlander, Henry. "The Judiciary and Nazi Crimes in Postwar Germany." *Simon Wiesenthal Center Annual* 1 (1982): 27–44.

————. "Nazi Crimes and the German Law." In *Nazi Crimes and the Law*, edited by Nathan Stoltzfus and Henry Friedlander, pp. 15–33. Cambridge: Cambridge University Press, 2008.

————. "The Perpetrators." In *Genocide: Critical Issues of the Holocaust*, edited by Alex Grobman, Daniel Landes, and Sybil Milton, pp. 155–158. New York: Rossel Books, 1983.

Friedländer, Saul. "From Anti-Semitism to Extermination: A Historiographical Study of Nazi Policies toward the Jews and an Essay in Interpretation." *Yad Vashem Studies* 16 (1984): 1–50.

————. *History and Psychoanalysis: An Inquiry into the Possibilities and Limits of Psychohistory*. Translated by Susan Suleiman. New York: Holmes and Meier, 1978.

————. *Kurt Gerstein: The Ambiguity of Good*. Translated by Charles Fullman. New York: Knopf, 1969.

————. *Nazi Germany and the Jews*. New York: HarperCollins, 1974.

————. *The Years of Extermination: Nazi Germany and the Jews 1939–1945*. New York: HarperCollins, 2008.

Friedman, Jonathan. "The Sachsenhausen Trials: War Crimes Prosecution in the Soviet Occupation Zone and in West and East Germany." In *Atrocities on Trial*, edited by Patricia Heberer and Jürgen Matthäus, pp. 159–184. Lincoln: University of Nebraska Press, 2008.

Friedman, Tuwiah, ed. *Tagebuch des SS-Hauptscharführers Felix Landau über seine Tätigkeit in Drohobycz 1941–1944*. Haifa: Historisches Institut für die Erforschung des Nazi Kriegsverbrechen, 1959.

Friedrich, Jörg. *Das Gesetz des Krieges: Das deutsche Heer in Russland 1941–1945. Der Prozess gegen das Oberkommando der Wehrmacht*. 3rd ed. Munich: Piper, 2003.

————. *Die kalte Amnestie: NS-Täter in der Bundesrepublik*. Rev. ed. Berlin: List, 2007.

————. *Freispruch für die Nazi-Justiz? Die Urteile gegen NS-Richter seit 1948: Eine Dokumentation*. Reinbek bei Hamburg: Rowohlt, 1983.

Fritsch, Gabriele. *Holocaust: Dokumente zum Verhalten der Täter*. Munich: Grin, 2013.

Fritz, Stephen G. *Frontsoldaten: The German Soldier in World War II*. Lexington: University Press of Kentucky, 1995.

————. *Ostkrieg: Hitler's War of Extermination in the East*. Lexington: University Press of Kentucky, 2011.

Fritz, Ulrich. "Wachmannschaften im KZ-Komplex Flossenbürg." In *Bewachung und Ausführung*, edited by Angelika Benz and MarijaVulesica, pp. 23–39. Berlin: Metropol, 2011.

Fritze, Lothar. *Anatomie des totalitären Denkens: Kommunistische und nationalsozialistische Weltanschauung im Vergleich*. Munich: Olzog, 2012.

———. "Die Moral der Täter: Über moralische Selbstlegitimierung in der Weltanschauungdiktatur." *Aufklärung und Politik* 10 (2003): 116–141.

———. "Täter und Gewissen: Zur Typologie des Täterverhaltens." *Aufklärung und Politik* 12 (2005): 82–94.

Fritzsche, Peter. "Holocaust and the Knowledge of Murder." *Journal of Modern History* 80 (2008): 594–613.

Fröhlich, Claudia. "Freispruch für Bonhoeffers Richter." In *Mit reinem Gewissen*, edited by Joachim Perels and Wolfram Wette, pp. 241–261. Berlin: Aufbau, 2011.

Frommel, Monika. "Taktische Jurisprudenz: Die versteckte Amnestie von NS-Schreibtischtätern 1969 and die Nachwirkung der damaligen Rechtsprechung bis heute." In *Gesellschaft und Gerechtigkeit*, edited by Matthias Mahlmann, pp. 458–473. Baden-Baden: Nomos, 2011.

Fuchs, Karl. *Your Loyal and Loving Son: The Letters of Tank Gunner Karl Fuchs 1937–1941.* Edited and translated by Horst Fuchs Richardson and Dennis E. Showalter. Washington, DC: Brassey's, 2003.

Fulbrook, Mary. *A Small Town near Auschwitz: Ordinary Nazis and the Holocaust.* Oxford: Oxford University Press, 2012.

Garbe, Detlef. "Absonderung, Strafkommandos und spezifischer Terror: Jüdische Gefangene in nationalsozialistischen Konzentrationslagern 1933 bis 1945." In *Verdrängung und Vernichtung der Juden unter dem Nationalsozialismus*, edited by Arno Herzig and Ina Lorenz, pp. 173–199. Hamburg: Hans Christians, 1992.

———. "Die Täter: Kommentierende Bemerkungen." In *Die nationalsozialistischen Konzentrationslager*, edited by Herbert Ullrich, Karin Orth, and Christoph Dieckmann, pp. 822–838. Göttingen: Wallstein, 1998.

———. "Von 'Furchtbaren Juristen' und ihrer Sorge um die 'Schlagkraft der Truppe': Deserteure der Wehrmacht und die Wehrmachtjustiz in der Nachkriegszeit." In *Der Krieg in der Nachkriegszeit*, edited by Michael Th. Greven and Oliver von Wrochem, pp. 51–76. Opladen: Leske und Budrich, 2000.

Gellately, Robert. *Backing Hitler: Consent and Coercion in Nazi Germany.* New York: Oxford University Press, 2001.

Gerlach, Christian. *Kalkulierte Morde: Die deutsche Wirtschafts und Vernichtungspolitik in Weissrussland 1941 bis 1944.* Hamburg: Hamburger Edition, 2000.

———. "Kontextualisierung der Aktionen eines Mordkommandos: Die Einsatzgruppe B." In *Täter im Vernichtungskrieg*, edited by Wolf Kaiser, pp. 85–95. Berlin: Propylaen, 2002.

Gerlach, Christian, ed. *"Durchschnittstäter."* Berlin: Assoziation, 2000.

Gerstenberger, Heide, and Dorothea Schmidt, eds. *Normalität oder Normalisierung? Geschichtswerkstätten und Faschismusanalyse.* Münster: Westfälisches Dampfboot, 1987.

Gilbert, Gustave M. *Nuremberg Diary.* New York: Da Capo Press, 1995.

Gilcher-Holtey, Ingrid. "Plädoyer für eine dynamische Mentalitätsgeschichte." *Geschichte und Gesellschaft* 24 (1998): 476–497.

Giordano, Ralph. *Der perfekte Mord: Die deutsche Justiz und die NS-Vergangenheit.* Göttingen: Vandenhoeck und Ruprecht, 2013.

———. *Die zweite Schuld oder von der Last Deutscher zu sein.* Hamburg: Rach und Röhring, 1987.

———. *Erinnerungen eines Davongekommenen: Die Autobiographie.* Cologne: Kiepenheuer und Witsch, 2007.

Glazar, Richard. *Trap with a Green Fence: Survival in Treblinka.* Translated by Roslyn Theobald. Evanston, IL: Northwestern University Press, 1995.

Gleichmann, Peter, and Thomas Kühne, eds. *Massenhaftes Töten: Kriege und Genozid im 20. Jahrhundert.* Essen: Klartext, 2004.

Glienke, Stephan Alexander, Volker Paulmann, and Joachim Perels, eds. *Erfolgsgeschichte Bundesrepublik? Die Nachkriegsgesellschaft im langen Schatten des Nationalsozialismus.* Göttingen: Wallstein, 2008.

Godau-Schüttke, Klaus-Detlev. "Entnazifizierung und Wiederaufbau der Justiz am Beispiel des Bundesgerichtshofes." In *Kontinuitäten und Zäsuren*, edited by Eva Schumann, pp. 189–212. Göttingen: Wallstein, 2008.

———. *"Ich habe nur dem Recht gedient." Die "Renazifizierung" der Schleswig-Holsteinschen Justiz nach 1945.* Baden-Baden: Nomos, 1993.

Goldensohn, Leon. *The Nuremberg Interviews Conducted by Leon Goldensohn*. Edited by Robert Gellately. New York: Alfred A. Knopf, 2004.

Goldhagen, Daniel Jonah. *Hitler's Willing Executioners: Ordinary Germans and the Holocaust*. New York: Alfred A. Knopf, 1996.

Golovchansky, Anatoly, ed. *"Ich will raus aus diesem Wahnsinn": Deutsche Briefe von der Ostfront 1941–1945 aus sowjetischen Archiven*. Wuppertal: Peter Hammer, 1991.

Gorscurth, Helmuth. *Tagebücher eines Abwehroffiziers 1938–1940*. Stuttgart: Deutsche Verlagsanstalt, 1970.

Görtemaker, Manfred, and Christoph Safferling, eds. *Die Rosenburg: Das Bundesjustizministerium der Justiz und die NS-Vergangenheit. Eine Bestandaufnahme*. 2nd ed. Göttingen: Vandenhoeck und Ruprecht, 2013.

Goshen, Seev. "Albert Battels Widerstand gegen die Judenvernichtung in Przemysl." *Vierteljahrshefte für Zeitgeschichte* 33 (1985): 478–488.

Gottwaldt, Alfred Bernd, Norbert Kampe, and Peter Klein, eds. *NS-Gewaltherrschaft: Beiträge zur historischen Forschung und juristischen Aufarbeitung*. Berlin: Hentrich, 2005.

Götz, Albrecht. *Bilanz der Verfolgung von NS-Straftaten*. Cologne: Bundesanzeiger, 1986.

Grabitz, Helge. *NS-Prozesse: Psychogramme der Beteiligten*. Heidelberg: C. F. Müller, 1985.

Grabitz, Helge, Klaus Bästlein, and Johannes Tuchel, eds. *Die Normalität der Verbrechen: Festschrift für Wolfgang Scheffler zum 65. Geburtstag*. Berlin: Hentrich, 1994.

Grabowski, Jan. *Hunt for the Jews: Betrayal and Murder in German-Occupied Poland*. Bloomington: Indiana University Press, 2013.

Grau, Fritz. *Wehrstrafrecht und allgemeines Strafrecht: Ihre wechselseitigen Beziehungen*. Berlin: R. v. Decker, 1936.

Greene, Joshua M. *Justice at Dachau: The Trials of an American Prosecutor*. New York: Broadway Books, 2003.

Greif, Gideon. *We Wept without Tears: Testimonies of the Jewish Sonderkommando from Auschwitz*. New Haven, CT: Yale University Press, 2005.

Greiser, Almut. *Der Kommandant Josef Schwammberger: Ein NS-Täter in der Erinnerung von Überlebenden*. Berlin: Aufbau, 2011.

Greve, Michael. "Amnestierung von NS-Gehilfen—eine Panne?" *Kritische Justiz* 33 (2000): 412–424.

———. *Der justitielle und rechtspolitische Umgang mit den NS-Gewaltverbrechen in den sechziger Jahren*. Frankfurt/M: Peter Lang, 2001.

———. "Neuere Forschungen zu NS-Prozessen: Ein Überblick." *Kritische Justiz* 32 (1999): 472–480.

———. "Täter oder Gehilfen? Zum strafrechtlichen Umgang mit NS-Gewaltverbrechen in der Bundesrepublik Deutschland." In *"Bestien" und "Befehlsempfänger"*, edited by Ulrike Weckel and Edgar Wolfrum, pp. 194–221. Göttingen: Vandenhoeck und Ruprecht, 2003.

———. "Von Auschwitz nach Ludwigsburg." In *Im Labyrinth der Schuld*, edited by Irmtrud Wojak and Susanne Meinl, pp. 41–64. Frankfurt/M: Campus, 2003.

Greven, Michael Th., and Oliver von Wrochem, eds. *Der Krieg in der Nachkriegszeit: Der zweite Weltkrieg in Politik und Gesellschaft der Bundesrepublik*. Opladen: Leske und Budrick, 2000.

Gross, Raphael. *Anständig geblieben: Nationalsozialistische Moral*. Frankfurt/M: Fischer, 2010.

———. "Die Ethik eines wahrheitssuchenden Richters: Konrad Morgen, SS-Richter und Korruptionsspezialist." In *Moralität des Bösen*, edited by Werner Konitzer and Raphael Gross, pp. 243–264. Frankfurt/M: Campus, 2009.

Gross, Raphael, and Werner Renz, eds. *Der Frankfurter Auschwitz-Prozess (1963–1965): Kommentierte Quellenedition*. 2 vols. Frankfurt/M: Campus, 2013.

Grossman, Dave. *On Killing: The Psychological Cost of Learning to Kill in War and Society*. Rev. ed. New York: Little Brown, 2009.

Grüttner, Michael, Rüdiger Hachtmann, and Heinz-Gerhard Haupt, eds. *Geschichte und Emanzipation*. Frankfurt/M: Campus, 1999.

Gutman, Yisrael, and Michael Berenbaum, eds. *Anatomy of the Auschwitz Death Camp*. Bloomington: Indiana University Press, 1998.

Haase, Norbert. "Oberleutnant Dr. Albrecht Battell und Major Max Liedtke: Konfrontation mit der SS im polnischen Przemyl im July 1942." In *Retter in Uniform*, edited by Wolfram Wette, pp. 181–208. Frankfurt/M: Fischer, 2002.

———. "Wehrmachtsangehörige vor dem Kriegsgericht." In *Die Wehrmacht*, edited by Rolf-Dieter Müller and Hans-Erich Volkmann, pp. 474–485. Munich: R. Oldenbourg, 1999.

Haberer, Erich. "History and Justice: Paradigm of the Prosecution of Nazi Crimes." *Holocaust and Genocide Studies* 19 (2005): 487–519.

Hackett, David A., ed. and trans. *The Buchenwald Report*. Boulder, CO: Westview Press, 1995.

Hamburger Institut für Sozialforschung. *Verbrechen der Wehrmacht: Dimensionen des Vernichtungskrieges 1941–1944*. Hamburg: Hamburger Institut für Sozialforschung, 2002.

Hammerschmidt, Helmut, ed. *Zwanzig Jahre Danach: Eine deutsche Bilanz 1945–1965*. Munich: Kurt Desch, 1965.

Hanack, Ernst-Walter. "Übergesetzlicher Schuldmachungsgrund wegen Verstrickung in staatlich befohlene Verbrechen." *Neue Juristische Wochenschrift* 29 (1976): 1756–1759.

———. "Zur Frage geminderter Schuld der vom Unrechtsstaat geprägten Täter." In *Probleme der Verfolgung und Ahndung von nationalsozialistischen Gewaltverbrechen*, edited by Deutscher Juristentag, pp. 53–58. Munich: C. H. Beck, 1967.

———. "Zur Problematik der gerechten Bestrafung nationalsozialistischer Gewaltverbrecher." *Juristenzeitung* 22 (1967): 329–338.

Haney, Craig. "A Study of Prisoners and Guards in a Simulated Prison." In *Readings about the Social Animal*, edited by Elliot Aronson, 7th ed., pp. 52–67. New York: Worth, 2004.

Hankel, Gerd. "Die NS-Militärjustiz in den Nürnberger Urteilen." In *Mit reinem Gewissen*, edited by Joachim Perels and Wolfram Wette, pp. 41–47. Berlin: Aufbau, 2011.

Hankel, Gerd, and Gerhard Stuby, eds. *Strafgerichte gegen Menschlichkeitsverbrechen: Zum Völkermord 50 Jahre nach den Nürnberger Prozessen*. Hamburg: Hamburger Edition, 1995.

Harrower, Molly. "Rorschach Records of the Nazi War Criminals: An Experimental Study after Thirty Years." *Journal of Personality Assessment* 40 (1976): 341–351.

Hartmann, Christian, ed. *Von Feldherren und Gefreiten: Zur biographischen Dimension des zweiten Weltkrieges*. Munich: R. Oldenbourg, 2008.

Headland, Ronald. *Messages of Murder: A Study of the Reports of the Einsatzgruppen of the Security Police and the Security Service 1941–1943*. London: Associated University Presses, 1992.

Heberer, Patricia, and Jürgen Matthäus, eds. *Atrocities on Trial: Historical Perspectives on the Politics of Prosecuting War Crimes*. Lincoln: University of Nebraska Press, 2008.

Heer, Hannes. "Bittere Pflicht: Der Rassenkrieg der Wehrmacht und seine Voraussetzungen." In *Die Wehrmacht im Rassenkrieg*, edited by Walter Manoschek, pp. 116–141. Vienna: Picus, 1996.

———. "Extreme Normalität: Generalmajor Gustav Freiherr von Mauchenheim gen. Bechtolsheim: Umfeld, Motive und Entschlussbildung eines Holocaust-Täters." *Zeitschrift für Geschichtswissenschaft* 51 (2003): 729–753.

———. "Killing Fields: Die Wehrmacht und der Holocaust." In *Vernichtungskrieg: Verbrechen der Wehrmacht*, edited by Hannes Heer and Klaus Naumann, pp. 57–77. Hamburg: Hamburger Edition, 1995.

———. *Vom Verschwinden der Täter: Der Vernichtungskrieg fand statt, aber keiner war dabei*. Berlin: Aufbau, 2004.

Heer, Hannes, and Klaus Naumann. *Vernichtungkrieg: Verbrechen der Wehrmacht, 1941–1944*. Hamburg: Hamburger Edition, 1995.

Heiber, Helmut. "Dokumentation: Aus den Akten des Gauleiters Kube." *Vierteljahrshefte für Zeitgeschichte* 4 (1956): 67–92.

———. *Reichsführer! Briefe an und von Himmler*. Munich: Deutscher Taschenbuch Verlag, 1970.

Heike, Irmtraud. "Johanna Langefeld: Die Biographie einer KZ-Oberaufseherin." *Werkstattgeschichte* 4 (1995): 7–19.

Heil, Johannes, and Reiner Erb, eds. *Geschichtswissenschaft und Öffentlichkeit: Der Streit und Daniel J. Goldhagen*. Frankfurt/M: Fischer, 1998.

Heilig, Bruno. *Man Crucified*. London: Eyre and Spottiswoode, 1941.

Heim, Susanne, and Götz Aly. "Sozialplanung und Völkermord: Thesen zur Herrschaftsrationalität der nationalsozialistischen Vernichtungspolitik." In *"Vernichtungspolitik": Eine Debatte über den Zusammenhang von Sozialpolitik und Genozid im nationalsozialistischen Deutschland*, edited by Wolfgang Schneider, pp. 11–23. Hamburg: Junius, 1991.

Heimannsberg, Barbara, and Christian J. Schmidt, eds. *The Collective Silence: German Identity and the Legacy of Shame*. Translated by Cynthia Oudejans Harris and Gordon Wheeler. San Francisco, CA: Jossey Bass, 1993.

Hein, Bastian. *Elite für Volk und Führer? Die Allgemeine SS und ihre Mitglieder 1925–1945*. Munich: R. Oldenbourg, 2012.

Heinrichs, Dirk. "Hauptmann d. R. Wilm Hosenfeld." In *Retter in Uniform*, edited by Wolfram Wette, pp. 69–87. Frankfurt/M: Fischer, 2002.

Heinsohn, Gunnar. *Warum Auschwitz? Hitlers Plan und die Ratlosigkeit der Nachwelt*. Reinbek bei Hamburg: Rowohlt, 1995.

Hellman, Peter. *The Auschwitz Album: A Book Based upon an Album Discovered by a Concentration Camp Survivor, Lili Meier*. New York: Random House, 1981.

Helm, Sarah. *If This Is a Woman: Inside Ravensbrück, Hitler's Concentration Camp for Women*. London: Little, Brown, 2015.

Henkys, Reinhard. *Die nationalsozialistischen Gewaltverbrechen: Geschichte und Gericht*. 2nd rev. ed. Stuttgart: Kreuz, 1965.

Herbert, Ulrich. "Arbeit und Vernichtung: Ökonomisches Interesse und Primat der 'Weltanschauung' im Nationalsozialismus." In *Ist der Nationalsozialismus Geschichte? Zu Historisierung und Historikerstreit*, edited by Dan Diner, pp. 198–236. Frankfurt/M: Fischer, 1987.

———. *Best: Biographische Studien über Radikalismus, Weltanschauung und Vernunft 1903–1989*. Bonn: I. H. W. Dietz, 1996.

———. "NS-Eliten in der Bundesrepublik." In *Verwandlungspolitik*, edited by Wilfried Loth and Bernd A. Rusinek, pp. 93–115. Frankfurt/M: Campus, 1998.

———. "Rassismus und rationales Kalkül: Zum Stellenwert utilitaristisch verbrämter Legitimationsstrategien in der nationalsozialistischen 'Weltanschauung.'" In *"Vernichtungspolitik": Eine Debatte über den Zusammenhang von Sozialpolitik und Genozid im nationalsozialistischen Deutschland*, edited by Wolfgang Schneider, pp. 25–35. Hamburg: Junius, 1991.

———. "Wer waren die Nationalsozialisten? Typologien des politischen Verhaltens im NS-Staat." In *Karrieren im Nationalsozialismus*, edited by Gerhard Hirschfeld and Tobias Jersak, pp. 17–42. Frankfurt/M: Campus, 2004.

———, ed. *Nationalsozialistische Vernichtungspolitik 1939–1945: Neue Forschungen und Kontroversen*. Frankfurt/M: Fischer, 1998.

Herf, Jeffrey. *The Jewish Enemy: Nazi Propaganda during World War II and the Holocaust*. Cambridge, MA: Harvard University Press, 2006.

Herzig, Arno, and Ina Lorenz, eds. *Verdrängung und Vernichtung der Juden unter dem Nationalsozialismus*. Hamburg: Hans Christians, 1992.

Hess, R. "Aus den Akten des Gauleiters Kube." *Vierteljahrshefte für Zeitgeschichte* 4 (1956): 67–92.

Heuer, Hans-Joachim. *Geheime Staatspolizei: Über das Töten und die Tendenzen der Entzivilisierung*. Berlin: Walter de Gruyter, 1995.

Hey, Bernd. "Die NS-Prozesse: Versuch einer juristischen Vergangenheitsbewältigung." *Geschichte in Wissenschaft und Unterricht* 32 (1981): 331–362.

Hilberg, Raul. "Das Goldhagen Phänomen." In *Geschichtswissenschaft und Öffentlichkeit*, edited by Johannes Heil and Reiner Erb, pp. 27–37. Frankfurt/M: Fischer, 1998.

———. *The Destruction of the European Jews*. Chicago: Quadrangle Books, 1961.

———. "Gehorsam oder Initiative? Zur arbeitsteiligen Täterschaft im Nationalsozialismus." Frankfurt/M: Arbeitsstelle zur Vorbereitung des Frankfurter Lern- und Dokumentationszentrum des Holocaust, 1991.

———. *Perpetrators, Victims, Bystanders: The Jewish Catastrophe 1933–1945*. New York: HarperCollins, 1992.

———. "Wehrmacht und Judenvernichtung." In *Die Wehrmacht im Rassenkrieg*, edited by Walter Manoschek, pp. 23–38. Vienna: Picus, 1996.

Hillgruber, Andreas. "Jürgen Habermas, Karl-Heinz Janssen, and the Enlightenment of 1986." In *Forever in the Shadow of Hitler?*, translated by James Knowlton and Truett Cates, pp. 222–236. Atlantic Highlands, NJ: Humanities Press, 1993.

Himmler, Heinrich. *Geheimreden 1933 bis 1945 und andere Ansprachen*. Edited by Bradley F. Smith and Agnes F. Peterson. Berlin: Prophyläen, 1974.

Hirsch, Günter E. "Die Strafzumessung bei nationalsozialistischen Gewalt- und Kriegsverbrechen." PhD diss., University of Erlangen-Nürnberg, 1973.

Hirschfeld, Gerhard, and Tobias Jersak, eds. *Karrieren im Nationalsozialismus: Funktionseliten zwischen Mitwirkung und Distanz*. Frankfurt/M: Campus, 2004.

Hoess, Rudolf. *Commandant of Auschwitz: The Autobiography of Rudolf Hoess*. Translated by Constantin Fitzgibbon. London: Phoenix, 2000.

Hoffmann, Christa. *Stunden Null? Vergangenheitsbewältigung in Deutschland 1945 und 1989*. Bonn: Bouvier, 1992.

Höhne, Heinz. *The Order of the Death's Head: The Story of Hitler's SS*. Translated by Richard Barry. New York: Coward-McCann, 1970.

Hölzl, Martin. "Grüner Rock und weisse Weste: Adolf von Bomhard und die Legende von der sauberen Ordnungspolizei." *Zeitschrift für Geschichtswissenschaft* 50 (2001): 22–43.

Homann, Ulrike. *Herausforderungen an den Rechtsstaat durch Justizunrecht: Die Urteile bundesdeutscher Gerichte zur strafrechtlichen Aufarbeitung von NS- und DDR-Justizverbrechen*. Berlin: Berliner Wissenschaftsverlag, 2003.

Homola, Victor. "Ex-Nazi Admits Complicity but Offers No Apology." *New York Times*, July 2, 2015.

Hördler, Stefan. "Aspekte der Täterforschung: Eine kritische Bilanz." In *Der Nationalsozialismus im Spiegel des öffentlichen Gedächtnisses*, edited by Petra Frank and Stefan Hördler, pp. 23–45. Berlin: Metropol, 2005.

———. *Ordnung und Inferno: Das KZ-System im letzten Kriegsjahr*. Göttingen: Wallstein, 2015.

Horstmann, Thomas, and Heike Litzinger, eds. *An den Grenzen des Rechts: Gespräche mit Juristen über die Verfolgung von NS-Verbrechen*. Frankfurt/M: Campus, 2006.

Horwitz, Gordon J. *In the Shadow of Death: Living Outside of the Gates of Mauthausen*. New York: Free Press, 1990.

Hosenfeld, Wilm. *"Ich versuche jeden zu retten": Das Leben eines deutschen Offiziers in Briefen und Tagebüchern*. Edited by Thomas Vogel. Munich: Deutsche Verlagsanstalt, 2004.

Hürter, Johannes. *Ein deutscher General an der Ostfront: Die Briefe und Tagebücher des Gotthard Heinrici 1941/42*. Erfurt: Sutton, 2001.

———. *Hitlers Heerführer: Die deutschen Oberbefehlshaber im Krieg gegen die Sowjetunion 1941/42*. Munich: R. Oldenbourg, 2007.

Hüttmann, Heiko, and Wolfgang Kopitzsch. *Das Polizeibataillon 307 (Lübeck) im Osteinsatz*. Essen: Schmidt-Römhild, 2002.

Ibach, Karl. *Kemna Wuppertaler Konzentrationslager 1933–1934*. Wuppertal: Peter Hammer, 1948.

Ingrao, Christian. *Believe and Destroy: Intellectuals in the War Machine*. Translated by Andrew Brown. Cambridge, MA: Polity, 2013.

———. *Hitlers Elite: Die Wegbereiter des nationalsozialistischen Massenmords*. Translated by Enrico Heinemann and Ursel Schäfer. Bonn: Bundeszentrale für politische Bildung, 2012.

International Military Tribunal. *Trial of the Major War Criminals*. Vol. 29. Nuremberg, 1948.

Jacobsen, Hans-Adolf. "Kommissarbefehl und Massenexekutionen sowjetischer Kriegsgefangener." In *Anatomie des SS-Staates*, edited by Hans Buchheim, Martin Broszat, and Helmut Krausnick, vol. 2, pp. 137–232. Munich: Deutscher Taschenbuchverlag, 1967.

Jäger, Herbert. "Die Widerlegung des funktionalistischen Täterbildes: Daniel Goldhagens Beitrag zur Kriminologie des Völkermordes." *Mittelweg 36* (1997): 73–85.

———. "Makroverbrechen als Gegenstand des Völkerstrafrechts: Kriminalpolitisch-Kriminologische Aspekte." In *Strafgerichte gegen Menschlichkeitsverbrechen*, edited by Gerd Hankel and G. Stuby, pp. 325–354. Hamburg: Hamburger Edition, 1995.

————. "Strafrecht und nationalsozialistische Gewaltverbrechen." *Kritische Justiz* 2 (1968): 143–157.

————. *Verbrechen unter totalitärer Herrschaft: Studien zur nationalsozialistischen Gewaltkriminalität*. Frankfurt/M: Suhrkamp, 1982.

Jaiser, Constanze. "Irma Grese: Zur Rezeption einer KZ-Aufseherin." In *Im Gefolge der SS*, edited by Simone Erpel, pp. 338–346. Berlin: Metropol, 2007.

Jarausch, Konrad N. *Reluctant Accomplice: A Wehrmacht Soldier's Letters from the Eastern Front*. Princeton, NJ: Princeton University Press, 2011.

Jaspers, Karl. *The Question of German Guilt*. Translated by E. B. Ashton. New York: Fordham University Press, 2000.

Jensen, Olaf, and Claus-Christian W. Szejnmann, eds. *Ordinary People as Mass Murderers: Perpetrators in Comparative Perspectives*. New York: Palgrave Macmillan, 2008.

Jersak, Tobias. "Die vermeintliche Ambivalenz des Bösen: Der SS-Offizier Karl Gerstein." In *Karrieren im Nationalsozialismus*, edited by Gerhard Hirschfeld and Tobias Jersak, pp. 255–262. Frankfurt/M: Campus, 2004.

Johnson, Eric A. *Nazi Terror: The Gestapo, Jews, and Ordinary Germans*. New York: Basic Books, 1999.

Jones, David H. *Moral Responsibility in the Holocaust: A Study in the Ethics of Character*. Lanham, MD: Rowman and Littlefield, 1999.

Just-Dahlmann, Barbara, and Helmut Just. *Die Gehilfen: NS-Verbrechen und die Justiz nach 1945*. Frankfurt/M: Athenäum, 1988.

Kaienburg, Hermann. "KZ-Terror und Kriegsgewalt: Zur Bedeutung von soldatischen Traditionen beim Aufbau von SS-Elitenverbänden." In *Entgrenzte Gewalt*, edited by Herbert Diercks and KZ-Gedenkstätte Neuengamme, pp. 37–49. Bremen: Temmen, 2002.

Kaiser, Wolf. *Täter im Vernichtungskrieg: Der Überfall auf die Sowjetunion und der Völkermord an den Juden*. Berlin: Propyläen, 2002.

Kamber, Richard. "Goldhagen and Sartre on Eliminationist Anti-Semitism: False Beliefs and Moral Culpability." *Holocaust and Genocide Studies* 13 (1999): 252–271.

Kaminer, Isidor J. "Normalität und Nationalsozialismus." *Psyche* 51 (1997): 385–409.

Kampling, Rainer. "Religiöse Motivation der Täter? Annäherungen an eine Fiktion des Entschuldigungsmythos." In *NS-Täter aus interdisciplinärer Perspektive*, edited by Helgard Kramer, pp. 243–251. Munich: Martin Meidenbauer, 2006.

Kastner, Heidi. *Schuldhaft: Täter und ihre Innenwelten*. Vienna: Kremayer und Scherlau, 2012.

Kater, Michael H. "Everyday Anti-Semitism in Prewar Nazi Germany: The Popular Bases." *Yad Vashem Studies* 16 (1984): 129–159.

Katz, Fred E. *Ordinary People and Extraordinary Evil: A Report on the Beguiling of Evil*. Albany: State University of New York, 1993.

Kautsky, Benedikt. *Teufel und Verdammte: Erfahrungen und Erkenntnisse aus sieben Jahren in deutschen Konzentrationslagern*. Vienna: Wiener Volksbuchhandlung, 1961.

Kay, Alex J. *The Making of an SS Killer: The Life of Colonel Alfred Filbert*. Cambridge: Cambridge University Press, 2016.

Keilig, Wolf. *Das deutsche Heer, 1939–1945: Gliederung, Einsatz, Stellenbesetzung*. Bad Nauheim: Hans Henning Podzun, 1957.

Kekes, John. *Facing Evil*. Princeton, NJ: Princeton University Press, 1990.

Kellenbach, Katharina von. "Vanishing Acts: Perpetrators in Postwar Germany." *Holocaust and Genocide Studies* 17 (2003): 305–329.

Kelley, Douglas M. *22 Cells in Nuremberg: A Psychiatrist Examines the Nazi War Criminals*. New York: Greenburg, 1947.

Kelman, Herbert C. "Violence without Moral Restraint: Reflections on the Dehumanization of Victims and Victimizers." *Journal of Social Issues* 29 (1973): 25–61.

Kelman, Herbert C., and V. Lee Hamilton. *Crimes of Obedience: Toward a Social Psychology of Authority and Responsibility*. New Haven, CT: Yale University Press, 1989.

Kempner, Robert. *Ankläger einer Epoche: Lebenserinnerungen*. Frankfurt/M: Ullstein, 1983.

————. *SS im Kreuzverhör*. Munich: Rütten und Loening, 1964.

Kenez, Peter. *The Coming of the Holocaust: From Antisemitism to Genocide.* New York: Cambridge University Press, 2013.

Kenkmann, Alfons, and Christoph Spieker, eds. *Im Auftrag: Polizei, Verwaltung und Verantwortung.* Essen: Klartext, 2001.

Kershaw, Ian. *Hitler 1889–1936: Hubris.* New York: W. W. Norton, 1998.

———. *Hitler, the Germans, and the Final Solution.* New Haven, CT: Yale University Press, 2008.

———. "The Persecution of the Jews and German Popular Opinion in the Third Reich." *Leo Baeck Institute Yearbook* 17 (1981): 261–289.

Kielar, Wieslaw. *Anus Mundi: Five Years in Auschwitz.* Translated by Susanne Flatauer. London: Allen Lane, 1981.

Kitterman, David H. "Those Who Said 'No!': Germans Who Refused to Execute Civilians during World War II." *German Studies Review* 11 (1988): 241–254.

Klausch, Hans-Peter. *Tätergeschichten: Die SS-Kommandanten der frühen Konzentrationslager im Emsland.* Bremen: Edition Temmen, 2005.

Klee, Ernst. *Auschwitz: Täter, Gehilfen, Opfer und was aus ihnen wurde: Ein Personallexikon.* Frankfurt/M: Fischer, 2013.

Klee, Ernst, and Willi Dressen, eds. *"Gott mit uns": Der deutsche Vernichtungskrieg im Osten 1939–1943.* Frankfurt/M: Fischer, 1989.

Klee, Ernst, Willi Dressen, and Volker Riess, eds. *"The Good Old Days": The Holocaust as Seen by the Perpetrators and Bystanders.* Translated by Deborah Burnstone. New York: Free Press, 1991.

Klein, Peter, ed. *Die Einsatzgruppen in der besetzten Sowjetunion 1941–42: Tätigkeits- und Lageberichte des Chefs der Sicherheitspolizei und des SD.* Berlin: Edition Hentrich, 1997.

———. "Die Erlaubnis zum grenzenlosen Massenmord: Das Schicksal der Berliner Juden und die Rolle der Einsatzgruppen bei dem Versuch Juden als Partisanen auszurotten." In *Die Wehrmacht*, edited by Rolf-Dieter Müller und Hans-Erich Volkmann, pp. 923–947. Munich: R. Oldenbourg, 1999.

Klemp, Stefan. *Freispruch für das "Mord-Bataillon": Die NS-Ordnungspolizei und die Nachkriegsjustiz.* Münster: LIT, 1998.

———. *Nicht ermittelt: Polizeibataillone und die Nachkriegsjustiz, ein Handbuch.* Essen: Klartext, 2005.

Klüger, Ruth. *Weiter leben: Eine Jugend.* Göttingen: Wallstein, 1992.

Knoch, Habbo. *Die Tat als Bild: Fotografie des Holocaust in der deutschen Erinnerungskultur.* Hamburg: Hamburger Edition, 2001.

Knoch, Habbo, and Thomas Rahe, eds. *Bergen-Belsen: Neue Forschungen.* Göttingen: Wallstein, 2014.

Kochinka, Alexander, and Jürgen Straub. "'Dämonologie' oder psychologisches Denken: Wie erklärt man, warum ganz gewöhnliche Angehörige der nationalsozialistischen Gesellschaft das Leben anderer auslöschten." *Analyse und Kritik* 20 (1998): 95–122.

Kogon, Eugen. "Das Recht auf den politischen Irrtum." *Frankfurter Hefte* 7 (1947): 641–655.

———. *The Theory and Practice of Hell: The German Concentration Camps and the System behind Them.* Translated by Heinz Norden. New York: Berkeley Books, 1998.

Kohl, Robert. "The Character of the Nazi SS." *Journal of Modern History* 34 (1962): 275–283.

Köhler, Thomas. "Anstiftung zu Versklavung und Völkermord: 'Weltanschauliche Schulung' der Literatur Lesestoff für Polizeibeamte des 'Dritten Reiches.'" In *Im Auftrag*, edited by Alfons Kenkmann and Christoph Spieker, pp. 130–156. Essen: Klartext, 2001.

Kolbert, Elizabeth. "The Last Trial: A Great-grandmother, Auschwitz, and the Arc of Justice." *The New Yorker*, February 16, 2015, pp. 24–30.

Konitzer, Werner, and Raphael Gross, eds. *Moralität des Bösen: Ethik und nationalsozialistische Verbrechen.* Frankfurt/M: Campus, 2009.

Koonz, Claudia. *The Nazi Conscience.* Cambridge, MA: Harvard University Press, 2003.

———. "On Reading a Document: SS-Mann Katzmanns Solution for the Jewish Question in the District of Galicia." Raul Hilbert Lecture, University of Vermont, November 2, 2005.

Koop, Volker. *Rudolf Höss: Der Kommandant von Auschwitz, eine Biographie.* Cologne: Böhlau, 2014.

Koppel, Wolfgang. *Justiz im Zwielicht: Dokumentation.* Karlsruhe: Im Selbstverlag, 1963.

Korn, Hans-Joachim. "Täterschaft oder Teilnahme bei staatlich organisierten Verbrechen." *Neue Juristischen Wochenschrift* 18 (1965): 1206–1210.

Krakowski, Samuel. "The Satellite Camps." In *Anatomy of the Auschwitz Death Camp*, edited by Yisrael Gutman and Michael Berenbaum, pp. 50–60. Bloomington: Indiana University Press, 1998.

Kramer, Helgard, ed. *NS-Täter aus interdisciplinärer Perspektive*. Munich: Martin Meidenbauer, 2006.

Kramer, Helmut. "Entlastung als System: Zur strafrechtlichen Aufarbeitung des Justiz- und Verwaltungsverbrechen des Dritten Reiches." In *Spuren des Unrechts*, edited by Martin Bennhold, pp. 101–130. Cologne: Pahl-Rugenstein, 1989.

Krannhals, Hanns von. "Die Judenvernichtung in Polen und die Wehrmacht." *Wehrwissenschaftliche Rundschau* 15 (1965): 570–581.

Krausnick, Helmut. "Hitler und die Morde in Polen: Ein Beitrag zum Konflikt zwischen Heer und SS um die Verwaltung der besetzten Gebiete." *Vierteljahrshefte für Zeitgeschichte* 11 (1963): 196–209.

———. "Kommissarbefehl und 'Gerichtsbarkeitserlass Barbarossa' in neuer Sicht." *Vierteljahrshefte für Zeitgeschichte* 25 (1977): 682–738.

Krausnick, Helmut, and Hans-Heinrich Wilhelm. *Die Truppe des Weltanschauungskrieges: Die Einsatzgruppen der Sicherheitspolizei und des SD 1938–1942*. Stuttgart: Deutsche Verlagsanstalt, 1981.

Kren, George M., and Leon Rappoport. *The Holocaust and the Crisis of Human Behavior*. New York: Holmes and Meier, 1980.

Kressel, Neil J. *Mass Hate: The Global Rise of Genocide and Terror*. New York: Plenum Press, 1996.

Kretzer, Annette. "'His or Her Special Job': Die Repräsentation von NS-Verbrechen im ersten Hamburger Ravensbrück Prozess und in der westdeutschen Täterschaft-Diskussion." In *Entgrenzte Gewalt*, edited by Herbert Diercks and KZ-Gedenkstätte Neuengamme, pp. 134–150. Bremen: Temmen, 2002.

———. *NS-Täterschaft und Geschlecht: Der erste britische Ravensbrück-Prozess 1946/47 in Hamburg*. Berlin: Metropol, 2009.

Kritische Justiz. *Die juristische Aufarbeitung des Unrechtsstaates*. Baden-Baden: Nomos, 1998.

Kruse, Flako. "Das Majdanak-Urteil: Von den Grenzen deutscher Rechtsprechung." *Kritische Justiz* 18 (1985): 140–158.

———. "NS-Prozesse und Restauration: Zur justitiellen Verfolgung von NS-Gewaltverbrechen in der Bundesrepublik." *Kritische Justiz* 11 (1978): 109–134.

———. "Zweierlei Mass für NS-Täter?" *Kritische Justiz* 11 (1978): 236–253.

Kühne, Thomas. "Der nationalsozialistische Vernichtungskrieg und die 'ganz normalen' Deutschen: Forschungsprobleme und Forschungstendenzen der Gesellschaftsgeschichte des Zweiten Weltkrieges." *Archiv für Sozialgeschichte* 39 (1999): 580–662 and 40 (2000): 440–486.

———. *Kameradschaft: Die Soldaten des nationalsozialistischen Krieges und das 20. Jahrhundert*. Göttingen: Vandenhoeck und Ruprecht, 2006.

———. "Male Bonding and Shame Culture: Hitler's Soldiers and the Moral Basis of Genocidal Warfare." In *Ordinary People as Mass Murderers*, edited by Olaf Jensen and Claus-Christian W. Szejnmann, pp. 55–77. New York: Palgrave Macmillan, 2008.

Kühnel, Sina, and Hans J. Markowitsch. *Falsche Erinnerungen: Die Sünden des Gedächtnisses*. Heidelberg: Spektrum, 2009.

Kulka, Dov, and Eberhard Jäckel, eds. *The Jews in the Secret Nazi Reports on Popular Opinion in Germany, 1933–1945*. Translated by William Templer. New Haven, CT: Yale University Press, 2010.

Kunz, Norbert. "Die Feld- und Ortskommandanten auf der Krim und der Judenmord 1941/42." In *Täter im Vernichtungskrieg*, edited by Wolf Kaiser, pp. 54–70. Berlin: Propyläen, 2002.

Küper, Wilfried. "Mittelbare Täterschaft, Verbotsirrtum des Tatmittlers und Verantwortungsprinzip." *Juristenzeitung* 44 (1989): 935–949.

Kurz, Thilo. "Paradigmenwechsel bei der Strafverfolgung des Personals in den deutschen Vernichtungslagern?" *ZiS* online, March 20, 2013, pp. 122–129. www.zis-online.com.

Kwiet, Konrad. "Erziehung zum Mord: Zwei Beispiele zur Kontinuität der deutschen 'Endlösung der Judenfrage.'" In *Geschichte und Emanzipation*, edited by Michael Grüttner, Rüdiger Hachtmann, and Gerhard Haupt, pp. 435–456. Frankfurt/M: Campus, 1999.

———. "From the Diary of a Killing Unit." In *Why Germany?*, edited by John Milfull, pp. 75–90. Providence, RI: Berghahn, 1993.

———. "Judenmord als Amtsanmassung: Das Feldurteil vom 12. März 1943 gegen Johannes Meisslein." *Dachauer Hefte* 16 (2000): 125–135.

———. "Paul Zapp: Vordenker und Vollstrecker der Judenvernichtung." In *Karrieren der Gewalt: Nationalsozialistische Täter-Biographien*, edited by Klaus-Michael Mallmann and Gerhard Paul, pp. 252–263. Darmstadt: Wissenschaftliche Buchgesellschaft, 2013.

———. "Von Tätern zu Befehlsempfängern: Legendenbildung und Strafverfolgung nach 1945." In *Ausbildungsziel Judenmord?*, edited by Jürgen Matthäus, Konrad Kwiet, Jürgen Förster, and Richard Breitmann, pp. 114–138. Frankfurt/M: Fischer, 2003.

Lampert, Tom. *Ein einziges Leben: Acht Geschichten aus dem Krieg.* Munich: Carl Hanser, 2001.

Lamprecht, Rolf. "Lesarten für Rechtsbeugung." *Neue Juristische Wochenschrift* 47 (1994): 562–563.

Langbein, Hermann. *Der Auschwitz-Prozess: Eine Dokumentation.* 2 vols. Frankfurt/M: Neue Kritik, 1995.

———. *Im Namen des deutschen Volkes: Zwischenbilanz der Prozesse wegen nationalsozialistischer Verbrechen.* Vienna: Europa, 1963.

———. *People in Auschwitz.* Translated by Harry Zohn. Chapel Hill: University of North Carolina Press, 2004.

———. *Wir haben es getan: Selbstportraits in Tagebüchern und Briefen 1939–1945.* Vienna: Europa, 1964.

Langerbein, Helmut. *Hitler's Death Squads: The Logic of Mass Murder.* College Station: Texas A&M University Press, 2004.

———. *Profiles of Mass Murder: The Einsatzgruppen Officers.* Santa Cruz: University of California Press, 1999.

Laqueur, Walter. *The Terrible Secret: An Investigation into the Suppression of Information about Hitler's "Final Solution."* London: Weidenfeld and Nicolson, 1980.

Large, David. "Reckoning without the Past: The HIAG of the Waffen-SS and the Problem of Rehabilitation in the Bonn Republic 1950–61." *Journal of Modern History* 59 (1987): 79–113.

Lasik, Alexander. "Historical Sociological Profile of the Auschwitz SS." In *Anatomy of the Auschwitz Death Camp*, edited by Yisrael Gutman and Michael Berenbaum, pp. 271–287. Bloomington: Indiana University Press, 1998.

———. "Postwar Prosecution of the Auschwitz SS." In *Anatomy of the Auschwitz Death Camp*, edited by Yisrael Gutman and Michael Berenbaum, pp. 588–600. Bloomington: Indiana University Press, 1998.

———. "Rudolf Höss: Manager of Crime." In *Anatomy of the Auschwitz Death Camp*, edited by Yisrael Gutman and Michael Berenbaum, pp. 288–300. Bloomington: Indiana University Press, 1998.

Lasker-Wallfisch, Anita. *Inherit the Truth: A Memoir of Survival and the Holocaust.* New York: St. Martin's Press, 2000.

Latzel, Klaus. *Deutsche Soldaten—nationalsozialistischer Krieg? Kriegserlebnis—Kriegserfahrung 1939–1945.* Paderborn: Ferdinand Schöningh, 1998.

———. "Wehrmachtsoldaten zwischen 'Normalität' und NS-Ideologie: Was sucht die Forschung in der Feldpost?" In *Die Wehrmacht*, edited by Rolf-Dieter Müller and Hans-Erich Volkmann, pp. 573–884. Munich: R. Oldenbourg, 1999.

Lenarczyk, Wojciech, ed. *KZ-Verbrechen: Beiträge zur Geschichte der nationalsozialistischen Konzentrationslager und ihrer Erinnerung.* Berlin: Metropol, 2007.

Lessing, Holger. *Der erste Dachauer Prozess (1945/46).* Baden-Baden: Nomos, 1993.

Levene, Mark. *The Meaning of Genocide.* London: I. B. Tauris, 2005.

Levi, Primo. *Survival in Auschwitz: The Nazi Assault on Humanity.* New York: Simon and Schuster, 1996.

Lewald, Walter. "Das Dritte Reich: Rechtsstaat oder Unrechtsstaat?" *Neue Juristische Wochenschrift* 17 (1964): 1658–1661.

Lewy, Guenter. *The Nazi Persecution of the Gypsies*. New York: Oxford University Press, 2000.

Ley, Robert. *Pesthauch der Welt*. Dresden: Franz Müller, 1944.

Lichtenstein, Heiner. *Himmlers grüne Helfer: Die Schutz- und Ordnungspolizei im "Dritten Reich."* Cologne: Bund, 1990.

———. *Im Namen des Volkes? Eine persönliche Bilanz der NS-Prozesse*. Cologne: Bund, 1984.

———. "NS-Prozesse: Ein nicht zu bewältigendes Stück deutscher Vergangenheit." *Tribüne* 37 (1998/1999): 165–173.

———. *Täter—Opfer—Folgen: Der Holocaust in Geschichte und Gegenwart*. Bonn: Bundeszentrale für politische Bildung, 1997.

Lifton, Robert Jay. *The Nazi Doctors: Medical Killing and the Psychology of Genocide*. New York: Basic Books, 1986.

Lifton, Robert Jay, and Eric Markusen. *The Genocidal Mentality and the Nuclear Threat*. New York: Basic Books, 1990.

Linck, Stephan. "Ernst Szymanowski alias Biberstein: Ein Theologe auf Abwegen." In *Karrieren der Gewalt: Nationalsozialistische Täter-Biographien*, edited by Klaus-Michael Mallmann and Gerhard Paul, pp. 219–230. Darmstadt: Wissenschaftliche Buchgesellschaft, 2013.

———. "Ordnung und Sauberkeit: Briefe Flensburger Ordnungspolizisten 1944." *Sozialwissenschaftliche Informationen* 26 (1997): 42–44.

Lingen, Kerstin von. "Partisanenkrieg und Wehrmachtjustiz am Beispiel: Italien 1943–1945." *Zeitschrift für Genozidforschung* 8 (2007): 8–40.

Lingens, Ella. "Als Ärztin in Auschwitz und Dachau." *Dachauer Hefte* 4 (1988): 22–58.

———. *Prisoner of Fear*. London: Victor Gollancz, 1948.

Liwerant, O. Sara. "Mass Murder: Discussing Criminological Perspectives." *Journal of International Criminal Justice* 5 (2007): 917–939.

Longerich, Peter. *"Davon haben wir nichts gewusst!" Die Deutschen und die Judenverfolgung 1933–1945*. Munich: Siedler, 2006.

———. *Der ungeschriebene Befehl: Hitler und der Weg zur "Endlösung."* Munich: Piper, 2001.

———. *Heinrich Himmler: Biographie*. Berlin: Siedler, 2008.

———. *Politik der Vernichtung: Eine Gesamtdarstellung der nationalsozialistischen Judenverfolgung*. Munich: Piper, 1998.

Loth, Wilfried, and Bernd A. Rusinek, eds. *Verwandlungspolitik: NS-Eliten in der westdeutschen Nachkriegsgesellschaft*. Frankfurt/M: Campus, 1998.

Lower, Wendy. *Hitler's Furies: German Women in the Nazi Killing Fields*. New York: Houghton Mifflin, 2013.

———. *Nazi Empire Building and the Holocaust in Ukraine*. Chapel Hill: University of North Carolina Press, 2005.

Lozowick, Yaacov. *Hitler's Bureaucrats: The Nazi Security Police and the Banality of Evil*. Translated by Haim Watzman. New York: Continuum, 2002.

Lüdtke, Alf. "Der Bann der Wörter: 'Todesfabriken' von Reden über NS-Völkermord, das auch Verschweigen ist." *Werkstattgeschichte* 13 (1996): 5–18.

———. "'Fehlgreifen in der Wahl der Mittel': Optionen im Alltag militärischen Handelns." *Mittelweg* 12 (2003): 61–75.

Lustiger, Arno. "Feldwebel Anton Schmid: Judenretter in Wilna 1941–1942." In *Retter in Uniform*, edited by Wolfram Wette, pp. 45–67. Frankfurt/M: Fischer, 2002.

MacLean, French L. *The Field Men: The SS Officers Who Led the Einsatzkommandos, the Nazi Mobile Killing Units*. Atglen, PA: Schiffer, 1999.

MacNair, Rachel. "Psychological Reverberations for the Killers: Preliminary Historical Evidence for Perpetration, Inducing Traumatic Stress." *Journal of Genocide Research* 3 (2001): 273–282.

MacQueen, Michael. "The Context of Mass Destruction: Agents and Prerequisites of the Holocaust in Lithuania." *Holocaust and Genocide Studies* 12 (1998): 27–48.

Mahlmann, Matthias. *Gesellschaft und Gerechtigkeit: Festschrift für Hubert Rottleuthner*. Baden-Baden: Nomos, 2011.

Mailänder, Elissa. *Female SS Guards and Workaday Violence: The Majdanek Concentration Camp 1942–1944*. Translated by Patricia Szobar. East Lansing: Michigan State University Press, 2015.

————. *Gewalt im Dienstalltag: Die SS-Aufseherinnen des Konzentrations- und Vernichtungslager Majdanek.* Hamburg: Hamburger Edition, 2009.

Mallmann, Klaus-Michael. "Der Einstieg in den Genozid: Das Lübecker Polizeibataillon 307 und das Massaker in Brest-Litowsk Anfang July 1941." *Archiv für Polizeigeschichte* 10 (1999): 82–88.

————. "Der qualitative Sprung im Vernichtungsprozess: Das Massaker von Kamenez-Podolsk Ende August 1941." *Jahrbuch für Antisemitismusforschung* 10 (2001): 239–264.

————. "Die Türöffner der 'Endlösung': Zur Genesis des Genozids." In *Die Gestapo im Zweiten Weltkrieg*, edited by Gerhard Paul and Klaus-Michael Mallmann, pp. 437–463. Darmstadt: Primus, 2000.

————. "Heinrich Hamann: Leiter des Grenzpolizeikommissariats Neu-Sandez." In *Karrieren der Gewalt: Nationalsozialistische Täter-Biographien*, edited by Klaus-Michael Mallmann and Gerhard Paul, pp. 104–114. Darmstadt: Wissenschaftliche Buchgesellschaft, 2013.

————. "'Mensch, ich feiere heute den tausendsten Genickschuss': Die Sicherheitspolizei in Westgalizien." In *Die Täter der Shoah*, edited by Gerhard Paul, pp. 109–136. Göttingen: Wallstein, 2002.

————. "Vom Fussvolk der 'Endlösung': Ordnungspolizei, Ostkrieg und Judenmord." *Tel Aviver Jahrbuch für deutsche Geschichte* 26 (1997): 355–391.

Mallmann, Klaus-Michael, Andrej Angrick, Martin Cuppers, Jürgen Matthäus, and Kwiet, Konrad, eds. *Die "Ereignismeldungen UdSSR" 1941: Dokumente der Einsatzgruppen in der Sowjetunion.* Vol. 1. Darmstadt: Wissenschaftliche Buchgesellschaft, 2011.

Mallmann, Klaus-Michael, Volker Riess, and Wolfram Pyta. *Deutscher Osten 1939–1945: Der Weltanschauungskrieg in Photos und Texten.* Darmstadt: Wissenschaftliche Buchgesellschaft, 2003.

Mann, Michael. *The Dark Side of Democracy: Explaining Ethnic Cleansing.* New York: Cambridge University Press, 2005.

————. "Were the Perpetrators of Genocide 'Ordinary Men' or 'Real Nazis'? Results from Fifteen Hundred Biographies." *Holocaust and Genocide Studies* 14 (2000): 331–366.

Manoschek, Walter. "'Gehst mit Juden erschiessen?': Die Vernichtung der Juden in Serbien." In *Vernichtungskrieg*, edited by Hannes Heer and Klaus Naumann, pp. 39–56. Hamburg: Hamburger Edition, 1995.

————. "'Wo der Partisan ist, ist der Jude, und wo der Jude ist, ist der Partisan': Die Wehrmacht und die Shoah." In *Die Täter der Shoah*, edited by Gerhard Paul, pp. 167–185. Göttingen: Wallstein, 2002.

————, ed. *Die Wehrmacht im Rassenkrieg: Der Vernichtungskrieg hinter der Front.* Vienna: Picus, 1996.

————. *"Es gibt nur eines für das Judentum—Vernichtung": Das Judenbild in deutschen Soldatenbriefen 1939–1944.* Hamburg: Hamburger Edition, 1995.

Matthäus, Jürgen. "Die Beteiligung der Ordnungspolizei am Holocaust." In *Täter im Vernichtungskrieg*, edited by Wolf Kaiser, pp. 166–185. Berlin: Propyläen, 2002.

————. "Die 'Judenfrage' als Schulungsthema von SS und Polizei: 'Inneres Erlebnis' und Handlungslegitimation." In *Ausbildungsziel Judenmord?*, edited by Jürgen Matthäus, Konrad Kwiet, Jürgen Förster, and Richard Breitman, pp. 35–86. Frankfurt/M: Fischer, 2003.

————. "Georg Heuser: Routinier des sicherheitspolizeilichen Osteinsatzes." In *Karrieren der Gewalt: Nationalsozialistische Täter-Biographien*, edited by Klaus-Michael Mallmann and Gerhard Paul, pp. 115–125. Darmstadt: Wissenschaftliche Buchgesellschaft, 2013.

————. "Operation Barbarossa and the Onset of the Holocaust." In *The Origins of the Final Solution*, edited by Christopher Browning, pp. 244–308. Lincoln: University of Nebraska Press, 2004.

————. "'Warum wird über das Judentum geschult?' Die ideologische Vorbereitung der deutschen Polizei auf den Holocaust." In *Die Gestapo im Zweiten Weltkrieg*, edited by Gerhard Paul and Klaus-Michael Mallmann, pp. 100–124. Darmstadt: Primus, 2000.

————. "What about the 'Ordinary Men'? The German Order Police and the Holocaust in the Occupied Soviet Union." *Holocaust and Genocide Studies* 10 (1996): 134–150.

Matthäus, Jürgen, Jochen Böhler, and Klaus-Michael Mallmann, eds. *War, Pacification and Mass Murder 1939: The Einsatzgruppen in Poland.* Lanham, MD: Rowman and Littlefield, 2014.

Matthäus, Jürgen, Konrad Kwiet, Jürgen Förster, and Richard Breitman, eds. *Ausbildungsziel Judenmord? "Weltasnschauliche Erziehung" von SS, Polizei und Waffen-SS im Rahmen der Endlösung.* Frankfurt/M: Fischer, 2003.

McKale, Donald M. *Nazis after Hitler: How Perpetrators of the Holocaust Cheated Justice and Truth.* Lanham, MD: Rowman and Littlefield, 2012.

McMillan, Dan. *How Could This Happen? Exploring the Holocaust.* New York: Basic Books, 2014.

Messerschmidt, Manfred. *Die Wehrmacht im NS-Staat: Zeit der Indoktrination.* Hamburg: R. v. Decker, 1969.

———. *Die Wehrmachtjustiz 1933–1945.* Paderborn: Ferdinand Schöningh, 2005.

———. *Militarismus, Vernichtungskrieg, Geschichtspolitik: Zur deutschen Militär- und Rechtsgeschichte.* Paderborn: Ferdinand Schöningh, 2006.

———. "Wehrmacht und Nationalsozialismus." In *"Ich musste selber etwas tun": Deserteure, Täter und Verfolgte im Zweiten Weltkrieg,* edited by Geschichtswerkstatt Marburg, pp. 11–33. Marburg: Schüren, 2000.

Miale, Robert, and Michael Selzer. *The Nuremberg Mind: The Psychology of the Nazi Leaders.* New York: Quadrangle, 1975.

Michael, Robert, and Karin Doerr. *Nazi Deutsch/Nazi German: An English Lexicon of the Language of the Third Reich.* Westport, CT: Greenwood Press, 2002.

Mildt, Dick de. "Getting Away with Murder: The Täubner Case." In *Nazi Crimes and the Law,* edited by Nathan Stoltzfus and Henry Friedlander, pp. 101–112. Cambridge: Cambridge University Press, 2008.

———. *In the Name of the People: Perpetrators of Genocide in the Reflection of Their Post-war Prosecutions in West Germany. The "Euthanasia" and "Aktion Reinhard" Trial Cases.* The Hague: Martinus Nijhoff, 1996.

———. "Memory on Trial: Eyewitness Testimony Assessment in West German 'Nazi Trials.'" In *Staatsverbrechen vor Gericht,* edited by Dick de Mildt, pp. 146–157. Amsterdam: Amsterdam University Press, 2003.

Milfull, John, ed. *Why Germany? National Socialist Anti-Semitism and the European Context.* Providence, RI: Berg, 1993.

Milgram, Stanley. *Obedience to Authority: An Experimental Study.* New York: Harper and Row, 1974.

Miller, Arthur G. "Explaining the Holocaust: Does Social Psychology Exonerate the Perpetrators?" In *Understanding Genocide,* edited by Leonard S. Newman and Ralph Erber, pp. 301–324. New York: Oxford University Press, 2002.

———. *The Obedience Experiments: A Case Study of Controversy in Social Science.* New York: Praeger, 1986.

Miller, Stephen. "A Note on the Banality of Evil." *Wilson Quarterly* (Autumn 1998): 54–59.

Miquel, Marc von. *Ahnden oder Amnestieren? Westdeutsche Justiz und Vergangenheitsbewältigung in den sechziger Jahren.* Göttingen: Wallstein, 2004.

———. "Juristen: Richter in eigener Sache." In *Karrieren im Zwielicht,* edited by Norbert Frei, pp. 181–237. Frankfurt/M: Campus, 2001.

———. "'Wir müssen mit den Mördern zusammenleben!' NS-Prozesse und politische Öffentlichkeit in den sechziger Jahren." In *"Gerichtstag halten über uns selbst...,"* edited by Irmtrud Wojak, pp. 97–116. Frankfurt/M: Campus, 2001.

Mitscherlich, Alexander, and Margarete Mitscherlich. *The Inability to Mourn: Principles of Collective Behavior.* Translated by Beverley R. Placzek. New York: Grove Press, 1978.

Möller, Robert G. "Germans as Victims? Thoughts on Post-Cold War History of World War II Legacies." *History and Memory* 17 (2005): 147–194.

Moller, Sabine, ed. *Abgeschlossene Kapitel? Zur Geschichte der Konzentrationslager der NS-Prozesse.* Tübingen: Edition Discord, 2002.

Mommsen, Hans. "Die Goldhagen Debatte: Zeithistoriker im öffentlichen Konflikt." *Zeitschrift für Geschichtswissenschaft* 54 (2006): 1063–1067.

———. "Probleme der Täterforschung." In *NS-Täter in interdisciplinärer Perspektive,* edited by Helgard Kramer, pp. 425–433. Munich: Martin Meidenbauer, 2006.

———. "The Thin Parting of Civilization: Anti-Semitism Was a Necessary, but by No Means a Sufficient Condition for the Holocaust." In *Unwilling Germans? The Goldhagen Debate*, edited by Robert R. Shandley, pp. 183–195. Minneapolis: University of Minnesota Press, 1998.

———. *Von Weimar nach Auschwitz: Zur Geschichte Deutschlands in der Weltkriegsepoche*. Stuttgart: Deutsche Verlagsanstalt, 1999.

Mommsen, Wolfgang J. "Vom 'Volkstumskampf' zur nationalsozialistischen Vernichtungspolitik in Osteuropa." In *Deutsche Historiker im Nationalsozialismus*, edited by Winfried Schulze and Otto Gerhard Oexle, pp. 183–214. Frankfurt/M: Fischer, 1999.

Montague, Patrick. *Chelmno and the Holocaust: The History of Hitler's First Death Camp*. Chapel Hill: University of North Carolina Press, 2012.

Morsch, Günter, and Agnes Ohm, eds. *Terror in der Provinz Brandenburg: Frühe Konzentrationslager 1933/34*. Berlin: Metropol, 2014.

Moses, A. D. "Structure and Agency in the Holocaust: The Case of Daniel Jonah Goldhagen." *History and Theory* 37 (1998): 194–219.

Mühlenberg, Jutta. *Das SS-Helferinnenkorps: Ausbildung, Einsatz und Entnazifizierung der weiblichen Angehörigen der Waffen-SS 1942–1949*. Hamburg: Hamburger Edition, 2011.

Müller, Filip. *Eyewitness Auschwitz: Three Years in the Gas Chambers*. Translated by Susanne Flatauer. New York: Ivan R. Dee, 1999.

Müller, Ingo. *Furchtbare Juristen: Die unbewältigte Vergangenheit unserer Juristen*. Munich: Kindler, 1987.

———. *Hitler's Justice: The Courts of the Third Reich*. Translated by Deborah Lucas Schneider. Cambridge, MA: Harvard University Press, 1991.

Müller, Monika. "Die Oberaufseherin Maria Mandl: Werdegang, Dienstpraxis und Selbstdarstellung nach Kriegsende." In *Im Gefolge der SS*, edited by Simone Erpel, pp. 48–58. Berlin: Metropol, 2007.

Müller, Rolf-Dieter, and Hans-Erich Volkmann, eds. *Die Wehrmacht: Mythos und Realität*. Munich: R. Oldenbourg, 1999.

Müller-Hohagen, Jürgen. *Verleugnet, verdrängt, verschwiegen: Seelische Auswirkungen der NS-Zeit und Wege zu ihrer Überwindung*. Munich: Kösel, 2005.

Musial, Bogdan. *Deutsche Zivilverwaltung und Judenverfolgung im Generalgouvernement: Eine Fallstudie zum Distrikt Lublin 1939–1944*. Wiesbaden: Harrassowitz, 1999.

Naujoks, Harry. *Mein Leben im KZ Sachsenhausen 1936–1942: Erinnerungen eines Lagerältesten*. Cologne: Röderberg, 1987.

Naumann, Bernd. *Auschwitz: A Report on the Proceedings against Robert Karl Ludwig Mulka and Others before the Court in Frankfurt*. Translated by Jean Steinberg. New York: Frederick A. Praeger, 1966.

Nehmer, Bettina. "Täter als Gehilfen? Zur Ahndung von Einsatzgruppenverbrechen." In *Die juristische Aufarbeitung des Unrechtsstaates*, edited by Kritische Justiz, pp. 635–668. Baden-Baden: Nomos, 1998.

Neitzel, Sönke, and Harald Walzer, eds. *Soldaten: On Fighting, Killing and Dying; The Secret World War II Transcripts of German POWs*. Translated by Jefferson Chase. New York: Alfred A. Knopf, 2012.

Neubacher, Frank. "How Can It Happen that Horrendous State Crimes Are Perpetrated? An Overview of Criminological Theories." *Journal of International Criminal Justice* 4 (2006): 787–799.

———. "Verbrechen aus Gehorsam: Folgerungen aus den Milgram-Experiment für Strafrecht und Kriminologie." In *Sozialpsychologische Experimente in der Kriminologie*, edited by Frank Neubacher and Michael Walter, pp. 43–67. Munich: LIT, 2002.

Neue Juristische Wochenschrift 8 (1963): p. 358

Neue Juristische Wochenschrift 49 (1996): p. 863.

Neumann, Ulfrid, Cornelius Prittwitz, and Paulo Abrão, eds. *Transitional Justice: Das Problem gerechter strafrechtlicher Vergangenheitsbewältigung*. Frankfurt/M: PL Academic Research, 2013.

Neurath, Paul Martin. *Die Gesellschaft der Terrors: Innenansichten des Konzentrationslager Dachau und Buchenwald.* Frankfurt/M: Suhrkamp, 2004.

Newman, Leonard S. "What Is a 'Social-Psychological' Account of Perpetrator Behavior? The Person versus the Situation in Goldhagen's *Hitler's Willing Executioners.*" In *Understanding Genocide,* edited by Leonard S. Newman and Ralph Erber, pp. 43–67. New York: Oxford University Press, 2002.

Newman, Leonard S., and Ralph Erber, eds. *Understanding Genocide: The Social Psychology of the Holocaust.* New York: Oxford University Press, 2002.

Noll, Peter. "Die NS-Verbrecherprozesse strafrechtsdogmatisch und gesetzgebungspolitisch betrachtet." In *Rechtliche und politische Aspekte der NS-Verbrecherprozesse,* edited by Fritz Bauer, Peter Schneider, and Hermann Meyer, pp. 38–49. Mainz: Johannes Gutenberg-Universität, 1968.

Nyiszli, Niklos. *Auschwitz: A Doctor's Eyewitness Account.* New York: Arcade, 2011.

Ogorreck, Ralf. *Die Einsatzgruppen und die "Genesis der Endlösung."* Berlin: Metropol, 1994.

Okroy, Michael. "Exzesstäter, Fanatiker, Karrieristen: Prozesse wegen nationalsozialistischer Gewaltverbrechen vor Wuppertaler Gerichte." *Romerike Berge* 47, no. 3 (1997): 24–31.

———. "'. . . kann nicht bezweifelt werden, dass er beim Aufbau eines freien Deutschland seine Kraft einsetzen wird.' NS-Täter aus Wuppertal. Auf Umwegen zurück in die Normalität." *Geschichte in Wuppertal* 8 (1999): 105–129.

———. "'Man will unserem Bataillon was tun . . .': Der Wuppertaler Bialystok-Prozess 1967/68 und die Ermittlung gegen Angehörige des Polizeibataillon 309." In *Im Auftrag,* edited by Alfons Kenkmann and Christoph Spieker, pp. 301–317. Essen: Klartext, 2001.

Oleschinski, Wolfgang. "Ein Augenzeuge des Judenmord desertiert: Der Füsilier Stefan Hampel." In *Zivilcourage,* edited by Detlef Bald and Wolfram Wette, pp. 51–59. Frankfurt/M: Fischer, 2004.

Orth, Karin. "Bewachung." In *Der Ort des Terrors,* edited by Wolfgang Benz and Barbara Distel, pp. 126–140. Munich: C. H. Beck, 2005.

———. "The Concentration Camp Personnel." In *Concentration Camps in Nazi Germany,* edited by Jane Caplan and Nikolaus Wachsmann, pp. 33–57. London: Routledge, 2010.

———. "Die 'Anständigkeit' der Täter: Texte und Bemerkungen." *Sozialwissenschaftliche Informationen* 25 (1996): 112–115.

———. "Die Kommandanten der nationalsozialistischen Konzentrationslager." In *Die nationalsozialistischen Konzentrationslager,* edited by Herbert Ullrich, Karin Orth, and Christoph Dieckmann, pp. 755–786. Göttingen: Wallstein, 1998.

———. *Die Konzentrationslager-SS: Sozialstrukturelle Analysen und biographische Studien.* Göttingen: Wallstein, 2000.

———. "Egon Zill: Ein typischer Vertreter der Konzentrationslager-SS." In *Karrieren der Gewalt: Nationalsozialistische Täter-Biographien,* edited by Klaus-Michael Mallmann and Gerhard Paul, pp. 264–273. Darmstadt: Wissenschaftliche Buchgesellschaft, 2013.

———. "Experten des Terrors: Die Konzentrationslager-SS und die Shoah." In *Die Täter der Shoah,* edited by Gerhard Paul, pp. 93–108. Göttingen: Wallstein, 2002.

———. "SS-Täter vor Gericht: Die strafrechtliche Verfolgung der Konzentrationslager SS nach Kriegsende." In *"Gerichtstag halten über uns selbst. . ." Geschichte und Wirkung des ersten Auschwitz-Prozesses,* edited by Irmtrud Wojak, pp. 43–60. Frankfurt/M: Campus, 2001.

Orth, Karin, and Michael Wildt. "Die Ordnung der Lager: Über offene Fragen und frühe Antworte in der Forschung zu Konzentrationslagern." *Werkstattgeschichte* 12 (1995): 51–56.

Osterloh, Jörg. "'Hier handelt es sich um die Vernichtung einer Weltanschauung. . .': Die Wehrmacht und die Behandlung der sowjetischen Gefangenen in Deutschland." In *Die Wehrmacht,* edited by Rolf-Dieter Müller and Hans-Erich Volkmann, pp. 783–802. Munich: R. Oldenbourg, 1999.

Paech, Norman. "Recht und Antifaschismus nach 1945." In *Spuren des Unrechts,* edited by Martin Bennhold, pp. 131–151. Cologne: Pahl-Rugenstein, 1989.

Paetel, Karl Otto. "Die SS: Ein Beitrag zur Soziologie des Nationalsozialismus." *Vierteljahrshefte für Zeitgeschichte* 2 (1954): 1–33.

Parker, Danny. *Hitler's Warrior: The Life and Wars of SS Colonel Jochen Peiper.* Boston: Da Capo Press, 2014.

Pauer-Studer, Herlinde, and James David Vellemann. *Konrad Morgen: The Conscience of a Nazi Judge.* New York: Palgrave Macmillan, 2015.

Paul, Gerhard. *Die Täter der Shoah: Fanatische Nationalsozialisten oder ganz normale Deutsche?* Göttingen: Wallstein, 2002.

———. *Landunter: Schleswig-Holstein und das Hakenkreuz.* Münster: Westfälisches Dampfboot, 2001.

———. "Rudolf Pallmann: Führer der Feldgendarmerieabteilung 683." In *Karrieren der Gewalt: Nationalsozialistische Täter-Biographien*, edited by Klaus-Michael Mallmann and Gerhard Paul, pp. 176–187. Darmstadt: Wissenschaftliche Buchgesellschaft, 2013.

———. "Von Psychopathen, Technokraten des Terrors und 'ganz gewöhnlichen' Deutschen': Die Täter der Shoah im Spiegel der Forschung." In *Die Täter der Shoah*, edited by Gerhard Paul, pp. 13–90. Göttingen: Wallstein, 2002.

Paul, Gerhard, and Klaus-Michael Mallmann. *Die Gestapo im Zweiten Weltkrieg: "Heimatfront" und besetztes Europa.* Darmstadt: Primus, 2000.

———. "Sozialisation, Milieu und Gewalt." In *Karrieren der Gewalt: Nationalsozialistische Täterbiographien*, edited by Klaus-Michael Mallmann and Gerhard Paul, pp. 1–32. Darmstadt: Wissenschaftliche Buchgesellschaft, 2004.

Pendras, Devin O. *The Frankfurt Auschwitz Trial 1963–65: Genocide, History, and the Limits of the Law.* Cambridge: Cambridge University Press, 2006.

Perels, Joachim. *Das juristische Erbe des "Dritten Reiches": Beschädigungen der demokratischen Rechtsordnung.* Frankfurt/M: Campus, 1999.

———. "Die Aushöhlung des Rechtsstaates durch die Umwandlung von NS-Tätern in Gehilfen." In *Passion Arbeitsrecht*, edited by Rainer Erd, pp. 203–221. Baden-Baden: Nomos, 2009.

———. *Entsorgung der NS-Herrschaft? Konfliktlinien im Umgang mit dem NS-Regime.* Hannover: Offizin, 2004.

Perels, Joachim, and Rolf Pohl, eds. *NS Täter in der deutschen Gesellschaft.* Hannover: Offizin, 2002.

Perels, Joachim, and Wolfram Wette. *Mit reinem Gewissen: Wehrmachttäter in der Bundesrepublik und ihre Opfer.* Berlin: Aufbau, 2011.

Peterson, Edward N. *The Limits of Hitler's Power.* Princeton, NJ: Princeton University Press, 1969.

Phillips, Raymond, ed. *The Trial of Joseph Kramer and Forty-Four Others: The Belsen Trial.* London: William Hodge, 1949.

Pick, Daniel. *The Pursuit of the Nazi Mind: Hitler, Hess and the Analysts.* Oxford: Oxford University Press, 2012.

Pingel, Falk. *Häftlinge unter SS-Herrschaft: Widerstand, Selbstbehauptung in Konzentrationslagern.* Hamburg: Hoffmann und Campe, 1978.

Pinker, Steven. *The Better Angels of Our Nature: Why Violence Has Declined.* New York: Viking, 2011.

Piper, Franciszek. "Gas Chambers and Crematoria." In *Anatomy of the Auschwitz Death Camp*, edited by Yisrael Gutman and Michael Berenbaum, pp. 157–182. Bloomington: Indiana University Press, 1998.

———. "The Number of Victims." In *Anatomy of the Auschwitz Death Camp*, edited by Yisrael Gutman and Michael Berenbaum, pp. 61–76. Bloomington: Indiana University Press, 1998.

Pohl, Dieter. "Die Holocaust-Forschung und Goldhagens Thesen." *Vierteljahrshefte für Zeitgeschichte* 45 (1997): 1–48.

———. "Die Trawniki-Männer im Vernichtungslager Belzec 1941–1943." In *NS-Gewaltherrschaft*, edited by Alfred Bernd Gottwaldt, Norbert Kampe, and Peter Klein, pp. 278–289. Berlin: Hentrich, 2005.

———. "Die Wehrmacht und der Mord and den Juden in den besetzten sowjetischen Gebieten." In *Täter im Vernichtungskrieg*, edited by Wolf Kaiser, pp. 39–53. Berlin: Propläen, 2002.

———. "Hans Krüger and the Murder of Jews in the Region of Stanislawow (Galicia)." *Yad Vashem Studies* 26 (1998): 239–264.

———. "Hans Krüger: Der 'König von Stanislau.'" In *Karrieren der Gewalt: Nationalsozialistische Täterbiographien*, edited by Klaus-Michael Mallmann and Gerhard Paul, pp. 134–144. Darmstadt: Wissenschaftliche Buchgesellschaft, 2004.

————. "The Holocaust and the Concentration Camps." In *Concentration Camps in Nazi Germany*, edited by Jane Caplan and Nikolaus Wachsmann, pp. 149–166. London: Routledge, 2010.

————. *Nationalsozialistische Judenverfolgung in Ostgalizien 1941–1944: Organisation und Durchführung eines staatlichen Massenverbrechens*. Munich: R. Oldenbourg, 1997.

————. "Ukrainische Hilfskräfte beim Mord an den Juden." In *Die Täter der Shoah*, edited by Gerhard Paul, pp. 205–234. Göttingen: Wallstein, 2002.

————. *Verfolgung und Massenmord in der NS-Zeit 1933–1945*. Darmstadt: Wissenschaftliche Buchgesellschaft, 2003.

Pohl, Jürgen. "Polizisten vor Gericht: Der Einsatz des Recklinghäuser Polizeibataillon 316 in Weissrussland." *Vestische Zeitschrift* 99 (2002): 363–402.

Pohl, Karl Heinrich. *Wehrmacht und Vernichtungspolitik: Militär im nationalsozialistischen System*. Göttingen: Vandenhoek and Ruprecht, 1999.

Pohl, Rolf. "Ganz normale Massenmörder? Zum Normalitätsbegriff in der neuen NS-Täterforschung." In *Volksgemeinschaft, Täterschaft und Nationalsozialismus*, edited by Markus Brunner, pp. 19–56. Giessen: Psychosozial-Verlag, 2011.

————. "Gewalt und Grausamkeit: Sozialpsychologische Anmerkungen zur NS-Täterforschung." In *NS-Täter in der deutschen Gesellschaft*, edited by Joachim Perels and Rolf Pohl, pp. 69–117. Hannover: Offizin, 2002.

Poliakov, Leon, and Josef Wulf, eds. *Das Dritte Reich und die Juden: Dokumente und Aufsätze*. Berlin: Arani, 1955.

Polian, Pavel. "First Victims of the Holocaust: Soviet-Jewish Prisoners of War in German Captivity." *Kritika* 6 (2005): 763–787.

Prusin, Alexander V. "A Community of Violence! The SiPo/SD and Its Role in the Nazi Terror System in the Generalbezirk Kiew." *Holocaust and Genocide Studies* 21 (2007): 1–30.

Przyrembel, Alexandra. "Ilse Koch: 'Normale' SS-Ehefrau oder 'Kommandeuse von Buchenwald.'" In *Karrieren der Gewalt: Nationalsozialistische Täter-Biographien*, edited by Klaus-Michael Mallmann and Gerhard Paul, pp. 126–133. Darmstadt: Wissenschaftliche Buchgesellschaft, 2013.

————. "Transfixed by an Image: Ilse Koch, the 'Kommandeuse of Buchenwald.'" *German History* 19 (2001): 369–399.

Radbruch, Gustav. "Statutory Lawlessness and Supra-Statutory Law." Translated by Bonnie Litschewski Paulson and Stanley L. Paulson. *Oxford Journal of Legal Studies* 26 (2006): 1–11.

Raim, Edith. "Der Wiederaufbau der westdeutschen Justiz unter allierter Aufsicht und die Verfolgung von NS-Verbrechen 1945 bis 1949/1950." In *Die lange Stunde Null*, edited by Hans Braun, Uta Gerhardt, and Everhard Holtmann, pp. 141–173. Baden-Baden: Nomos, 2007.

————. *Justiz zwischen Diktatur und Demokratie: Wiederaufbau und Ahndung von NS-Verbrechen in Westdeutschland 1945–1949*. Munich: R. Oldenbourg, 2013.

Raine, Adrian. *The Anatomy of Violence: The Biological Roots of Crime*. New York: Pantheon Books, 2013.

Rajchman, Chil. *The Last Jews of Treblinka: A Survivor's Memory 1942–43*. Translated by Solon Beinfeld. New York: Praeger, 2011.

Ratz, Michael, ed. *Die Justiz und die Nazis: Zur Strafverfolgung von Nazismus und Neonazismus seit 1945*. Frankfurt/M: Röderberrg, 1979.

Reemtsma, Jan Philipp. "Über den Begriff Handlungsspielraum." *Mittelweg* 36 (2002): 5–23.

Rees, Laurence. *Auschwitz: A New History*. New York: Public Affairs, 2005.

Reese, Willy Peter. *Mir selber seltsam fremd: Die Unmenschlichkeit des Krieges in Russland 1941–44*. Munich: Classen, 2003.

Reichardt, Sven. "Vergemeinschaftung durch Gewalt: Das Beispiel des SA-'Mördersturms 33' in Berlin-Charlottenburg zwischen 1928 und 1932." In *Entgrenzte Gewalt*, edited by Herbert Diercks and KZ-Gedenkstätte Neuengamme, pp. 20–23. Bremen: Temmen, 2002.

Reichel, Peter, Harald Schmid, and Peter Steinbach, eds. *Der Nationalsozialismus: Die zweite Geschichte, Überwindung, Deutung, Erinnerung*. Munich: C. H. Beck, 2009.

Reichelt, Katrina. "Kollaboration und Holocaust in Lettland 1941–1945." In *Täter im Vernichtungskrieg*, edited by Wolf Kaiser, pp. 110–124. Berlin: Propyläen, 2002.

Reichsführer SS und Chef der Deutschen Polizei, SS Hauptamt. *Der Untermensch.* Berlin: Nordland, 1943.

Reichsorganisationsleiter der NSDAP. *Organisationsbuch der NSDAP.* 4th ed. Munich: Franz Eher, 1937.

———. *30 Jahre Justiz und NS-Verbrechen: Die Aktualität einer Urteilssammlung.* Frankfurt/M: Peter Lang, 1998.

Reiter, Raimond. *Nationalsozialismus und Moral: Die "Pflichtenlehre" eines Verbrecherstaates.* Frankfurt/M: Peter Land, 1996.

Reitlinger, Gerald. *The SS: Alibi of a Nation 1922–1945.* New York: Da Capo Press, 1989.

Renz, Werner. *Fritz Bauer und das Versagen der Justiz: Nazi-Prozesse und ihre "Tragödie."* Hamburg: Europäische Verlagsanstalt, 2015.

Reuters World News. "'Bookkeeper of Auschwitz' Found Guilty by German Court." July 15, 2015. www.reuters.com.

Richardi, Hans-Günter. *Schule der Gewalt: Die Anfänge des Konzentrationslager Dachau 1933–1934. Ein dokumentarischer Bericht.* Munich: C. H. Beck, 1983.

Richter, Timm. "Die Wehrmacht und der Partisanenkrieg in den besetzten Gebieten der Sowjetunion." In *Die Wehrmacht,* edited by Rolf-Dieter Müller and Hans-Erich Volkmann, pp. 837–857. Munich: R. Oldenbourg, 1999.

Riedel, Dirk. *Ordnungshüter und Massenmörder im Dienst der "Volksgemeinschaft": Der KZ-Kommandant Hans Loritz.* Berlin: Metropol, 2010.

Riedle, Andrea. *Die Angehörigen des Kommandostabs im KZ Sachsenhausen: Sozialstruktur, Dienstwege und biografische Studien.* Berlin: Metropol, 2011.

Rieger, Berndt. *Creator of Nazi Death Camps: The Life of Odilo Globocnik.* London: Vallentine Mitchell, 2007.

Rippl, Susanne. *Autoritarismus: Kontroverse und Aufsätze der aktuellen Autoritarismusforschung.* Opladen: Leske und Budrich, 2000.

Rittau, Martin. *Militärstrafgesetzbuch in der Fassung der Verordnung vom 10. Oktober 1940 . . . und Kriegssonderstrafrechtsordnung.* Berlin: Walter de Gruyter, 1944.

Ritzler, Barry A. "The Nuremberg Mind Revisited: A Quantitative Approach to Nazi Rorschachs." *Journal of Personality Assessment* 42 (1978): 344–353.

Rohd, Florian. "Hauptmann Dr. Fritz Fiedler, Ortskommandant: Der gute Mann von Horodenka." In *Retter in Uniform,* edited by Wolfram Wette, pp. 142–156. Frankfurt/M: Fischer, 2002.

Rohrkampf, René. "'Weltanschaulich gefestigte Kämpfer': Die Soldaten der Waffen-SS 1933–1945." Thesis, Universität Paderborn, 2010.

Rossi, Lauren Faulkner. *Wehrmacht Priests: Catholicism and the Nazi War of Annihilation.* Cambridge, MA: Harvard University Press, 2015.

Rossino, Alexander. "Nazi Anti-Jewish Policy during the Poland Campaign: The Case of the Einsatzgruppe von Woyrsch." *German Studies Review* 24 (2001): 35–53.

Rossolinski-Liebe, Grzegorz. "Der Verlauf und die Täter des Lemberger Pogroms vom Sommer 1941: Zum aktuellen Stand der Forschung." *Jahrbuch für Antisemitismusforschung* 22 (2013): 207–243.

Roth, Paul R. "Hearts of Darkness: 'Perpetrator History' and Why There Is No Why." *History of the Human Sciences* 17 (2004): 211–251.

Rothfels, Hans. "Augenzeugenbericht zu den Massenvergasungen." *Vierteljahrshefte für Zeitgeschichte* 1 (1953): 177–194.

Rottleuthner, Hubert. *Karrieren und Kontinuitäten deutscher Justizjuristen vor und nach 1945.* Berlin: Berliner Wissenschaftsverlag, 2010.

Roxin, Claus. "Straftaten im Rahmen organisatorischer Machapparate." *Goltdammers Archiv für Strafrecht* 7 (July 1963): 193–207.

Rückerl, Adalbert. *The Investigation of Nazi Crimes 1945–1978: A Documentation.* Translated by Derek Rutter. Heidelberg: Müller, 1979.

———. *Nationalsozialistische Vernichtungslager im Spiegel deutscher Strafprozesse: Belzec, Sobibor, Treblinka, Chelmno.* 2nd ed. Munich: Deutscher Taschenbuchverlag, 1978.

———. *NS-Verbrechen vor Gericht: Versuch einer Vergangenheitsbewältigung.* Heidelberg: C. F. Müller, 1982.

———. "Statistische Angaben über Verfahren betreffend nationalsozialistische Gewaltverbrechen und Analysen von Strafzurechnungsgründen." In *Probleme der Verfolgung und Ahndung von nationalsozialistischen Gewaltverbrechen*, edited by Deutscher Juristentag, pp. 33–44. Munich: C. H. Beck, 1967.

———, ed. *NS-Prozesse nach 25 Jahren: Strafverfolgung, Möglichkeiten, Grenzen, Ergebnis*. Karlsruhe: C. F. Müller, 1971.

Rümer, Felix. *Kameraden: Die Wehrmacht von innen*. Munich: Piper, 2012.

———. "Truppenführer als Täter: Das Beispiel des Majors Günther Drange." In *Von Feldherren und Gefreiten*, edited by Christian Hartmann, pp. 69–80. Munich: R. Oldenbourg, 2008.

Rupnow, Dirk. "Das unsichtbare Verbrechen: Beobachtungen zur Darstellung des NS-Massenmordes." *Zeitgeschichte* 29 (2002): 87–97.

Rüter, Christian Frederic. *Die westdeutschen Strafverfahren wegen nationalsozialistischen Tötungsverbrechen 1945–1997*. Munich: K. G. Saur, 1998.

Rüthers, Bernd. "Die Gesetzgebung: Vom 'Dritten Reich' zur Bundesrepublik Deutschland." In *Die Rosenburg*, edited by Manfred Görtemaker and Christoph Safferling, pp. 119–144. Göttingen: Vandenhoeck und Ruprecht, 2013.

———. *Geschönte Geschichte—Geschonte Biographien: Sozialisationskohorten in Wendeliteraturen*. Tübingen: Mohr Siebeck, 2001.

Sa'adah, Anne. *Germany's Second Chance: Trust, Justice, and Democratization*. Cambridge, MA: Harvard University Press, 1998.

Sachslehner, Johannes. *Der Henker: Leben und Tod des SS-Hauptsturmführers Amon Leopold Göth*. Graz: Styria Premium, 2013.

Safrian, Hans. "Komplizen des Genozids: Zum Anteil der Heeresgruppe Süd an der Verfolgung und Ermordung der Juden in der Ukraine 1941." In *Die Wehrmacht im Rassenkrieg*, edited by Walter Manoschek, pp. 90–115. Vienna: Picus, 1996.

Sakowska, Ruta. *Die zweite Etappe ist der Tod: NS-Ausrottungspolitik gegen die polnischen Juden gesehen mit den Augen der Opfer*. Berlin: Edition Hentrich, 1993.

Sandkühler, Thomas. "Die Täter des Holocaust: Neuere Überlegungen und Kontroversen." In *Wehrmacht und Vernichtungspolitik*, edited by Karl-Heinrich Pohl, pp. 39–65. Göttingen: Vandenhoek und Ruprecht, 1999.

Sax, Walter. "Der BGH und die Täterlehre: Gedanken zum Stachynskij-Urteil." *Juristenzeitung* 19 (1963): 329–338.

Schäfer, Torsten. *"Jedenfalls habe ich auch mitgeschossen": Das NSG-Verfahren gegen Johann Josef Kuhr und andere Angehörige des Polizeibataillons 306*. Hamburg: CIT, 2007.

Scheffler, Wolfgang. *Die Normalität des Verbrechens: Bilanz und Perspektiven der Forschung zu den nationalsozialistischen Gewaltverbrechen*. Berlin: Edition Hentrich, 1994.

———. "Zur Praxis des SS- und Polizeigerichtsbarkeit im Dritten Reich." In *Klassenjustiz und Pluralismus*, edited by Günther Doeker, pp. 224–236. Hamburg: Hoffmann und Campe, 1973.

Schleunes, Karl A. *The Twisted Road to Auschwitz: Nazi Policy toward German Jews 1933–1939*. Urbana: University of Illinois Press, 1990.

Schmid, Hans. "Otto Moll: 'Der Henker von Auschwitz.'" *Zeitschrift für Geschichtswissenschaft* 54 (2006): 118–138.

Schmid, Jeanette. "Freiwilligkeit der Gewalt? Von der Psychologie der Täter zur Psychologie der Tat." *Analyse und Kritik* 20 (1998): 27–45.

Schmidt, Eberhard. *Militärstrafrecht*. Berlin: Julius Springer, 1936.

Schnabel, Reimund. *Macht ohne Moral: Eine Dokumentation über die SS*. 2nd rev. ed. Frankfurt/M: Röderberg, 1958.

Schneider, Christian. "Reinheit und Ähnlichkeit: Anmerkungen zum psychischen Funktionieren ganz normaler deutscher Massenmörder." *Mittelweg* 36 (1998): 21–30.

Schneider, Karl. *"Auswärts eingesetzt": Bremer Polizeibataillone und der Holocaust*. Essen: Klartext, 2011.

Schneider, Peter, and Hermann Meyer, eds. *Rechtslehre und politische Aspekte der NS-Verbrecherprozesse*. Mainz: Johannes Gutenberg-Universität, 1968.

Schoenberner, Gerhard, ed. *Wir haben es gesehen: Augenzeugenberichte über Terror und Judenverfolgung im Dritten Reich*. Hamburg: Rütten und Loening, 1962.

Schoeps, Julius H. *Das Gewaltsyndrom: Verformungen und Brücken im deutsch-jüdischen Verhältnis.* Berlin: Aragon, 1998.

———, ed. *Ein Volk von Mördern? Die Dokumentation zur Goldhagen Kontroverse um die Rolle der Deutschen im Holocaust.* Hamburg: Campe, 1996.

Schramm, Percy Ernst, ed. *Kriegstagebuch des Oberkommando der Wehrmacht.* Vol. 1, 1940–41. Munich: Bernard and Graefe, 1982.

Schueler, Hans. "Schuldig ist nur, wer grausam mordet." *Die Zeit,* May 22, 1992.

Schulte, Jan Erik, Peter Lieb, and Bernd Wegner, eds. *Die Waffen-SS: Neue Forschungen.* Paderborn: Ferdinand Schöningh, 2014.

Schulze, Winfried, and Otto Gerhard Oexle, eds. *Deutsche Historiker im Nationalsozialismus.* Frankfurt/M: Fischer, 1999.

Schumann, Eva. *Kontinuitäten und Zäsuren: Rechtswissenschaft und Justiz im Dritten Reich und in der Nachkriegszeit.* Göttingen: Wallstein, 2008.

Schwan, Gesine. *Politics and Guilt: The Destructive Power of Silence.* Translated by Thomas Dunlap. Lincoln: University of Nebraska Press, 2001.

———. *"Wussten sie nicht, was sie tun?" Die Deutschen in der Zeit des Nationalsozialismus.* In *Moralität des Bösen,* edited by Werner Konitzer und Raphael Gross, pp. 140–167. Frankfurt/M: Campus, 2009.

Schwan, Heribert, and Helgard Heindrichs. *Der SS-Mann: Leben und Sterben eines Mörders.* Munich: Knaur, 2005.

Schwarberg, Günther. *The Murders at Bullenhuser Damm: The SS Doctor and the Children.* Translated by Erna Baber Rosenfeld. Bloomington: Indiana University Press, 1984.

Schwarz, Gudrun. "SS-Aufseherinnen in Konzentrationslagern." *Dachauer Hefte* 10 (1994): 32–49.

Segev, Tom. *Soldiers of Evil: The Commandants of the Nazi Concentration Camps.* Translated by Haim Watzman. New York: McGraw Hill, 1987.

Sellert, Wolfgang, and Hinrich Rüping. *Studien- und Quellenbuch zur Geschichte der deutschen Strafrechtspflege.* Vol. 2. Aalen: Scientia, 1994.

Sereny, Gitta. *Into the Darkness: An Examination of Conscience.* New York: Vintage Books, 1983.

Shandley, Robert R. *Unwilling Germans? The Goldhagen Debate.* Minneapolis: University of Minnesota Press, 1998.

Shils, Edward. "Authoritarianism, 'Right' and 'Left.'" In *Studies in the Scope and Method of "The Authoritarian Personality,"* edited by Richard Christie and Marie Jahoda. Glencoe, IL: Free Press, 1954.

———. *A Fragment of a Sociological Autobiography: The History of My Pursuit of a Few Ideas.* New Brunswick, NJ: Transaction Books, 2006.

Sigel, Robert. *Im Interesse der Gerechtigkeit: Die Dachauer Kriegsverbrecherprozesse 1945–1948.* Frankfurt/M: Campus, 1992.

Simmel, Johannes Mario. "Wir haben nur unsere Pflicht getan." In *Die Wehrmacht im Rassenkrieg,* edited by Walter Manoschek, pp. 16–22. Vienna: Picus, 1996.

Smale, Alison. "Judging the Guilt of a Man Who Admits Complicity at Auschwitz." *New York Times,* April 23, 2015.

———. "Survivors of Auschwitz Seek Action in New Case." *New York Times,* August 18, 2016.

Smelser, Neil J. "Some Determinants of Destructive Behavior." In *Sanctions for Evil,* edited by Neville Sanford, pp. 15–24. San Francisco: Jossey-Bass, 1971.

Smelser, Ronald M., and Enrico Syring, eds. *Die SS-Elite unter dem Totenkopf: 30 Lebensläufe.* Paderborn: Ferdinand Schöningh, 2000.

Smith, David Livingstone. *Less than Human: Why We Demean, Enslave, and Exterminate Others.* New York: St. Martin's Press, 2011.

Snyder, Timothy. *Black Earth: The Holocaust as History and Warning.* New York: Tim Duggan Books, 2015.

———. *Bloodlands: Europe between Hitler and Stalin.* New York: Basic Books, 2010.

Sofsky, Wolfgang. "An der Grenze des Sozialen: Perspektiven der KZ-Forschung." In *Die nationalsozialistischen Konzentrationslager,* edited by Herbert Ullrich, Karin Orth, and Everhard Dieckmann, pp. 1141–1169. Göttingen: Wallstein, 1998.

———. *The Order of Terror: The Concentration Camp.* Translated by William Templer. Princeton, NJ: Princeton University Press, 1997.

———. *Violence: Terrorism, Genocide, War.* Translated by Anthea Bell. London: Granta, 2003.

Spendel, Günter. *Rechtsbeugung durch Rechtsprechung.* Berlin: Walter de Gruyter, 1984.

Spiegel Online. "'Holocaust': Die Vergangenheit kommt zurück." January 29, 1979. www. spiegel.de.

SS-Hauptamt. *Lehrplan für die weltanschauliche Erziehung in der SS und Polizei.* N.p., 1943.

Staff, Ilse, ed. *Justiz im Dritten Reich: Eine Dokumentation.* Frankfurt/M: Fischer, 1964.

Stahl, Friedrich-Christian. "Generaloberst Johannes Blaskowitz." In *Hitlers militärische Elite,* edited by Gerd R. Ueberschär, vol. 1, pp. 20–27. Darmstadt: Primus, 1998.

Stang, Knut. "Dr. Oskar Dirlewanger: Protagonist der Terrorkriegsführung." In *Karrieren der Gewalt: Nationalsozialistische Täter-Biographien,* edited by Klaus-Michael Mallmann and Gerhard Paul, pp. 66–75. Darmstadt: Wissenschaftliche Buchgesellschaft, 2013.

———. *Kollaboration und Massenmord: Die litauische Hilfspolizei, das Rollkommando Hamann und die Ermordung der litauischen Juden.* Frankfurt/M: Peter Lang, 1996.

Stargardt, Nicholas. *The German War: A Nation under Arms 1939–1945. Citizens and Soldiers.* New York: Basic Books, 2015.

Staub, Ervin. "The Psychology of Bystanders, Perpetrators, and Heroic Helpers." In *Understanding Genocide,* edited by Leonard S. Newman and Ralph Erber, pp. 11–42. New York: Oxford University Press, 2002.

———. *The Roots of Evil: The Origins of Genocide and Other Group Violence.* Cambridge: Cambridge University Press, 2014.

Stehmann, Siegbert. *Die Bitternis verschweigen wir: Feldpostbriefe 1940–1945.* Hannover: Lutherisches Verlagshaus, 1992.

Stein, George H. *The Waffen-SS: Hitler's Elite Guard at War 1939–1945.* Ithaca, NY: Cornell University Press, 1966.

Steinbach, Lothar. *Ein Volk, ein Reich, ein Glaube? Ehemalige Nationalsozialisten und Zeitzeugen berichten über ihr Leben im Dritten Reich.* Bonn: J. H. W. Dietz, 1983.

Steinbacher, Sybille. *Der Frankfurter Auschwitz Prozess.* Frankfurt/M: Campus, 2013.

Steiner, Johann M., and Jochen Fahrenberg. "Autoritäre Einstellung und Statusmerkmale von ehemaligen Angehörigen der Waffen-SS und SS und der Wehrmacht." *Köllner Zeitschrift für Soziologie und Sozialpsychologie* 52 (2000): 329–348.

Steinweis, Alan E., and Robert D. Rachlin. *The Law in Nazi Germany: Ideology, Opportunism and the Perversion of Justice.* New York: Berghahn, 2013.

Stern, Frank. *The Whitewashing of the Yellow Badge: Antisemitism and Philosemitism in Postwar Germany.* Translated by William Temple. Oxford: Pergamon Press, 1992.

Sternberg, Robert J., ed. *The Psychology of Hate.* Washington, DC: American Psychological Association, 2005.

Steur, Claudia. *Theodor Dannecker: Ein Funktionär der "Endlösung."* Essen: Klartext, 1997.

Stipani, Ute. "Die Dachauer Prozesse und ihre Bedeutung im Rahmen der alliierten Strafverfolgung von NS-Verbrechen." In *Der Nationalsozialismus vor Gericht,* edited by Gerd R. Ueberschär, pp. 227–239. Frankfurt/M: Fischer, 1999.

Stockhorst, Erich, ed. *5000 Köpfe: Wer war was im 3. Reich.* Kiel: Blick und Bild, 1967.

Stoffels, Hans. "Vexierbilder der Vergangenheit: Die Täter als Opfer?" *Sozialwissenschaftliche Informationen* 20 (1991): 73–77.

Stoll, Katrina. "Hitler's Unwilling Executioners? The Representation of the Holocaust through the Bielefeld Bialystok Trial of 1965–1967." In *Holocaust and Justice,* edited by David Bankier, pp. 159–193. Jerusalem: Yad Vashem, 2010.

———. "Walter Sonntag: Ein SS-Arzt vor Gericht." *Zeitschrift für Geschichtswissenschaft* 50 (2002): 918–939.

Stoltzfus, Nathan, and Harry Friedlander, eds. *Nazi Crimes and the Law.* Cambridge: Cambridge University Press, 2008.

Streim, Alfred. "Zum Beispiel: Die Verbrechen der Einsatzgruppen in der Sowjetunion." In *NS-Prozesse nach 25 Jahren,* edited by Adalbert Rückerl, pp. 66–106. Karlsruhe: C. F. Müller, 1971.

Streit, Christian. *Keine Kameraden: Die Wehrmacht und die sowjetischen Kriegsgefangenen 1941– 1945.* Stuttgart: Deutsche Verlagsanstalt, 1978.

Strobl, Ingrid. "Vernichtung ohne Vernichter." *Konkret* 5 (1992): 45–47.

Strzelcki, Andrzej. "The Plunder of the Victims and Their Corpses." In *Anatomy of the Auschwitz Death Camp,* edited by Yisrael Gutman and Michael Berenbaum, pp. 246–266. Bloomington: Indiana University Press, 1998.

Suedfeld, Peter, and Murk Schaller. "Authoritarianism and the Holocaust: Some Cognitive and Affective Implications." In *Understanding Genocide,* edited by Leonard S. Newman and Ralph Erber, pp. 68–90. New York: Oxford University Press, 2002.

Swaan, Abram de. *The Killing Compartments: The Mentality of Mass Murder.* New Haven, CT: Yale University Press, 2015.

Sydnor, Charles. W. "The History of the SS Totenkopfverbände and the Postwar Mythology of the Waffen SS." *Central European History* 6 (1973): 339–362.

———. *Soldiers of Destruction: The SS Death's Head Division 1933–1945.* Princeton, NJ: Princeton University Press, 1977.

Szejnmann, Claus-Christian W. "Perpetrators of the Holocaust: A Historiography." In *Ordinary People as Mass Murderers,* edited by Olaf Jensen and Claus-Christian W. Szejnmann, pp. 25– 54. New York: Palgrave Macmillan, 2008.

Tec, Nechama. *In the Lion's Den: The Life of Oswald Rufeisen.* New York: Oxford University Press, 1990.

Tellenbach, Gerd. *Die deutsche Not als Schuld und Schicksal.* Stuttgart: Deutsche Verlagsanstalt, 1947.

Tillion, Germaine. *Frauenkonzentrationslager Ravensbrück.* Translated by Barbara Glassman. Lüneburg: Klampen, 1998.

Todorov, Tzvetan. *Facing the Extreme: Moral Life in the Concentration Camp.* Translated by Arthur Denner and Abigail Pollak. New York: Metropolitan Books, 1996.

Töpperwien, August. *"Erschiessen will ich nicht!" Als Offizier und Christ im totalen Krieg: Das Kriegstagebuch der Dr. August Töpperwien. 3. September 1939 bis 6. Mai 1945.* Düsseldorf: Gaasterland, 2006.

Totten, Samuel, William S. Parsons, and Israel W. Charny, eds. *Century of Genocide: Eyewitness Accounts and Critical Views.* New York: Garland, 1997.

Tregenza, Michael. "Belzec: Das vergessene Lager des Holocaust." *Jahrbuch zur Geschichte und Wirkung des Holocaust* 4 (2000): 241 267.

Trials of War Criminals before the Nuernberg Military Tribunals under Control Council Law No. 10. Vol. 4, *The Einsatzgruppen Case.* Washington, DC: GPO, 1946–49.

Tuchel, Johannes. "Die Wachmannschaften der Konzentrationslager 1939 bis 1945: Ergebnisse und offene Fragen der Forschung." In *NS-Gewaltherrschaft,* edited by Alfred Bernd Gottwald, Norbert Kampe, and Peter Klein, pp. 135–151. Berlin: Hentrich, 2005.

———. *Konzentrationslager: Organisationsgeschichte und Funktion der "Inspektion der Konzentrationslager" 1934–1938.* Boppard: Harald Boldt, 1991.

Ueberschär, Gerd R. "Der Polizeioffizier Klaus Hornig: Vom Befehlsverweigerer zum KZ-Häftling." In *Zivilcourage,* edited by Detlef Bald and Wolfram Wette, pp. 77–93. Frankfurt/M: Fischer, 2004.

———. *Hitlers militärische Elite.* Vol. 2. Darmstadt: Primus, 1998.

———, ed. *Der Nationalsozialismus vor Gericht: Die alliierten Prozesse gegen Kriegsverbrechen und Soldatern 1943–1952.* Frankfurt/M: Fischer, 1999.

Ullrich, Herbert, Karin Orth, and Christoph Dieckmann, eds. *Die nationalsozialistischen Konzentrationslager: Entwicklung und Struktur.* Göttingen: Wallstein, 1998.

Ullrich, Volker. "'Wir haben nichts gewusst'—ein deutsches Trauma." *1999: Zeitschrift für Sozialgeschichte des 20. und 21. Jahrhunderts* 6 (1991): 11–46.

United States Holocaust Memorial Museum. "John Demjanjuk: Prosecution of a Nazi Collaborator." www.ushmm.org.

University of Amsterdam. *Justiz und NS-Verbrechen: Sammlung deutscher Strafurteile wegen nationalsozialistischen Tötungsverbrechen 1945–2012.* 49 vols. Amsterdam: Amsterdam University Press, 1968–2012.

Venezia, Shlomo. *Inside the Gas Chambers: Eight Months in the Sonderkommando of Auschwitz.* Cambridge: Polity, 2009.

Vest, Hans. *Genozid durch organisatorische Machtapparate: An der Grenze von individueller und kollektiver Verantwortlichkeit.* Baden-Baden: Nomos, 2002.

———. *Völkerverbrecher verfolgen: Ein abgestuftes Mehrebenenmodell systemischer Täterschaft.* Bern: Stömpfli, 2011.

Vieregge, Bianca. *Die Gerichtsbarkeit einer "Elite": Nationalsozialistische Rechtsprechung am Beispiel der SS- und Polizei-Gerichtsbarkeit.* Baden-Baden: Nomos, 2002.

Von der Ohe, Axel. "Der Bundesgerichtshof und die NS-Justizverbrechen." In *Erfolgsgeschichte Bundesrepublik?*, edited by Stephan Alexander Glienke, Volker Paulmann, and Joachim Perels, pp. 293–318. Göttingen: Wallstein, 2008.

Vormbaum, Thomas. "Die 'strafrechtliche Aufarbeitung' der nationalsozialistischen Justizverbrechen in der Nachkriegszeit." In *Die Rosenburg*, edited by Manfred Görtemaker and Christoph Safferling, pp. 142–168. Göttingen: Vandenhoeck und Ruprecht, 2013.

Wachsmann, Nikolaus. *KL: A History of the Nazi Concentration Camps.* New York: Farrar, Straus and Giroux, 2015.

Wagner, Jean-Christoph. *Produktion des Todes: Das KZ Mittelbau.* Göttingen: Wallstein, 2001.

Waller, James. *Becoming Evil: How Ordinary People Commit Genocide and Mass Killing.* New York: Oxford University Press, 2002.

———. "Perpetrators of the Holocaust: Divided and Unitary Self-Conception of Evildoing." *Holocaust and Genocide Studies* 10 (1996): 11–33.

Wallner, Peter. *By Order of the Gestapo: A Record of Life in Dachau and Buchenwald Concentration Camps.* Translated by Lawrence Wolfe. London: John Murray, 1941.

Wall Street Journal. "Woman, 91, Charged over Auschwitz Role." September 22, 2015.

Walter, Michael. "Über Machtstrukturen, aus denen Kriminalität entsteht: Folgerungen aus dem 'Stanford-Prison Experiment' für Kriminologie und Kriminalpolitik." In *Sozialpsychologische Experimente in der Kriminologie*, edited by Frank Naubacher and Michael Walter, pp. 93–101. Münster: LIT, 2002.

Webb, Chris, and Michal Chocholaty. *The Treblinka Death Camp: History, Biographies, Remembrance.* Stuttgart: Ibidem, 2014.

Weber, Jason. "Normalität und Massenmord: Das Beispiel des Einsatzgruppenleiters Otto Ohlendorf." In *NS-Täter in der deutschen Gesellschaft*, edited by Joachim Perels and Rolf Pohl, pp. 41–68. Hannover: Offizin, 2002.

Weber, Jürgen, and Peter Steinbach, eds. *Vergangenheitsbewältigung durch Strafverfahren? NS-Prozesse in der Bundesrepublik Deutschland.* Munich: G. Olzog, 1984.

Weckel, Ulrike, and Edgar Wolfrum, eds. *"Bestien" und "Befehlsempfänger": Frauen und Männer in NS-Prozessen nach 1945.* Göttingen: Vandenhoeck und Ruprecht, 2003.

Wefing, Heinrich. *Der Fall Demjanjuk: Der letzte grosse NS-Prozess.* Munich: C. H. Beck, 2011.

Wegner, Bernd. "Anmerkungen zur Geschichte der Waffen-SS aus organisatorischer- und funktionsgeschichtlicher Sicht." In *Die Wehrmacht*, edited by Rolf-Dieter Müller and Hans-Erich Volkmann, pp. 405–419. Munich: R. Oldenbourg, 1999.

———. "Die Sondergerichtsbarkeit von SS und Polizei: Militärjustiz oder Grundlegung einer SS-gemässen Rechtsordnung?" In *Das Unrechtsregime: Internationale Forschung über den Nationalsozialismus*, edited by Ursula Büttner, vol. 1, pp. 243–259. Hamburg: Hans Christians, 1986.

———. *The Waffen-SS: Organization, Ideology and Function.* Oxford: Basil Blackwell, 1999.

Wegner, Gregory Paul. *Anti-Semitism and Schooling under the Third Reich.* New York: Routledge Falmer, 2002.

Wehner, Hans-Ulrich. "Nationalsozialismus und Historiker." In *Deutsche Historiker im Nationalsozialismus*, edited by Winfried Schulze and Otto Gerhard Oexle, pp. 306–339. Frankfurt/M: Fischer, 1999.

Weinberg, Gerhard L. *Crossing the Line in Nazi Genocide: On Becoming and Being a Professional Killer.* Burlington, VT: University of Vermont Center for Holocaust Studies, 1997.

Weingartner, James J. "Law and Justice in the Nazi SS: The Case of Konrad Morgen." *Central European History* 16 (1983): 276–294.

Weiss-Wendt, Anton. *Murder without Hatred: Estonians and the Holocaust.* Syracuse: Syracuse University Press, 2009.

Welzer, Harald. "Härte und Rollendistanz: Zur Sozialpsychologie des Verwaltungsmassenmordes." *Leviathan* 21 (1993): 358–373.

———. *Täter: Wie aus ganz normalen Menschen Massenmörder werden.* Frankfurt/M: Fischer, 2005.

———. "Wer waren die Täter? Anmerkungen zur Täterforschung aus sozialpsychologischer Sicht." In *Die Täter der Shoah,* edited by Gerhard Paul, pp. 237–253. Göttingen: Wallstein, 2002.

Wenck, Eileen. "Verbrechen als 'Pflichterfüllung'? Die Strafverfolgung nationalsozialistischer Gewaltverbrechen am Beispiel des Konzentrationslagers Bergen-Belsen." *Beiträge zur Geschichte der nationalsozialistischen Verfolgung in Norddeutschland* 3 (1997): 38–55.

Wenzel, Mario. "Die SS-Kommandanten von Zwangsarbeitslagern für Juden im Distrikt Krakau des Generalgouvernement 1942–1944." In *Bewachung und Ausführung,* edited by Angelika Benz and Marija Vulesica, pp. 40–51. Berlin: Metropol, 2011.

Werle, Gerhard. "Der Holocaust als Gegenstand der bundesdeutschen Strafjustiz." *Neue Juristische Wochenschrift* 45 (1992): 2529–2535.

Werle, Gerhard, and Thomas Wandres. *Auschwitz vor Gericht: Völkermord und bundesdeutsche Strafjustiz.* Munich: C. H. Beck, 1995.

Westberg, Lennart. "Zwei Polizeischicksale im Zweiten Weltkrieg: Befehlsverweigerung und Widerstand." *Archiv für Polizeigeschichte* 2 (1991): 80–83.

Westermann, Edward B. *Hitler's Police Battalions: Enforcing Racial War in the East.* Lawrence: University of Kansas, 2005.

———. "'Ordinary Men' or 'Ideological Soldiers'? Police Battalion 310 in Russia 1942." *German Studies Review* 21 (1998): 41–68.

———. "Stone-Cold Killers or Drunk with Murder? Alcohol and Atrocity during the Holocaust." *Holocaust and Genocide Studies* 30 (2016): 1–19.

Westernhagen, Dörte von. *Die Kinder der Täter: Das Dritte Reich und die Generation danach.* Munich: Kösel, 1987.

Wette, Wolfram. "Das Bild der Wehrmacht Elite nach 1945." In *Hitlers militärische Elite,* edited by Gerd R. Ueberschär, vol. 2, pp. 293–308. Darmstadt: Primus, 1998.

———. "Der Krieg gegen die Sowjetunion: Ein rassenbiologisch begründeter Vernichtungskrieg." In *Täter im Vernichtungskrieg,* edited by Wolf Kaiser, pp. 15–38. Berlin: Propyläen, 2002.

———. *Feldwebel Anton Schmid: Ein Held der Humanität.* Frankfurt/M: Fischer, 2013.

———. "'Rassenfeind.'" In *Die Wehrmacht im Rassenkrieg,* edited by Walter Manoschek, pp. 55–73. Vienna: Picuss, 1996.

———. *Retter in Uniform: Handlungsspielräume im Vernichtungskrieg der Wehrmacht.* Frankfurt/M: Fischer, 2002.

Wette, Wolfram, and Detlef Vogel, eds. *Das letzte Tabu: NS-Militärjustiz und "Kriegsverrat."* Berlin: Aufbau, 2007.

Wiesel, Elie. *Night.* Translated by Marion Wiesel. New York: Hill and Wang, 2006.

Wiggeshaus, Rolf. *The Frankfurt School.* Cambridge, MA: MIT Press, 1994.

Wildt, Michael. *Generation des Unbedingten: Das Führungskorps des Reichssicherheitshauptamtes.* Hamburg: Hamburger Edition, 2002.

———. *Nachrichtendienst, politische Elite, und Mordeinheit: Der Sicherheitsdienst des Reichsführers-SS.* Hamburg: Hamburger Edition, 2003.

———. "Von Apparaten zu Akteuren." In *Bewachung und Ausführung,* edited by Angelika Benz and Marija Vulesica, pp. 11–22. Berlin: Metropol, 2011.

Wilhelm, Hans-Heinrich. "The Holocaust in National-Socialist Rhetoric and Writing." *Yad Vashem Studies* 16 (1984): 95–127.

———. *Rassenpolitik und Kriegsführung: Sicherheitspolizei und Wehrmacht in Polen und in der Sowjetunion.* Passau: Richard Rothe, 1991.

Wilhelm, Heinz. *Aus meinem Leben.* Speyer: Evangelischer Presseverlag, 1996.

Wittke, Stefan. "Teilexkulpation von NS-Tätern?" In *Die juristische Aufarbeitung des Unrechtsstaates,* edited by Kritische Justiz, pp. 547–594. Baden-Baden: Nomos, 1998.

Wittmann, Rebecca. *Beyond Justice: The Auschwitz Trial.* Cambridge, MA: Harvard University Press, 2005.

————. "Tainted Law: The West German Judiciary and the Prosecution of Nazi War Criminals." In *Atrocities on Trial*, edited by Patricia Heberer and Jürgen Matthäus, pp. 211–243. Lincoln: Nebraska University Press, 2008.

Wojak, Irmtrud, and Susanne Meinl. *Im Labyrinth der Schuld: Täter, Opfer, Ankläger.* Frankfurt/M: Campus, 2003.

Wojak, Irmtrud, ed. *"Gerichtstag halten über uns selbst . . .": Geschichte und Wirkung des ersten Auschwitz-Prozesses.* Frankfurt/M: Campus, 2001.

Wolfe, Alan. *Political Evil: What It Is and How to Combat It.* New York: Alfred A. Knopf, 2011.

Wolff, Jeanette. *Sadismus oder Wahnsinn: Erlebnisse in den deutschen Konzentrationslagern im Osten.* Dresden: Sachsenverlag, 1947.

Wolfrum, Edgar. "Täterbilder: Die Konstruktion der NS-Täter durch die deutsche Nachkriegsjustiz." In *Die lange Stunde Null*, edited by Hans Braun, Uta Gerhardt, and Everhard Holtmann, pp. 117–139. Baden-Baden: Nomos, 2007.

Wollenberg, Jörg, ed. *The German Public and the Persecution of the Jews 1933–1945: "No One Participated, No One Knew."* Atlantic Highlands, NJ: Humanities Press, 1996.

Wüllner, Fritz. *Die NS-Militärjustiz und das Elend der Geschichtsschreibung.* Baden-Baden: Nomos, 1997.

Wünschmann, Kim. *Before Auschwitz: Jewish Prisoners in the Pre-war Concentration Camps.* Cambridge, MA: Harvard University Press, 2015.

Zapf, Wolfgang, ed. *Beiträge zur Analyse der deutschen Oberschicht.* Tübingen: Soziologisches Seminar der Universität Tübingen, 1964.

Zarusky, Jürgen. "Die juristische Aufarbeitung der KZ-Verbrechen." In *Der Ort des Terrors*, edited by Wolfgang Benz and Barbara Distel, pp. 345–362. Munich: C. H. Beck, 2005.

Zeiler, Joachim. "Psychogramm der Kommandanten von Auschwitz: Erkenntnis und Begegnung durch Zerstörung: Zur Autobiographie des Rudolf Höss." *Psychen* 45 (1991): 335–362.

Zieba, Anna. "'Wirtschaftshof Babitz': Nebenlager bei dem Gut Babice." *Hefte von Auschwitz* 11 (1970): 73–87.

Ziemann, Benjamin. "Fluchten aus dem Konzens zum Durchhalten: Ergebnisse, Probleme und Perspektiven der Erforschung soldatischer Verweigerungsform in der Wehrmacht 1939–1945." In *Die Wehrmacht*, edited by Rolf-Dieter Müller and Hans-Erich Volkmann, pp. 589–613. Munich: R. Oldenbourg, 1999.

Zillmer, Eric A. *The Quest for the Nazi Personality: A Psychological Investigation of Nazi War Criminals.* Hillsdale, NJ: Lawrence Erlbaum, 1995.

Zimbardo, Philip G., Frank Neubacher, and Michael Walter. "Psychologie der Gefangenschaft: Deprivation, Macht und Pathologie." In *Sozialpsychologische Experimente in der Kriminologie*, edited by Frank Naubacher and Michael Walter, pp. 69–92. Münster: LIT, 2002.

Zukier, Henri. "The 'Mindless Years'? A Reconsideration of the Psychological Dimension of the Holocaust 1938–1945." *Holocaust and Genocide Studies* 11 (1997): 190–212.

INDEX